MW00711650

FLOYD D. CAREY

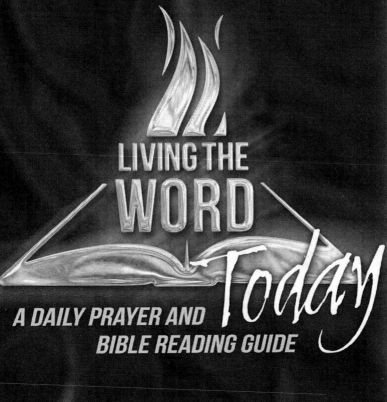

LIVING THE WORD Today

A DAILY PRAYER AND BIBLE READING GUIDE

FOREWORD
MARK L. WILLIAMS

All Scripture quotations, unless otherwise indicated, are taken from the Holy Bible, *New King James Version*. Copyright © 1982 by Thomas Nelson, Inc. Used by permission. All rights reserved.

Scripture quotations marked NIV are taken from the Holy Bible, *New International Version* ®. NIV®. Copyright © 1973, 1978, 1984, 2011 by International Bible Society. Used by permission of Zondervan Publishing House. All rights reserved.

Scripture quotations marked KJV are taken from the King James Version of the Holy Bible.

Scripture quotations marked NLT are taken from the Holy Bible, *New Living Translation*, copyright © 1996, 2004, 2007. Used by permission of Tyndale House Publishers, Inc., Wheaton, Illinois 60189. All rights reserved.

Scripture quotations marked MSG are taken from *The Message*. Copyright © 1993. Used by permission of NavPress Publishing Group.

Verses marked TLB are taken from *The Living Bible* © 1971. Used by permission of Tyndale House Publishers, Inc. Wheaton, IL 60189. All rights reserved.

Scripture quotations marked NCV are taken from The Holy Bible, *New Century Version*, copyright © 2007 by Thomas Nelson Publishers. Used by permission.

Scripture quotations marked CEV are taken from the *Contemporary English Version* of the Bible. Copyright © 1991, 1992, 1995 by American Bible Society. Used by permission.

Cover Design by Michael McDonald
Interior Design by Tom George

ISBN: 978-1-59684-732-3

Copyright © 2012 by Floyd D. Carey

Printed by Pathway Press, Cleveland, Tennessee

MISSION STATEMENT

To provide elevating support
and scriptural resources
to maintain a life
of purpose and purity
through an influential pattern
of prevailing prayer and
daily Bible reading.

FOREWORD

Early in the history of our movement, we declared that we accept "the whole Bible rightly divided, and . . . the New Testament as the only rule for government and discipline." For more than a century, we have revered the Word of God as an indispensable "lamp to [our] feet and a light to [our] path" (Psalm 119:105 NASB).

Skeptics have attacked the Bible and retreated in confusion. Agnostics have scoffed at its teaching, but are unable to produce an intellectually honest refutation. Atheists have denied its validity, but must surrender to its historical accuracy and archaeological verification.

Empires rise and fall and are forgotten, but the Word of God still stands. Kings are crowned and uncrowned, but the Word of God still stands. The Word of God is "forever . . . settled in heaven" (Psalm 119:89 NKJV). "The grass withers, the flower fades, but the word of our God stands forever" (Isaiah 40:8 NKJV).

Today, the legacy of the Church of God and the stewardship of its history, values, and mission are being placed in the hands of a new generation—a generation that must rediscover the power of Scripture.

Researchers George Gallup and Jim Castelli said, "Americans revere the Bible but, by and large, they don't read it. And because they don't read it, they have become a nation of biblical illiterates."

I believe God is calling us to make a covenant with Him to read the Word of God, but not only to read the Word but to live the Word, to covenant with Him and with each other to keep His Word with all of our heart and soul.

I urge you to make the Word of God a part of your life each day and I pray that you will find the Word to indeed be a lamp to your feet and a light to your path.

— Mark L. Williams
General Overseer
Church of God

INTRODUCTION

God reveals Himself to us through prayer and daily Bible reading. We grow in grace, we grow in the likeness of Christ, and we grow in ministry wisdom as we steadfastly embrace His plan.

The material in this book, *Living the Word Today*, will guide you along a personal path of daily interaction with God and daily instructions from His Word — the Holy Bible.

The plan for daily prayer and Bible reading is simple! The key factor is a guiding threefold "I Will" attitude:

1. **I Will Be Committed.** I will make my time with God and His revealed Word a priority.

2. **I Will Be Consistent.** I will plan my daily schedule to include a set time for intercession and to receive instructions from the Bible.

3. **I Will Be Contagious.** I will live my prayer and Bible study life with daily Christlike behavior, compassion for the distressed and suffering, and visible concern for the unchurched.

An "I Will" attitude will prepare you to receive answers to your petitions and to be anointed for God-honoring ministry.

There are three transforming steps to take in the daily plan of action:

1. **RESPOND** to the written prayer — personalize it, activate it in daily discipline, and visualize God's response to it.

2. **READ** the listed Bible chapter(s) at the lower section of the page for a journey through the New Testament. Focus on the highlighted verse(s) and the admonition or prayer listed. Many of the prayers will address the responsibilities of your pastor and how you can partner with him in ministry. In some cases, the same chapter will be read twice; in others instances, you will be asked to read two or three chapters.

3. **RECORD** your commitment to prayer and Bible reading. Place a check in the box in the upper left corner of the page following completion of the daily assignments. If you are following the plan to read the entire Bible outlined in the Resource Section, place a check in the box indicating the assigned chapter(s) has been read.

DAILY PRAYER

Our heavenly Father has given us a divine pattern to please Him and to live a productive, faith-anchored life:

> "Call [pray] to Me, and I will answer you, and show you great and mighty things, which you do not know" (Jeremiah 33:3).

In this passage, we have the assurance that God will hear and answer our prayers and will reveal His supernatural strength, direct our steps in paths of righteousness, and develop us into spiritually mature believers.

The following threefold action plan will guide you in a refreshing and rewarding daily prayer life.

1. **READ** the prayer for the day. What is the message? How can it strengthen your walk with the Lord and your understanding of His will for your life?
2. **RELATE** the message to your life. Personalize how it applies to your growth in Christ, your daily lifestyle, and your relationship with God the Father.
3. **RESPOND** with positive steps of action. Outline ways to practice and to enjoy the close interaction you experience with the Lord.

As you read, relate, and respond through prayer, you will be ready and spiritually empowered, to represent God as a committed, consistent, and contagious follower of His Son, Jesus Christ.

DAILY BIBLE READING

Through divine wisdom and oversight, God has provided a clear pathway to understand His will, to receive divine wisdom, and to walk closely with Him:

> "All scripture is given by inspiration of God, and is profitable for doctrine, for reproof, for correction, for instruction in righteousness" (2 Timothy 3:16).

All we need to live a pleasing and acceptable life in the presence of our Lord is contained in the Bible. God's Word empowers us to live and be "complete, thoroughly equipped for every good work" (v. 17).

The following threefold guidance outline will lead you in following an impactful, inspirational, and instructional daily Bible reading plan:

1. **DECIDE** on a plan. At the conclusion of each daily prayer, there is a chapter(s) and verse(s) to read that will take you on a spiritual journey through the New Testament. In the Resources Section, there is a plan to read the entire Bible in one year. **Decide** on one of the plans.

2. **DEVELOP** a routine. The most effective method of Bible reading is to create a daily system that includes a specific time, place, and approach. Consistency will play a major role in generating enthusiasm and in staying motivated. **Develop** a consistent daily routine.

3. **DEMONSTRATE** the fruit. Follow the advice of the writer, James: "Be doers of the word" (1:22). Set forth

ways for God's Word to come alive in Your life — understanding truth, practicing truth, and sharing truth. **Demonstrate** the fruit of Bible reading in daily life.

As you decide, develop, and demonstrate through daily Bible reading, you will grow stronger in faith and works and will show forth the virtues of a committed, consistent, and contagious follower of Jesus Christ.

Ministry Commitment and Personal Diary

On Saturday and Sunday of each week the Daily Prayer has been replaced with a Ministry Commitment and a Personal Diary.

The Ministry Commitment consists of pledges, covenants, and challenges to foster faithfulness to God, your family, your church, and your pastor, as well as sharing Christian love and support in your daily life.

The Personal Diary is to record answers to prayer, patterns of spiritual growth, participation in ministry projects, and the results of sharing the good news of light, love, and liberty in Jesus Christ.

The following threefold instructional steps will assist you in setting spiritual goals and in remembering Christian duties, God's guidance, and abundant blessings.

1. **REVIEW** the five personal prayers that you offered to God during the week. What do they reveal about your goals and commitment to Christ?

2. **RESPOND** to God's provisions and guidance. Be open, willing, and ready to respond to God's leadership and plans for your spiritual health, growth, and happiness.

3. **RECORD** experiences and achievements that happen during the week. Your diary will preserve and remind you of how God has overshadowed your life.

Accept the Challenge

The challenge is to pray and read the Bible daily. The challenge embodies both commitment and consistency. It is a personal choice, a choice that will please God and bear the fruit of closeness with Him.

To undergird you in accepting the outlined challenges and in making them a priority, a Daily Prayer Pledge, a Daily Bible Reading Pledge, and a Ministry Commitment and Personal Diary have been prepared. Read them, mediate on them, and accept them as a foundation for faithfulness, spiritual fruit, and fullness in Christ.

MY PLEDGE

DAILY PRAYER

I realize daily prayer is the pathway for living a blessed and balanced Christian life. Prayer guides me to . . .

Establish a consistent pattern for spending life-transforming time with my Lord and Master.

Depend on the illuminating oversight of the Holy Spirit to communicate honestly, clearly, and expectantly in my time with God Jehovah.

Share the fulfilling reward of total lifestyle commitment and the promise of abundant life through prevailing prayer.

Therefore, I Pledge

To pray daily, voicing praise for God's gifts, for divine guidance, and for grace to be an effective witness. I make this pledge in faith, hope, and charity.

Signed _____

MY PLEDGE

DAILY BIBLE READING

I understand daily Bible reading is God's method to . . .

Lead me to a deeper appreciation for His leadership and provisions and to **Teach** me self-discipline in following His plan for my life.

Reveal to me the Spirit's guidance in visualizing, trusting in, and obeying scriptural truths to **Guide** me in developing faith and uncompromising dedication.

Provide me with the resources to grow in wisdom and spiritual maturity and to **Receive** supportive enablement to fulfill the Great Commission with faith, authority, and persistence.

Therefore, I Pledge

To read my Bible daily with the goal of reading the New Testament or the entire Bible in the time frame of one year. I make this pledge depending upon the overshadowing ministry of the Holy Spirit.

Signed ————————————————————

MINISTRY COMMITMENT AND PERSONAL DIARY

I am spiritually aware that my ministry commitment and my personal diary are avenues to . . .

Provide me with plans to show my allegiance to Jesus Christ and to embrace methods to live harmoniously and victoriously in daily life.

Protect me from the snares of Satan and to give me Holy Spirit power to develop skills to advance the kingdom of God.

Preserve how God has protected me, provided for me, and performed His will in my life.

Therefore, I Pledge

To stay alert to how God desires to develop my spiritual nature, to direct me in performing ministry, and to experience His works of grace in my life.

Signed _____

A 20/20 VISION TODAY

Father of the present and future, You provide insights and energy for achievements today and to anticipate the possibilities of tomorrow. You are holy! You are high and lifted up! I want to see You clearly so I can follow a pattern of pure purpose and principle-centered daily conduct. I ask You to give me a . . .

CLEAR vision of the unity of the Holy Trinity. Total togetherness in mission! Harmony in all aspects of duties to achieve heaven-sent purposes. This unity sets the example for me and the members of my church to be in harmony, to be together in mission, and to understand Your divine will, Father.

CLEAR vision of the magnitude of Your kingdom. Fathomless Father, Your kingdom has no boundaries or limitations. It is expansive beyond comprehension. Thank You for including me in Your kingdom family and for the honor to experience and enjoy Kingdom resources. I will keep my eyes focused on the unlimited benefits of belonging to Your family.

CLEAR vision of my heritage as a believer. I have a beautiful and boundless heritage—beautiful in scope, sacredness, and eternal security; boundless in personal fulfillment, spiritual fruitfulness, and daily enjoyments. I embrace my heritage!

BIBLE READING—MATTHEW

1. Understanding—1:19. Our pastor is "a just man" (upright), sensitive to the needs and crisis situations of church members. Father, I ask You to let me, and the people of our congregation, be "just" and "upright" in respecting him, in our relationship with him, and in responding to his challenges.

A BIG DAY TODAY

Bigness! Father, I see Your bigness in creation — the sky, oceans, and land masses. I see Your bigness in the beauty of heaven, Your gifts of grace, and Your bonding with me through redemption. I see Your bigness in providing me with a big day every day. I am . . .

Surrounded by BEAUTY. I will have a big day today because I am surrounded by beauty — beautiful people in the church, beautiful people in the community who are friends of the church, and beautiful people in the city who are receptive to the good news. I will embrace and love all three of these beautiful gifts.

Surrounded by BLESSINGS. I will have a big day today because I am surrounded by blessings — blessings through the operation of the gifts of the Spirit, blessings through the guidance of my pastor, and blessings through the richness of scriptural worship. I will enjoy and share God's flow of blessings in my life.

Surrounded by BOUNDLESS Opportunities. I will have a big day today because I am surrounded by opportunities — opportunities to learn lessons on how to live successfully, opportunities to relate to the needs and goals of others, and opportunities to cultivate guiding convictions. I will express thanksgiving for the glorious privileges that surround me.

BIBLE READING — MATTHEW

2. Warning — 2:7-12. Lord, You know Herod wanted to destroy the future of Christ and nullify His mission. People in high places today, inspired by our adversary Satan, desire to kill the influence of our pastor. I ask You to divinely protect him, give him spiritual armor, and let Your Spirit guide him around temptations and traps.

A BLESSED DAY TODAY

Father of all blessings, You have blessed me today — possibilities, adventure, bountiful surroundings. You have also blessed me to experience and enjoy Your magnificent blessings. I will count my blessings, one by one, and go about my activities with singing in my soul and praise on my lips. Today has . . .

BRIMMING possibilities. Master, You have given me a mind to think, hands to work, and feet to walk. I will use the skills You have given me to see and seize the possibilities before me — possibilities to use my time more effectively, to work more creatively, and to worship more enthusiastically.

BOUNTIFUL adventure. Life with You, Father, is never dull or boring. Every day is filled with adventure — adventure to uncover new thought patterns, to unlock new doors of expressing feelings and faith, and to discover new scriptural treasures.

BEAUTIFUL surroundings. Father, Your creative genius in nature is ever before me. I am surrounded by beauty — the beauty of clouds during the day and stars at night; the beauty of trees, flowers, and vegetation; and the beauty of different times of the year sparkling with new shades of color and seasonal expressions.

BIBLE READING — MATTHEW

3. Submitting — 3:13-17. Submission is a holy virtue, and John set a sterling example (v. 14). Father, let me be submissive to Christ and to my pastor, both in attitude and actions, even when I don't clearly understand the reasons or the restrictions.

A BOLD TRUST TODAY

Faithful Father, You are always on time to meet every challenge I face, every conflicting encounter, and every confusing ordeal. I trust You! I trust You with a bold trust, an unfailing trust, an unmovable trust because You have proven to always be faithful. I will . . .

TALK about Your love. Your love reaches around the world and it also reaches around me. Your love is permanent and always available through bold trust. Father, I trust You! I will talk about Your love, depend on Your love, and share Your love.

TRANSFER talk into action. My trust in You, Father, leads me to talk and train and then to turn talk and training into action; positive action of serving my church and sharing my testimony. Touch my spirit so I can minister trustworthily, aggressively, compassionately, and enthusiastically

TURN negative situations into positive possibilities. Today, I will face pitfalls, problem people, and perplexing confrontations. I will look to You, Lord, and think thoughts of trust—acting and reacting with positive scriptural integrity, positive personal discipline, positive inspirational action, and positive uplifting encouragement.

BIBLE READING—MATTHEW

4. Following—4:18-22. Christ calls us to leave "our nets" (old lifestyle), follow Him, and "fish for men" (v. 19). Let me actively do this by always seeking Your will, walking hand in hand with my pastor, and witnessing boldly to the unchurched.

My Personal Pledge

TO FERVENT PRAYER

I understand through prayer I connect with God; I connect with His purposes, purity, protection, and provisions. Therefore, I will give prayer top priority in my daily schedule!

I pledge to be loyal in fervent prayer by . . .

EMBRACING the privilege of prayer with joyful excitement and life-changing anticipation.

EXPRESSING love and thanksgiving for God's abundant blessings and daily grace gifts.

EXPLAINING my need for support and guidance in standing strong as a Christian witness.

EXPLORING the wonders of God and talking with Him about my spiritual health.

EXAMINING my relationship with God's Holy Word and His ideal will for my life.

BIBLE READING — MATTHEW

5. Blessings — 5:1-12. Lord of Precious Gifts, I want to be blessed, I want our church to be blessed, and I want my pastor to be blessed. I ask that the Beatitudes be active in my life, directing my loyalty and allegiance, my personal attitude and my spiritual actions.

My Journal

FOR THE WEEK

Praise reports, answered prayers, divine provisions, and
spiritual plans.

_____

_____

_____

_____

_____

_____

_____

_____

_____

_____

BIBLE READING — MATTHEW

6. Praying — 6:9-13. Jesus taught us to call You "Father"
and to pray: "Your Kingdom come." I do that today by
being faithful in church attendance, by being consistent in
my prayer life, and by joining with my pastor in achieving
the ministry objectives of my church.

A CARING SPIRIT TODAY

Caring Comforter, I want to follow Your example and show a caring spirit to members of my family, friends, and those facing difficulties. Your caring spirit comforts, provides peace, and solves problems. Today, let my actions . . .

Show UNITY — "I am with You!" In times of need, people feel all alone, forsaken, and down-and-out. Father, I want Your caring Spirit to be reflected in my attitude and actions, to show unity in getting through and getting over trying times.

Offer UNDERSTANDING — "I feel your pain! I want to give a supportive hand to help, heal, and restore through understanding." Father, let your Spirit show me and overshadow me to do this. Through understanding I can give restoring support.

Reveal UNCTION — "I will pray with you for God's anointing to overcome and for a pleasant spirit to cover you!" As I stand with and support others, I will depend on You, Lord, to stand with me and support me. You are my source of strength! I will depend on Your caring Spirit.

BIBLE READING — MATTHEW

7. Judging — 7:1-5. Father, my pastor is often judged regarding the church budget, music, committee meetings, leadership, personnel, and the contents or length of his sermons. Give our church a nonjudgmental spirit, and let it begin with me. I want to be a joy to him, not a judge.

ACCEPTING RESPONSIBILITY TODAY

God of saving grace, Your will is that people of every country and culture experience new life in Jesus Christ; this is Your will and the mission of Your Church. It is also Your plan for me to accept personal responsibility in embracing Your will and mission. Guide and empower me to . . .

Develop VISION. Father, create a clear vision in me of joining You in ministering to the unchurched. With a clear vision, I also need commanding convictions to act. Today, give me the eyes of Christ to see the condition of people in my community and city, and to weep with compassion (Matthew 9:36).

Form VALUES. Father, one lost sheep is valuable to You (Matthew 18:10-14; Luke 15:4-7). I want one lost person to be valuable to me—to seek for, to pray for, and to witness to today. I will accept responsibility to be an active witness of Your generous grace and goodness.

Achieve VICTORY! Today, Father, I accept victory in Christ—receiving spiritual gifts, reaching the unchurched, and the rewards of mission obedience and church growth.

BIBLE READING—MATTHEW

8. Cleansing—8:1-4. Jesus said to the man with leprosy, "I am willing; be cleansed" (v. 3). Lord of glory, these are life-shaping words. Today, I am willing to place my personal life, my church life, and my life with my pastor in the willing hands of my Lord and Savior, Jesus Christ.

ACCEPTING VISITORS TODAY

Lord, I am reminded of the shepherd who left the ninety-nine to search for one lost sheep (Luke 15:4). This story illustrates the pattern and vision of Your Church. Lost sheep, visitors, guests, and friends need attention and affection. Help me and my church to . . .

RECOGNIZE Their Value. People, both young and the old, are valuable to You, Lord—their faith, their fulfillment, and their future. Both the young and the old must be valuable to me and my church—accept them, love them, and care for them. I will recognize the value of every person today!

RESPECT Their Individuality. Every person needs Christ. Every person has a different personality. In accepting visitors to my church, I will recognize their uniqueness and understand that God has a personalized, unique plan for their lives. Father, give me wisdom to do this. I will respect the individuality of every person today!

RESPOND to Their Needs. Visitors to my church are different and their needs are different. Father, let me and my church be open to addressing these needs and not locked into one style or approach to meet all needs. I will respond to different needs in different ways today!

BIBLE READING—MATTHEW

9. Forgiving—9:1-8. Forgiving and healing go hand in hand. Lord, You forgive sins and failures and heal broken and bruised hearts. With our pastor, may our church be known as a healing, forgiving, accepting, and restoring church, always following the pattern of Christ.

A CLEAR MIND TODAY

What a wonderful privilege, Father, to meditate, antici-pate, and activate thoughts about Your purity, perfection, and daily provisions. In this process, I receive clarity in staying close to You and drawing wisdom to walk accord-ing to Your will for my life. Anoint my thinking so I can . . .

Think like CHRIST. Father, the thinking of Christ was wrapped around pleasing You and performing the minis-try You outlined for Him—providing hope, healing, and the promise of heaven. I will embrace the thinking pattern of Christ and share hope in overcoming life's difficulties, in emotional healing, and in the glories of heaven.

Think CREATIVELY. Master, You are the author of de-sign and form. You created all things and all things are under Your care and control. Work Your creative powers in and through me so I can think constructively, act differ-ently, and relate to the unchurched compassionately.

Think COURAGEOUSLY. I do not want to be timid in my thinking. I want to think boldly, out-of-the-box, and progressively. I will think new thoughts today, and I will follow creative paths of personal development and coura-geous service.

BIBLE READING—MATTHEW

10. Receiving—10:40-42. Father, when You speak of re-ceiving "a prophet" and "giving a cup of cold water to one of these little ones," you are talking about how I should embrace my pastor, provide for him, follow his leadership, and team up with him in ministry. I will do this because You have promised both present and future rewards for this action.

ACTION STEPS TODAY

Mighty Conqueror, You offer new opportunities every day to learn, grow, and experience. My walk with You is filled with great adventure. You give me courage to take action steps and to . . .

Set Stretching GOALS. Thank You, Father, for urging me to bypass the ordinary and reach for the extraordinary; to set goals that stretch my faith and vision. I will set goals that generate greater devotional habits, greater communication skills, and greater sharing of values.

Develop Creative GUIDELINES. In order to set stretching goals, I must develop and follow creative guidelines. This calls for order, systems, and accountability. I know, Father, You are a God of order, and I will depend on You for spiritual strategy and supervision.

Properly Direct GLORY. Father, all good things come from You—I give You glory! Many individuals assisted me in reaching my goals—I express love to them! My church provides support to keep me grounded through teaching, training, and fellowship—I convey thanksgiving for my church!

BIBLE READING—MATTHEW

11. Telling—11:1-6. When we "go and tell" people about the mercy of Christ, the mission of love of our church, and the compassionate ministry of our pastor, doubt will be dissolved, and the good news will be received and God's kingdom will be advanced. Lord, make our church a "go-and-tell" church.

PERSONAL AFFIRMATION – GROWTH

To be a member of the family of God is a holy honor. To increase in wisdom and knowledge and to grow in the likeness of Christ is a sacred process that requires full-life devotion:

I Will . . .

- **EXAMINE** past growth patterns.

- **ASK** for divine oversight for growth.

- **DESIGN** a path for biblical growth.

- **PINPOINT** qualities required for growth.

- **RESEARCH** instructions for growth.

- **CONSISTENTLY** practice growth principles.

- **OFFER** praise for growth assistance.

BIBLE READING – MATTHEW

12. Standing – 12:22-30. Father, You tell us that a "house [church] divided against itself will not stand" (v. 25). In our church, with my pastor, let me be a peacemaker by always standing with integrity, by showing a spirit of understanding, and by focusing on Your plan for harmony and church health..

My Journal

FOR THE WEEK

Praise reports, answered prayers, divine provisions, and
spiritual plans.

BIBLE READING — MATTHEW

13. Sowing — 13:1-8, 18-23. Father of mercy and compassion, You have called us to be wise sowers of Your Word. Show us the "good ground" so that we will use our gifts effectively and reap an abundant harvest.

A DOVE TOUCH TODAY

God of constant care, You are always in control — always! Throughout history, You have demonstrated Your presence in unique ways. You sent a dove to broadcast Your pleasure with the ministry of Christ. I need a dove touch today to show . . .

I am Your PROPERTY. I belong to You, Father. As Your property, I am under Your protection. You provide for me and surround me with protective care, defensive awareness, divine anointing, and daily inspirational briefings.

I have Your PEACE. A dove in the Bible represents a divine presence, holy pleasure, and heavenly peace. Peace from You, Father, brings calmness, closeness, and companionship. I raise Your banner of peace! I rejoice for the gift of Your peace! I will enjoy the fruit of Your peace today!

I am following Your PLAN. Your plan for me is perfect, providing leadership and anointing, and it nurtures faith, hope, and love. Father, I will honor the plan You have designed for my life. I will cherish it, guard it, delight in it, and fulfill it in the power of the Holy Spirit.

BIBLE READING — MATTHEW

14. Feeding — 14:14-21. Lord, by a divine miracle, Jesus, Your Son, provided both spiritual bread and physical bread for the hungry multitude. We realize we must do the same. Our pastor gives spiritual bread; let us work with him in giving physical bread to the people in our community and city — food, clothing, shelter, counseling, and encouragement.

A DREAMER TODAY

God who births dreams, I am open, receptive, and ready for You to birth dreams in me. Dreams open minds, reveal possibilities, and picture life-changing plans. I want to be a dreamer! Birth dreams in me that . . .

DEMONSTRATE Your leadership. Lord, I need Your leadership to inspire holy dreams to fulfill Your plans for my life. Your plans include dreams for my career, my church, and my community. Direct me . . . Refresh me . . . Educate me . . . Anoint me . . . Motivate me. I will follow Your leadership today!

DEVELOP a productive trust. Yes, I desire to be a dreamer; a dreamer who dreams with trust that is active and merits results. Trust positions me for productivity. Father, develop me . . . renew me . . . ensure me . . . advance me . . . mobilize me. I will be a trustworthy dreamer today!

DIRECT me in paths of righteousness. For my dreams to honor You, Master, they must lead me along the path that is right in Your eyes, that respect Your holiness, and that respond to scriptural responsibilities. Dispatch me . . . reinforce me . . . empower me . . . assure me . . . monitor me. I will follow Your directions and walk in paths of righteousness today!

BIBLE READING — MATTHEW

15. Realizing — 15:21-28. Father of mercy and healing, we show "great faith" by humbling ourselves, realizing our smallness and Your greatness. If we dedicate, You will deliver. Let us continually give ourselves to the Holy Spirit and the love-based leadership of our pastor.

AFFIRM TODAY

Affirming Advocate, You affirm my value as a member of Your worldwide family. You speak on my behalf. You arrange for my well-being. You prepare the way before me. In response to Your unfailing grace, I will affirm my loyalty through . . .

SEPARATION—Living a life of focus. Lord, in order to live a life of spiritual focus, I must separate myself from distractions—sights, sounds, and stumbling blocks. By Your strength, I will keep my eyes focused "on the prize of the high calling of God in Christ" (Philippians 3:14).

SACRIFICE—Living a life of service. My words must be supported by works. Kingdom service always requires sacrifice—time, talents, and treasures. By Your oversight, Lord, I will maintain an attitude of serving others with honor.

SENSITIVITY—Living a life of understanding. Father, I want to understand the personality and problems of those around me so I can offer guidance and support. I also want to be transparent so others can understand me. By Your Holy Spirit, I will express a sensitive spirit in my character and conduct.

BIBLE READING—MATTHEW

16. Confessing—16:13-19. Confessing that Jesus Christ is Your Son, Holy Father, is the foundation for the mission and ministries of our church. Let us be faithful in this as our pastor guides us through teaching, training, and reaching the unchurched.

A FIRM GRIP TODAY

There is no change in You, mighty Master. You are always the same (Hebrews 13:8). Unchangeable, totally reliable in Your promises, oversight, and provisions. I am subject to change because of my surroundings. I need a firm grip by Your grace to . . .

HOLD ON to holy help. You are always present, Father, all the time, everywhere, and every time I need care or counsel. I will hold on to Your help and believe I am safe, secure, and stable in Your loving arms.

HOLD UP holy standards. I represent You, wonderful King, my family, and my church. I have a Savior to share, a church to support, and a glorious cause to live for. I ask You for "hold- up" initiative, instructions, and empowerment, so I can "hold up" holy standards and serve You with pure integrity and with influence that transforms.

HOLD TOGETHER my family in serving You, Father. You have given me a beautiful family to love and to hold together in unity. I am grateful! I will help hold together my family by my commitment to You, by my spiritual conduct in home life, and by my lifestyle in everyday life — godly character, worthy goals, and graceful attitude.

BIBLE READING — MATTHEW

17. Transfiguring — 17:1-5. As Christ was transfigured on the mountain, His "face shone like the sun" (v. 2), and the lives of Peter, James, and John were changed. Jesus, let Your glory be reflected in my life so those around me will be influenced, transformed, and transferred to a new position of spiritual wholeness.

A FIRM STAND TODAY

Lord of assurance and accountability, I stand on a firm foundation — Your authority, Your unbroken promises, and Your delivering power. This foundation provides a biblical backbone to stand without wavering and with maximum loyalty. Therefore, I will not . . .

Shut UP. No, never! I will not shut up within me the talents and skills You, Father, have blessed me with. I will stand on the firm foundation You have provided and release them, rejoice while using them, and honor You for the results of using them. I will not shut up!

Give UP. No, absolutely not! I will not give up on ministering to my unchurched friends. I will not give up on reaching young people in my community and in motivating my friends to trust You, Father, for supplying special needs. I will not give up!

Back UP. No, not me! I will not back up in standing up for truth, liberty, and total life in Christ. I will not back down in boldly confessing my faith. I will not back up in embracing the doctrine of forgiveness, holiness, righteousness, and completeness in Jesus Christ. I will not back up!

BIBLE READING — MATTHEW

18. Measuring — 18:1-5. Master, to truly walk with You and serve You, I must cultivate a childlike attitude of trust, daily dependence, and loyalty. This same spirit must be reflected in my relationship with my pastor. Today, I "humble myself" so I can be great in Your kingdom (v. 4).

PRAYER PATTERN — YEAR

- **YIELDED**. Lord, throughout the year I will be **YIELDED** to your will and ways and to my pastor's leadership.

- **ENCIRCLE**. I ask You to **ENCIRCLE** me, my pastor, and my church with protective grace and love gifts.

- **ARRIVE**. I believe You want us to blend our skills and **ARRIVE** at some specific spiritual destinations.

- **RENEW**. I also ask You to **RENEW** our strength so we can see clearly, love tenderly, and minister gracefully.

BIBLE READING — MATTHEW

19. Guiding — 19:13-15. Lord of love, we know children have a special place in Your Kingdom. With our pastor, let us "lay our hands on them" like Christ (v. 15), and "bless them" through love-based programs of teaching, training, and tutoring in Your ways.

My Journal

FOR THE MONTH

Praise reports, answered prayers, divine provisions, and spiritual plans.

BIBLE READING — MATTHEW

20. Serving — 20:20-26. Lord, I believe our pastor is a "servant" (v. 26). His lifestyle and work among us testify of this. May our church be made up of servants — serving one another, serving our community, and serving faithfully with our pastor to fulfill Your will for our church.

A LAMP TODAY

Lord of everlasting light, You illuminate the path I walk and dispel darkness, fear, and anxiety. You are the way, the truth, and the source of salvation in Christ. You guide me by Your Word. Your Word is a lamp (Psalm 119:105) that . . .

Shows the WAY. Lord, sometimes I am directionally dysfunctional. Sights, sounds, and surroundings distract me, and I lose a clear view of my destination. You have provided Your Word to show me the way. I will read it, study it, and trust You to guide me to live by it. Your Word will show me the way today!

Shows How to WALK. Lord, the Bible tells us that Enoch walked with You (Genesis 5:22, 24). Your plan is for believers to walk with You. I'm a believer and my goal is to walk with You. Your Word instructs me about how to walk in step with You. I will keep it close, protect it, and follow its directions. Your Word will show me how to walk today!

Shows Available WISDOM. I need wisdom, Lord, and I ask You for it (2 Chronicles 1:10). Your Word provides wisdom to plan strategically, to trust obediently, and to advance victoriously. Your Word will show me available wisdom today!

BIBLE READING—MATTHEW

21. Cleaning—21:12-13. Heavenly Father, our actions and activities in Your house must be holy, clean, and edifying. We cannot condone shady or borderline events. As a team—pastor, leaders, members—let us uphold high standards in our approach to worship and in our personal accountability to You.

A LIGHT TODAY

Lord of light and liberty, I walk an illuminated path today. Your love lights the way—reveals true directions, releases walking-power energy, and provides power to overcome faintheartedness. I will depend on Your light to . . .

SHOW me the way. Lord, there are many paths before me today. I need to know the right one to walk on; the path that keeps me close to You and that connects me within Your will. Show me the way! I will respond! I will follow Your leadership!

SHINE through me as a witness. Father, I want those around me to see You in me. Let Your light release love through my conversations, my spirit of care, and my involvement in the ministries of the church. Make me a shining witness today!

SECURE my destination. Lord, You have prepared a place for me in heaven—my final destination. You have also prepared things for me to see and achieve now—my earthly destinations. I will trust Your light to warm me and lead me today!

BIBLE READING—MATTHEW

22. Inviting—22:1-10. Your Word tells us, Father, that You love all people. You "show no partiality" (Acts 10:34). You want us to love people without regard to background or color and to personally invite them to attend church. This means building relationships with sinners.

A MESSENGER TODAY

Sending Father, You sent Your Son, Jesus Christ, into the world as a messenger of Your restoring grace. I heard the message, accepted it, and it remade my life. In response, Father, I am committed to being Your messenger, a messenger of . . .

TRUTH. Life without truth, Master, is shallow, subpar, and shaky. Your Word is truth. I can anchor my life on it. I will embrace truth! I will be a messenger today, relating how truth shows the way, molds to follow the way, and holds in the way.

TRANSFORMATION. Lord, when I responded to the message of repentance, it transformed my life — my values and my vision for the future. Today, I will be a messenger of repentance, and I will tell how it can transform a person to follow a new course in life.

TOGETHERNESS. I will be a messenger of unity, bonding, and togetherness in the body of Christ. This message will bring harmony and wholeness, and it will reflect the nature of the Holy Trinity. I will be a messenger today!

BIBLE READING — MATTHEW

23.   Lamenting — 23:37-39. Lord, You lamented and wept over the city of Jerusalem (v. 37) because of unbelief and unresponsiveness. May our vision and burden for our city be intensified. Let us lament and weep, but let us also go out and minister and lead people to understand Your love for them.

A NEW DAY TODAY

Lord of new beginnings, each morning You set a new day before me to experience new things, to explore new avenues of possibilities, and to express new measures of thanksgiving. Today, I will . . .

DREAM Big Dreams. In the Bible, Joseph was called a dreamer (Genesis 37:19). I want to be known as a believer who dreams big dreams—dreams to experience a powerful flow of Holy Spirit power, dreams to explore new spiritual horizons, and dreams to express contagious zeal for the ministries of my church. Father, big dreams are made possible by You! I will receive them from You!

DEVELOP Service Skills. Jesus Christ came into the world "not . . . to be served, but to serve" (Matthew 20:28; Mark 10:45). I want to follow His pattern and "serve myself into the hearts of people." Today, Lord, I ask You to guide me in developing service skills—pleasing personality traits, productive work patterns, and performance praise and integrity.

DEMONSTRATE Loving Care. Lord, I can be Your representative today, demonstrating loving care—lifting up the fallen, loving the suffering, and leading the spiritually blind. Empower me, equip me, and energize me to do this. I will demonstrate loving care to reflect Your nature!

BIBLE READING—MATTHEW

24. Preaching—24:1-14. Lord, we know people are converted by the preaching of Your Word and that, "the gospel of the kingdom will be preached in all the world" (v. 14). Let us support our pastor in his pulpit ministry, and let us support world missions so the gospel can be preached in all the world.

AN EXAMPLE TODAY

Father, Your nature is characterized by compassion—compassion that informs, transforms, and reforms. Your compassion has changed my life—my purpose, my priorities, and the center of my praise. In response to Your compassion, I want to honor and serve You as an example . . .

By My DEDICATION. Lord and Master, I will show compassion in my life. I will be an example of dedication to You, of exalting Jesus Christ, and of performing ministry that focuses on Your compassion that informs, transforms, and reforms. I will be an example of dedication today!

By My DOCTRINE. What I believe, what I practice, and what I share as a witness, Father, will be firmly established on Your Word, the Holy Bible. Your Word releases my spirit and guides me in living Bible-based convictions. I will be an example by my doctrine today!

By My DEVELOPMENT. Father, I want to develop daily in the nature of Your Son, Jesus Christ. I desire to grow in wisdom, knowledge, and understanding. Guide me by Your Spirit to act with wisdom, to serve with knowledge, and to make decisions with understanding. I will be an example of personal development today!

BIBLE READING—MATTHEW

25. Watching—25:1-13. Lord, I want to be awake, to be watchful, and to have my spiritual lamp burning bright every day, so I will be prepared for the return of Your Son, Jesus Christ. I commit to living soberly, righteously, and godly so I can be prayed up, packed up, and ready to go up.

BEATITUDES FOR CHURCH MEMBERS FOR THE PASTOR

- Blessed are those who . . .
  LOVE the pastor unconditionally, without complaining about his weaknesses or work patterns.

- Blessed are those who . . .
  LOOK to the pastor as God's shepherd to oversee them, feed them, and nurture them.

- Blessed are those who . . .
  LISTEN to the pastor and receive instruction and inspiration to live life God's way.

- Blessed are those who . . .
  LEARN from the pastor's leadership and develop their gifts to perform Kingdom service

- Blessed are those who . . .
  LIFT up the pastor in prayer, who help **LIFT** his ministry load, and who join him in **LIFTING** up Christ in the community.

BIBLE READING—MATTHEW

26. Anointing—26:6-13. The act of Mary in anointing Your feet, Jesus, showed humility, sacrifice, and courage. I ask today that I will show humility in serving with my pastor and other church members, that I would reflect a spirit of sacrifice, and that I would be courageous in attempting great things in living for You and in bringing the unchurched to You.

My Journal
FOR THE WEEK

Praise reports, answered prayers, divine provisions, and spiritual plans.

_____

_____

_____

_____

_____

_____

_____

_____

_____

_____

BIBLE READING — MATTHEW

27. Carrying — 27:32-35. Simon was "compelled " to carry the cross of Christ (v. 32). Lord, may my pastor, church members, friends, and neighbors know me as a person who "willingly" carries the cross of Christ. May this be denoted in my full surrender, my service to others, and my spiritual maturity.

AN "I WILL" ATTITUDE TODAY

Situation-changing Savior, I will face challenges, conflict, and confusion in many areas of life today. I will respond to each one with a positive attitude. I will also recognize and respond to opportunities, possibilities, and open doors with an "I will" positive attitude.

I will not SIT DOWN. No! I will stand up boldly for truth, righteousness, and the mission of my church. To do this, mighty Master, I need supernatural strength, heavenly wisdom, and Bible-based discipline. I trust You to supply these needs.

I will not BREAK DOWN. No! There will be pressure to give in and to give up. There will be invitations to loosen up and free up standards and guiding principles. Father, I will accept and depend on Your oversight to stand up, to offer up praise, and to stand out with the shining armor of holy anointing.

I will BREAK THROUGH. Yes! In Your name, Father, under Your authority, and by Your mighty power, I will break through every barrier of spiritual lukewarmness and laziness. I will break through every barrier that hinders liberty in Christ and a life of faith and satisfying fulfillments.

BIBLE READING—MATTHEW

28. Worshipping—28:1-10, 18-20. Father, we praise You today because we worship a living Savior (v. 9). Let this be reflected in a happy, joyful, victorious attitude and lifestyle. May it also be reflected in our obedience to the Great Commission—baptizing, teaching, and making disciples.

ANOTHER WAY TODAY

Lord of daily directions, I know You have new and intriguing paths for me to follow. I am open to going another way today — new adventure, new attitude, and new allocations of energy. After the Wise Men presented gifts to Christ they returned home "another way" (Matthew 2:12), a different way. Guide me today to . . .

VIEW Differently. Father, anoint my eyes to see possibilities, not problems; to see growth opportunities, not limitations; and to see potential in church growth, not stagnation. I will open my eyes to view the beauty of today and your unlimited power to renew, restore, and reward faithfulness.

VALUE Differently. Sometimes my values get misdirected — a focus on getting instead of giving. Today, Master, raise up in me a giving spirit that springs from Your love, a desire to share Your love, and a commitment to live by the laws of Your love.

VOICE Differently. I will speak positive words today — words of encouragement, words of inspiration, and words of instructions. I will voice words of praise that denote freshness and zeal in walking with You, Lord.

BIBLE READING — MARK

1. Fishers — 1:16-20. When Christ called Peter, Andrew, James, and John, they left everything (routines and patterns of the old life) and immediately (positive action) followed Him to "become fishers of men" (v. 17). **Prayer Question:** In what ways can I more effectively join my pastor in being a "fisher of men"?

A RADIANT LIFE TODAY

Glowing Giver of gifts, You provide me with a radiant life — full, rich, and flowing with heavenly abundance. I'm thankful! I'm grateful! I'm honored! With heart-pounding appreciation, I . . .

RECEIVE Your gift of radiant life with thanksgiving. Every day, giving Father, my heart is filled, to overflowing with thanksgiving. I am thankful for the exciting walk of the Christian life and for the adventures of spiritual growth. I am thankful for the thrill of discovering divine truths and for the inspiration of tracing miracles recorded in Your Word.

RESPOND to the radiant life You give by sharing with others. Today, I will "show and share" the sparkling beauty of sins forgiven — Salvation, Security, Safety, and Sufficiency. I will radiate joy and contentment in my life today.

RESPECT Your gifts and guidelines for my life. Your gifts, Master, are precious and priceless. I will respect them, honor them, and protect them. I will enjoy them in my daily life in ways that reflect wholeness and wellness. I will also use my gifts as avenues to advance the nurturing and outreach ministries of my church.

BIBLE READING — MARK

2. Preach — 1:35-39. Christ got up early and went out to a solitary place to pray (v. 35). When the disciples found Him, He said to them, "Let us go . . . so I can preach . . . that is why I have come" (v. 38). **Prayer Question:** My pastor is commissioned to preach. He needs time and a solitary place to pray. How can I assist him?

A RENEWED SPIRIT TODAY

Father of beginning again, You never leave me sinking or stranded. Every day is a new day, a day to begin again, to be revived, to be renewed in spirit. The challenges before me today offers unique opportunities for self-expression and self-fulfillment. I will respond by . . .

Total SURRENDER. No secret sins! No hidden evil pursuits! No twisted worldly thinking! Lord, I will be totally surrendered and live a life of daily partnership with You, a life of purity, and a life of Kingdom-building productivity. Total surrender—I will!

A bold STANCE. No backwardness! No timid approach! No weak posture! Father, I will take a bold stance and be a witness of living a life that reflects conquering courage, creative ambition, and a Christ-exalting attitude in home life, work life, and social life. A bold stance—I will!

Spiritual STRETCHING. No sitting around! No happy-go-lucky disposition! No mediocre motivation! Master, I will stretch spiritually by cultivating a deeper devotional life, a greater comprehension of spiritual truths, and a broader awareness of how to share love with the wounded, the wayward, and the weary. Spiritual stretching—I will!

BIBLE READING—MARK

3. Creative—2:1-5. The church workers in Capernaum found a way to bring the paralytic to Christ (v. 4). They were focused and creative. **Prayer Question:** We must be creative in attracting and bringing people to church to receive healing and forgiveness (v. 5). How can I be an example and a leader in this?

ARMS OF SUPPORT TODAY

Uplifting and upholding Father, I am thankful for Your unfailing arms of support. As I go about my responsibilities, I know You will be present to provide and protect. Your arms in the Bible represent matchless grace and mighty power — miracle-working and mountain-moving power that will . . .

ENCIRCLE me. Father, the Enemy seeks to surround me and separate me from Your protection. Block his advances! Encircle me! Build a wall around me — a wall of wisdom to unite faith and works to stand boldly against the Enemy and defend the good news of protection and deliverance in Christ.

ENRICH me. Every day with You, Master, is an opportunity to excel, to open new doors that lead to self-improvement and closeness with You. I depend on You to encircle me and to enrich me. Let both of these work in me, through me, and around me for completeness in Christ.

EMPOWER me. I need Your power, Father! Power to achieve worthy goals. Power to be spiritually productive. Power to partner with my pastor in ministry. Power to stand, shine, and serve. I rejoice today in Your restoring and renewing power.

BIBLE READING — MARK

4. Relationships — 2:13-17. Christ mixed with sinners and formed relationship with them so He could lead them to repentance (v. 17). **Prayer Question:** How can I form relationships with unchurched neighbors, friends, and co-workers to influence them for Christ?

My Personal Pledge

TO REGULAR DAILY DEVOTIONS

I believe I draw close to God by meeting with Him through meditating on His Word, memorizing passages of Scripture, and expressing praise for His abundant grace, divine goodness, and life-enriching gifts. Therefore, I will cherish my daily appointment with my Lord!

I pledge to be loyal in safeguarding my time for daily devotion by . . .

1. **RESPECTING** the glorious opportunity to meet daily with my Master, Life-giver, and Guide.
2. **REMOVING** any barrier or activity that would hinder my faithfulness in studying and applying God's instructions.
3. **READING** my Bible with open ears, an open mind, and an open heart to hear God speak, impart wisdom, and inspire me to live victoriously.
4. **RENEWING** my commitment to grow daily in wisdom, knowledge, and understanding in performing God's ideal will.
5. **REMEMBERING** my strength comes from the Lord and by staying close to Him in my devotional life.

BIBLE READING — MARK

5. Divide — 3:20-25. Satan wants to divide the local church over issues and procedures, thereby reducing influence and outreach. **Prayer Question:** How can I work with my pastor and other church members in maintaining harmony and teamwork?

My Journal

FOR THE WEEK

Praise reports, answered prayers, divine provisions, and
spiritual plans.

_____

_____

_____

_____

_____

_____

_____

_____

_____

BIBLE READING — MARK

6. Together — 3:31-35. Doing the will of God as a body
of believers brings the church together as a family (v. 20).
Prayer Question: How can I work with brothers and sisters in the church in performing the will of God — loving
Him, loving my church, and loving my neighbor?

A SUCCESS JOURNEY TODAY

Shepherd of my soul, guide me today in experiencing an eye-opening success journey. Your Word reveals the way, provides strength for the journey, and keeps me in step with Your will. I will follow Your directions and depend on You for instructions, insights, and inspiration. I will . . .

DREAM big dreams that demonstrate Your supernatural power, Lord, and Your provisions for total life success. I will dream about maximizing my contribution to church growth. I will dream about developing my skills for personal success. I will dream about modeling the virtues of pure commitment to Christ.

DECLARE my allegiance to Christ, His Church, and to improving conditions in my community. I will take a positive stance against anything that damages or restricts religious freedom, the wholesome environment for children and youth, and assistance for those in need—food, housing, health, counseling, and security.

ACHIEVE possibilities and walk through the open doors that are set before me. I will be an achiever! I will accept challenges! I will embrace opportunities! I will be successful—spiritually, in family life, in my career, and in honoring You, Lord, in all I do.

BIBLE READING—MARK

7. **Sowing—4:1-20.** Sowing gospel seeds on "good ground" must be the top priority of the church (v. 20). **Prayer Question:** How can our church, with our pastor, come together and specialize in ministries that sow seeds on fertile ground?

AUTHENTIC WORSHIP TODAY

Lord of heaven and earth, You deserve worship that is holy, honorable, and that flows from a heart of commitment. I will foster authentic worship in my life that reveals my devotion to You — worship that is . . .

WORD-Centered. Father, You set forth in Holy Scripture how I am to worship You — sincerely, in spirit, and in truth. I will study how Your people worshiped You in both the Old Testament and the New Testament and will establish patterns that You honored and approved. My worship will be guided by Your Word!

WISDOM-Centered. You grant wisdom to know how to come into Your presence to offer praise and thanksgiving. Master, issue me wisdom — understanding, awareness, reverent protocol — to engage in authentic worship that is honorable and acceptable unto You. My worship today will be Word-centered and wisdom-centered!

WHOLE-Life-Centered. I understand, Master, that worship is not just for Sunday or church services. You call for whole-life, everyday worship. In everything I do — duties, planning, and relationships — I will look to You, ask You for guidance, and will honor You with words and biblical works. My worship today will be Word-centered, wisdom-centered, and whole-life-centered!

BIBLE READING — MARK

8. Storms — 4:35-41. Storms in life, personal and spiritual, will arise (v. 37). **Prayer Question:** How can I, and my church, recognize that Christ is always present and that we need not fear or fight these storms alone, but steadfastly look to Him?

AWARENESS TODAY

Father of all wisdom and grace, You know what I will face today. I will be aware of Your presence to give me wisdom to seize opportunities and grace to face opposition. Satan will come against me and attempt to obstruct my view of Your presence. Make me aware of the . . .

TRAPS of Satan. Father, as I walk with You, Satan will set traps to hinder my progress — ruts of compromise, misleading directional signs, and energy-draining obstacles. Guide me! I will stay close to You and keep my eyes focused on my Christian duties and my heavenly destination.

TESTS of Satan. My faith and trust in Christ will be tested in many ways — misunderstanding between church members, doctrinal questions, and unanswered prayers. Empower me! I will stand on the promises of Your Word, Father, that assure me of wisdom to understand and power to stand with confidence.

TEMPTATIONS of Satan. I will encounter temptations today — to take dedication shortcuts, to engage in spiritually weakening practices, and to bypass consistent time in prayer. Counsel me! Lord, I will put on Your full armor and overcome the advances of Satan.

BIBLE READING — MARK

9. Witness — 5:1-19. The cured and converted man of Gadara wanted to leave the people who knew him and travel with Christ (v. 18). **Prayer Question:** Christ told the delivered, demon-possessed man to "stay home and witness and work for Him" (v. 19). How can I witness and work among people who really know me instead of just marching in victory parades?

A WATCHMAN TODAY

Giver of grace and glory, You stand watch over me to guide me into all truth, to lead me around the traps of Satan, to fortify me against deceiving temptations. I'm fully protected! In response to Your watchful care, I will be a watchman to . . .

WARN of WICKEDNESS. I will be a watchman today and warn of the evil intentions of the adversary, Satan. He seeks to deceive, destroy integrity, and divert attention from God's plan of wholeness in Christ. I will warn faithfully today!

WORK to WIN. I will be a winner today by experiencing a positive faith in the love and power of my Savior, Jesus Christ. He will equip me with the skills to win, the strength to endure, and the standards to uphold. I will work with faith and fortitude today!

WITNESS for WHOLENESS. I will be a witness today to signify wholeness and completeness in Christ. I ask for discipline to display the characteristics of Christ in my pursuits and practices. I will witness of transforming and keeping grace today!

BIBLE READING—MARK

10. Courage—5:25-34. It took great courage for the woman with the flow of blood to press through the crowd and touch the garment of Jesus (v. 27). **Prayer Question:** In what ways can I mix great courage and faith to touch Christ for miracles in my church?

A WITNESS TODAY

All-seeing Advocate, I praise You for upholding me and molding me into a person who can represent You with purity and dignity. I am a witness of Your wonder-working might—transformed, empowered, and commissioned. Today, I want to represent You as a witness—a walking witness, a Word witness, and a winning witness.

A WALKING witness. Father, I desire that my daily walk with You will be a witness of my conformity to Your will and Your control of my life. Infuse me with divine energy to walk worthy of Your calling and to demonstrate heaven-bound characteristics.

A WORD witness. Today, Lord, I will speak with authority about Your nature of love, acceptance, and forgiveness. I will share the good news! I will witness of my personal relationship with You. I will share Your plan of salvation and new life in Christ.

A WINNING witness. Father, Your Son, Jesus Christ, triumphed over death, hell, and the grave. He was, and is, a winner! In Christ, You have placed a winning spirit in me—a spirit of adoration, advancement, and achievement. Today, I will walk worthily of this winning spirit and will honor You with a lifestyle of Christ-exalting witnessing.

BIBLE READING—MARK

11. Honor—6:1-4. The people of Nazareth, the hometown of Jesus, were offended by His teaching and authority (v. 3). Christ said, "A prophet [pastor] doesn't have honor among his people" (v. 4). **Prayer Question:** How can I honor my pastor and increase respect and support for him among church members?

PERSONAL AFFIRMATION —

WORKERS

The Scriptures state that "workers are few" (Matthew 9:37). My first responsibility is to be a worker. My second responsibility is to help recruit and support workers.

I Will . . .

- Pledge to be a willing worker.

- Respect the contribution of church workers.

- Assist in recruiting members for ministry.

- Stand with individuals called to be missionaries.

- Support programs to train workers.

- Continually increase skills for impact.

- Honor workers for life-changing performance.

BIBLE READING — MARK

12. Food — 6:34-44. The people followed Christ and listened to His teaching without thought of food (v. 33). Christ said to the disciples, "You give them something to eat" (v. 37). **Prayer Question:** How can I give spiritual food to the hungry with my pastor under the direction of Jesus Christ?

My Journal

FOR THE WEEK

Praise reports, answered prayers, divine provisions, and spiritual plans.

BIBLE READING — MARK

13. Tradition — 7:1-9. The religious leaders asked Christ why His disciples did not follow the tradition of the elders (v. 5). Christ said, "You reject the commandment of God, that you may keep your tradition" (v. 9). **Prayer Question:** Father, how can I recognize traditions dealing with form, procedures, and observances in my church and in the lives of believers that obstruct communion with You and the performance of Your ideal will? Free me, and my church, from any tradition or worship habit that is not scriptural and that does not exalt Jesus Christ.

A YIELDED SPIRIT TODAY

Great and awesome God, You have plans for my life — noble, fantastic, beyond-imagination plans. I have a responsibility to respond to Your plans by showing a yielded, receptive spirit. I will respond to Your leadership.

I will submit and CONFESS. Father, I confess my dependence on You to walk worthy of Your companionship. I confess my dependence on You for strength to stand up, stand out, and stand against the continual assaults of Satan. *Accept my confession!*

I will embrace Your COVENANTS. Lord, Your covenants cover all my pursuits and practices. Your covenant of grace is my salvation. Your covenant of Your presence is my security. Your covenant of hearing my prayers is my serenity. Your oversight is my shelter. You have blessed me with Your covenants. *Accept my gratefulness!*

I will follow Your COMMANDMENTS. Your commands, Master, do not restrict me; they do not confine me; they do not limit me; they **ignite me!** They do not rebuff me; they **refresh me!** Your commandments keep me in check and on the right road. They **shape me** and share glory, grace, and grit with me. *Accept my loyal commitment!*

BIBLE READING — MARK

14. Unusal — 7:24-30. In unusual circumstances and among unrecognized people groups, God honors humility and faith and gives blessings and deliverance (vv. 27-30). **Prayer Question:** Lord, we often overlook some people because we have been isolated from them as a result of faith and finances. How can I be more sensitive to these people and touch them with Your heart?

BEAR FRUIT TODAY

Lord of endless love, You supply daily oversight to keep me on the path of productivity. Walking with You enables me to learn, to grow, and to be a faithful, fruit-bearing member of Your family. Send spiritual sunshine on my life, so I can bear fruit that honors You in my . . .

CONDUCT. Father, I desire that my attitude, actions, and activities attest to my commitment to honor You in all I do. I ask You to "let the words of my mouth and the meditation of my heart be acceptable in Your sight" (Psalm 19:14). You are my strength and my redeemer!

COMPASSION. I also desire that my spirit of concern for the welfare of others will reflect my daily walk with You, Father—empathizing, encouraging, and assisting. To do this, I need compassion that is visible and active. You are my strength and my redeemer!

CONNECTIVITY. First, Lord of glory, I must be connected with You through prayer. Then, I can be connected with my church and my community by bearing fruit. You are my strength and my Redeemer!

BIBLE READING—MARK

15. Clear Vision—8:22-26. Christ often used strange and unorthodox methods to "open eyes" and to "clear vision" (vv. 23-25). We can become restricted in our vision for wholeness and wellness in the church. **Prayer Question:** How can our church, both leaders and members, become more open to out-of-the-box revelations and acts from You?

BLESS THE CHILDREN OF MY CHURCH TODAY

Lord of glory, children are a beautiful part of Your family. You have a special love for them and a plan to guide them in becoming mature followers of Christ. Empower my church to embrace Your plan and provide . . .

LOVING Environment. Children need to know they are loved by the actions of the church: a loving, caring environment; teaching that entertains and educates; expressions that build self-esteem; and oversight that shows they are special to You, Father, and to the local church.

LEARNING Experiences. Father, my church has an enormous responsibility to provide biblical and life-related learning experiences for our children. May we all respond to this challenge with delight and devotion—members, teachers, workers, leaders. Give us a vision of our children growing in Christlikeness.

LIFE-SUPPORTING Models. Models are valuable to children to assist in developing life-shaping values. I want to be a model! I want to invest in the lives of children! I will strive to do this by backing the children's ministry of my church, by expressing appreciation to workers, and by personal touches of care and love.

BIBLE READING—MARK

16. Influence—8:27-29. We cannot permit the thinking and attitudes of others to influence our solid stance for Christ (v. 29). **Prayer Question:** How can our church be bolder in proclaiming the identity, nature, and character of Jesus Christ—Messiah, Savior, Lord, and Master?

BLESS THE LEADERS OF MY CHURCH TODAY

Guiding Father, You have placed leaders in my church to direct me and support me in following You, trusting You, and representing You by my lifestyle of liberty and loving service. Bless my church leaders.

ANOINT Them. Father, anoint my church leaders to perform with Your authority and with the power of the Holy Spirit. Let Your gifts operate in their ministry to raise up mature disciples and for the outreach impact of the church. Give them connecting favor, clear vision, and bold courage.

ANCHOR Them. There will be difficulties and differences of opinion. Satan will seek to divide loyalty and set up roadblocks to stymie spiritual renewal and aggressive plans. Father, anchor my church leaders with supportive wisdom from Your Word. Give them partnership favor to create harmony, teamwork, and endurance.

ADVANCE Them. Giving Master, You do not withhold honor and gifts from leaders who follow Your plan and fulfill Your will. Advance my church leaders with congregational support and vision. Give them appreciation favor with respect, tributes of honor, and expressions of thanksgiving.

BIBLE READING — MARK

17. Revelation — 9:2-7. Peter, James, and John had a "mountain-top" experience with Christ (v. 2). **Prayer Question:** Mighty heavenly Father, it is Your will to reveal Your Son to us in mighty unusual ways. How do You want us to prepare to receive Your glorious revelations?

BLESS THE MEN OF MY CHURCH TODAY

Many men in the Bible are set forth as models of commitment and courage—defending the faith, developing people in the faith, and sharing the fruit of faith. Bless the men of my church to follow their example and be . . .

MIGHTY Men—defending the faith. Lord, You have commissioned men to be leaders at home and in the church. May they accept the role of being mighty men leading under Your supervision with scriptural authority and compassionate care.

MOTIVATED Men—leading with vision. Father, endow the men of my church with awareness of spiritual resources and to accept leadership responsibilities. May they cultivate the characteristics of mighty men in the Bible—being steadfast in faith, yielding to spiritual authority, and being aggressive in pursuing Christ-centered goals.

MESSAGE-BEARING Men—proclaiming the good news. The good news is salvation in Christ, security in Christ, and stability in Christ. May the men of my church be leaders, examples, and promoters of sharing the good news through witnessing, worshiping, and supporting the ministries of the church.

BIBLE READING—MARK

18. Encounters—9:16-27. The disciples of Christ faced many head-on encounters with the devil (v. 18). But Christ said to them, "If you can believe, all things are possible to him who believes" (v. 23). **Prayer Question:** Lord, I believe! How can I combine belief, faith, works, and trust together to overcome the tricks and traps of the Evil One?

PRAYER PATTERN — Revival

R – RELEASE, Lord, an awakening flow of Your quickening power in our church.

E – ENLIVEN us with a new vision of Your splendor and matchless majesty.

V – VISUALIZE: Let us join our pastor in visualizing a churchwide, citywide revival.

I – INCREASE our desire and fervency to be instruments for revival.

V – VALUE liberty in You, and let us be a channel for Your love to others.

A – ANSWER by fire, Father; send the refining and restoring impact of revival.

L – LOVE: We love You; we **LOVE** our pastor; and we **LOVE** the lost people in our community.

BIBLE READING — MARK

19. Children — 10:13-16. Children are a gift from the Lord and a vital part of His kingdom (v. 14). **Prayer Question:** How can our church give special attention to our children in raising them in Your ways? Also, give us an extra portion of love to embrace the children of the neighborhood and inner city.

My Journal

FOR THE WEEK

Praise reports, answered prayers, divine provisions, and spiritual plans.

_____

_____

_____

_____

_____

_____

_____

_____

_____

BIBLE READING — MARK

20. Slave — 10:35-45. Jesus Christ came to serve, not to be served (v. 45). He is our model. **Prayer Question**: Lord, what does it mean to "be slave of all"? I want to serve; I want to have the right attitude toward other church members and my pastor regarding ministry support and involvement. Teach me; train me!

BLESS THE WOMEN OF MY CHURCH TODAY

Father, You chose women in the Bible to set an example for women in the church today—leading for just causes, raising children to be spiritual champions, and serving in ministries that transform lives. Bless the women of my church to follow their example and be . . .

GODLY Women—setting an example of love and faith. Lord, You have given women a unique disposition of love, faith, and caring. Bless them as they influence and shape the lives of individuals in the home, the church, and the community by their godly characteristics and care.

GRACIOUS Women—showing a generous spirit of support. Father, thank You for the gracious spirit of women—tenderness in guiding, kindness in relationships, and thoroughness in showing understanding and care.

GIVING Women—sharing special talents and skills. Master, You have given women unique talents of serving—giving time to train, giving time to mend and heal, giving time to mold character, and giving time to shape values. I ask You to bless the women of my church with heavenly gifts as they tutor the young and serve the church.

BIBLE READING—MARK

21. Sidetracked—11:15-19. The local church is to do the business of the church—worship and work with God—and not be sidetracked by practices or activities that distract from this mission (v. 17). **Prayer Question:** How can we weed out those things in our church that divert attention from our main mission?

BLESS THE YOUTH OF MY CHURCH TODAY

In Your plans, Master Designer, youth occupy a place of prominence because they represent the future lifeline of the church — vision of the resources of heaven, values that stabilize, and vitality that attracts and impacts. Bless them with . . .

EXPERIENCES that Mold Character. Direct my church, guiding Father, in providing experiences for young people that develop strong faith, sterling character, contagious zeal, and an understanding of their role in the mission of the church.

EXPRESSIONS of Affirmation. Lead me and the members of my church, loving Father, to affirm the value of our youth, to express confidence in their ability, and to surround them with support — prayer for guidance, encouragement, opportunities to accept responsibility, and praise for achievements.

EXAMPLE-SETTING Leaders. Anoint the leaders of my church, equipping Father, to be examples and models for young people — carrying the cross of Christ, confessing Christ as Lord of their lives, conveying commitment through works of righteousness, and displaying the caring, loving, and protective characteristics of Christ.

BIBLE READING — MARK

22. Fruitful — 11:20-24. Christ desires that we be fruitful and release our faith to see, believe, and receive (v. 24). **Prayer Question:** What can I do, Lord, to look at my mountains (obstacles and opposition), trust You "without doubt," and say, "Be removed and be cast into the sea"? (v. 23).

BLESSED TODAY

Father of faith and spiritual fruit, I am richly and abundantly blessed, having closeness with You, companionship with Christ, and the comfort of the Holy Spirit. I am under Your favor. I am blessed to . . .

Bear FRUIT. Father, You have blessed me to bear fruit—graciousness, goodness, and gentleness. This fruit identifies me as a true follower of Christ and a true servant manifesting the characteristics of Christ. Today, I will inspect my fruit, protect my fruit, and share my fruit!

Lift the FALLEN. Father, I realize there are people around me who have experienced major falls in life—broken promises, disgraceful relationships, unlawful dreams, and disrespectful encounters. They are looking for restoration and to be reconnected with love, hope, and peace. Today, I will lift up the fallen with the love of Christ, with hope from Christ, and the peace that exceeds understanding found in Christ!

Live on a sure FOUNDATION. I'm blessed, Master, to live on a sure foundation—Your unchanging Word, the unchanging love of Christ, and the unchanging leadership of the Holy Spirit. Today, I will live on a sure foundation, bear fruit, and lift up the fallen!

BIBLE READING—MARK

23. Impact—12:13-17. The church can make a strong impact in the community by embracing political leaders and social projects that foster integrity, goodwill, moral standards, and assistance for the poor, hungry, and needy (v. 17). **Prayer Question:** How can our church "render to Caesar the things that are Caesar's" and in the process, exalt You and expand the ministry of the church?

BLESSINGS OF HEAVEN TODAY

Father of bountiful blessings, every day You overflow my life with blessings—big, beautiful, abundant blessings. You have also reserved blessings for me in heaven that are eternal. These blessings focus on You as . . .

My SAVIOR—Your presence. I will be in the presence of my Savior, Jesus Christ—everlasting joy, celebration, rejoicing. Father, in heaven there will be no pain, problems, distressing pressure. I praise You, Father, for the assurance of heaven!

My SECURITY—Your provisions. I will be totally secure by Your provisions—spiritual food, heavenly sunshine, Trinity interaction. There will be no limitations in fellowship with the saints of all ages and in singing songs of redemption. I will be surrounded by beauty beyond description. I honor You, Father, for the riches of heaven!

My SERENITY—Your pledge. I will have everlasting serenity—peace forevermore, praise that is pure, and majestic gifts. Your pledge of serenity, Father, is sacred and cannot be broken. I worship You, Father, for the rewards of heaven!

BIBLE READING—MARK

24. Neighbor—12:28-31. Father, I do love You with all my heart, mind, and strength (v. 30). But I cannot say fully that I love my neighbor as myself (v. 31). **Prayer Question:** In my lifestyle and church work, how can I develop a love for my neighbor? I need Your help . . . guidance . . . wisdom.

BOLDNESS TODAY

Master of might and glory, You grant boldness to be a convincing witness of Your authority and Your promises (Acts 4:31). Today, according to Your Word, I will . . .

SPEAK with Boldness. Father I will not be reluctant or backward in speaking about eternal truths or the transformation that has taken place in my life. You have endowed me with boldness to speak about and to practice gospel truths in love.

SHOW Boldness. I will not stand still or stand back in showing my commitment to Christ or demonstrating my convictions about the Christian life. Lord, I will stand on Your Word, receive authority from Your Word, and show boldness in relaying the liberating message of Your Word.

SERVE with Boldness. Father, serving with You and for You is an honor and a privilege. I will serve with vision and vitality—with boldness that nets spiritual victory. Today, I will speak, show, and serve with heaven-sent, Kingdom-building boldness.

BIBLE READING—MARK

25. Signs—13:32-37. Jesus explained the signs of the times in this chapter. He told us to "take heed, watch and pray" (v. 33). **Prayer Question:** Father, only You know the time of the end (v. 32). How can my church and my pastor strive for excellence in ministry and at the same time be ready and alert for the return of Your Son?

A PASTOR'S DREAM

To see church members . . .

- Developing in Christian maturity.

- Demonstrating God's love to others.

- Displaying the fruit of the Spirit.

- Dancing in their heart in worship.

- Dealing fairly in business practices.

- Declaring God's truths in personal testimony.

- Dedicating time to outreach ministries.

- Deferring one to another in sincere love.

- Defusing conflict in the church.

- Delighting in the ways of the Lord.

BIBLE READING — MARK

26. Fragrance — 14:1-9. Mary poured costly oil of spikenard on the head of Christ (v. 3). A sweet fragrance filled the room. Christ said, "She [Mary] has done a beautiful thing to me" (v. 6 NIV). **Prayer Question:** Father, the purpose of the church is to do "beautiful things for You." How can I be a partner with my pastor and other members in filling the environment with a sweet fragrance that denotes love, sacrifice, and service?

My Journal

FOR THE WEEK

Praise reports, answered prayers, divine provisions, and spiritual plans.

_____

_____

_____

_____

_____

_____

_____

_____

_____

BIBLE READING — MARK

27. Compelled — 15:21-26. Simon from Cyrene was "compelled" or "forced" to carry the cross of Christ (v. 21). **Prayer Question:** How can our church show the community and the unchurched that we willingly carry the cross of Christ, because it is a symbol of new life, love, and liberty?

BOUNDLESS BLESSINGS TODAY

Everlasting Lord of boundless blessings, I abide under Your watchful care. I am guided by Your unmatched wisdom. I'm blessed, blessed, blessed! I feel safe and secure, and satisfied. I am blessed, blessed, blessed by . . .

The BEATITUDES. I am blessed by the "blessed-are" virtues, outlined in Luke 6:20-22, that offer a pattern for pleasing You, Father, and for a positive and productive daily walk with You. I will purpose to be "pure in heart" and to be a "peacemaker." **I am blessed.**

Your BOUNTIFULNESS. God of glory, You give, and give, and give—bountifully, lovingly, and generously. When I am in need, You are there! Whatever I need, You supply! Wherever I am, You are there! Whatever I face, You are there to defend, to deliver, to develop. **I'm blessed!**

The BEAUTY of Peace. Peace comes from You, Father, Your **PEACE** gives — Purpose, Energy, Affirmation, Courage, Endearment. I'm blessed! Today, I will pass the peace by emphasizing strength of community, opportunities for growth, and loyalty to Your Church. **I'm blessed — super blessed!**

BIBLE READING — MARK

28. Confirm — 16:19-20. Following the resurrection and ascension of Christ, the disciples "preached everywhere, the Lord working with them , and confirming the word with signs (miracles)" (v. 20 KJV). **Prayer Question:** Lord of the Resurrection, how can our church follow the pattern of the disciples and depend on You to confirm Your Word with miracles? We are available for Your guidance and enablement.

BREAD TODAY

"Bread of heaven, feed me till I want no more." That's my request! Bread from heaven gives me nourishment for today—aliveness, energy, stamina. Father, I receive Your bread with eagerness and excitement, it is . . .

Baked Fresh—ENLIGHTMENT. Every day I receive enlightenment from You—understanding the tactics of Satan, techniques on how to face temptation, and how to live triumphantly. Fresh bread from You, Father, will build a healthy and strong spiritual body. *I will receive, learn, and grow today!*

Baked to Perfection—ENCIRCLEMENT. Every day I feel Your surrounding strength—a wall of protection, will-power to stand strong, and wisdom to act wisely. Baked-to-perfection bread from You, Master Baker, will fortify my faith and fill me with resisting energy. *I will develop, dedicate, and grow today!*

Baked for Me—ENRICHMENT. Every day I receive special favors from You—faith-building experiences, the impact of the fruit of the Spirit, and guiding fullness through prayer. Bread baked for me, all-knowing Father, will meet my personal need for acceptance and affirmation. *I will receive, rejoice, and grow today.*

BIBLE READING—LUKE

1. Acceptance—1:38. "Mary responded, 'I am the Lord's servant, and I am willing to accept whatever He wants. May everything you have said come true'" (NLT). **Prayer Application:** Lord, Your will contains miracles, spiritual motivation, and mighty revelations. As a team, our pastor and the congregation, let us accept Your specific plans for our church, trust You, and work with You for the total fulfillment of the plans.

BUILDING TODAY

Energy-giving Master, You provide strength to stand on a solid foundation and build a life of stability, durability, and availability for ministry. I will look to You to be a trustworthy builder—mentally alert, physically responsive, and spiritually devoted. I will enlist and build through . . .

FAITH Connections. Father, my vision is to be connected with people of faith, policies founded on faith, and programs propelled by faith. Active faith, Scriptural faith, builds a structure for my vision to become a reality. Guide me to see, grow, and stay connected to these principles.

FRIENDSHIP Trust. My trust is in You, Father, and I will employ this trust to build friendships in my church, in my community, and in my social contacts. I will honor these friendships by being sensitive to personality differences, personal challenges, and understanding the potential for productive outreach ministry.

FOUNDATIONAL Values. I will build my life, my influence, and my future on foundational values—biblical values, integrity values, and faith values. I praise You, Master, for the privilege to build under Your divine direction.

BIBLE READING—LUKE

2. Business—2:49. "And He said to them, 'Why is it that you sought Me? Did you not know that I must be about My Father's business?'" **Prayer Application:** Father, Your Son set the example early in His ministry to be engaged in Your business¬—reaching, teaching, mending, sending. May our church be known as an alive church, conforming to the pattern set by Christ.

BUILD A FIRM FOUNDATION TODAY

Father, scriptural, Savior-based, and salvation-assurance qualities constitute a firm foundation on which to build my life—a life that honors You. Thank You for energy, skills, and equipment to build on this foundation.

SCRIPTURAL—*Instructional Manual*. Father, I will build my life and ministry in my church according to the instructions outlined in the Bible. Holy scriptures provide a framework for building creatively, impressively, and honorably.

SAVIOR-BASED—*Standard for Construction*. The completed work of Christ—death, burial, resurrection, and ascension—is the message, motivation, and standard for building. All construction must be Savior-based. Master, I will build my life under your supervision on the righteousness and lordship of Jesus Christ.

SALVATION ASSURANCE—*Guaranteed Performance*. Father, I am grateful, indebted, and overwhelmed at the magnitude of Your mercy, grace, and love. You give me the assurance of Your nearness that births unity in fellowship, understanding in mission, and unflinching courage to stand strong on a firm foundation.

BIBLE READING—LUKE

3. Word of God—3:2. "During the high priesthood of Annas and Caiaphas, the Word of God came to John, son of Zechariah, in the desert" (NIV). **Prayer Application:** God, You speak, whatever the circumstances or location, to lead Your people. Let our church recognize this. Let Your Word come to our pastor so he can preach, baptize, and focus attention on Christ the Lamb of God who takes away the sin of the world!

CHANGE AGENT TODAY

Father of dynamic change, You change problems into possibilities, change perplexities into performance power, and change pitfalls into pathways. You have changed me and transformed my nature and my position in Your presence. I want to represent You by being a change agent through . . .

ENCOURAGEMENT. Lord of change, You have changed my thinking! My thinking is positive, uplifting, and edifying. This equips me to be an encourager; a change agent that encourages friends and church members to look up and see Your gifts on the way and to look around and see opportunities to achieve, grow, and learn.

ENRICHMENT. I want to enrich the lives of others by sharing scriptural guidance, personal growth experiences, and new pathways of productivity and prosperity. I can do this by the enriching anointing of Your Spirit, Father.

ENLIGHTMENT. Father, Your Word strengthens, stabilizes, and secures. Your Word enlightens, inspires, and instructs. Lead me as I read, study, and apply Your Word to every aspect of my life. Also, direct me in sharing the enlightening and delivering message of Your Word with others. By Your wisdom and witness in my life, I will be a change agent!

BIBLE READING — LUKE

4. Filled — 4:1. "Then Jesus, being filled with the Holy Spirit, returned from the Jordan and was led by the Spirit into the wilderness." **Prayer Application:** Sometimes, Lord, my pastor has to go into the "wilderness" areas of ministry. Fill him, cover him, and lead him by Your Spirit. Use Your Word and my support to overcome every temptation or trial he may encounter.

My Pledge of Loyalty

SOUND SCRIPTURAL BEHAVIOR

I am fully convinced that my conduct is a picture of my commitment to Jesus Christ and displays my values of serving my church, my community, and my country. Therefore, I will center on being consistent in my conduct!

I pledge to develop and demonstrate sound scriptural behavior by . . .

1. **SEARCHING** the scriptures to establish a firm base to guide my daily behavior.
2. **SECURING** scriptural behavior by depending on the supervision and empowerment of the Holy Spirit.
3. **SHOWING** my faith and conveying holy standards by my consistent behavior.
4. **SELECTING** Bible verses to memorize and to utilize in facing both opposition and opportunities.
5. **STANDING** firmly on scriptures to guide my behavior in all facets of life — worship, relationships, work-related aspirations, and Kingdom outreach.

BIBLE READING — LUKE

5. Deep — 5:4. "He [Christ] said to Simon, 'Launch out into the deep, and let down your nets for a catch.'" **Prayer Application:** Blessed Lord, Your instructions only require obedience; You do the rest. Let me, with my pastor and the people of our church, follow the path of obedience in claiming Your promises, in promoting church ministries, and in participating in "deep-water" outreach events.

My Journal

FOR THE WEEK

Praise reports, answered prayers, divine provisions, and spiritual plans.

_____

_____

_____

_____

_____

_____

_____

_____

_____

_____

BIBLE READING — LUKE

6. Sabbath — 6:9. "Then Jesus addressed them, 'Let me ask you something: What kind of action suits the Sabbath best? Doing good or doing evil? Helping people or leaving them helpless?'" (MSG). **Prayer Application:** Guide my pastor and church in making Sunday a day of "doing good" and "helping people," not a time of self-centered activities, ritualism, and leaving harvest fields unattended.

CHRISTIAN WALK TODAY

All-seeing, vision-casting Master, it is in Your divine plan that all Your family members go forward in life — achieving goals and growing in Christlikeness. I am a member of Your family and I want Your plan to unfold daily in my life through . . .

TRUST — personal reliability. Lord of every situation, I trust Your judgment implicitly. You are just, righteous, and reliable in all Your practices and precepts. May Your example guide and guard my life. May I be known as a trustworthy and reliable follower of Christ.

TESTIMONY — authentic witness. I want to be straightforward in my Christian testimony, but warmly sincere. Father, give me a compassionate, caring, and understanding attitude and let it be evident in my approach and in the manner I communicate eternal truths.

TEMPERAMENT — natural disposition. Every day I want to be smooth, relaxed, and natural in my Christian walk, in my expressions of trust, and in the manner I treat my family, friends, and neighbors. This foundation will propel me forward to grip possibilities and to be successful.

BIBLE READING — LUKE

7. Great Faith — 7:9. "When Jesus heard these things, He marveled and turned around, and said to the crowd that followed Him, 'I say to you, I have not found such great faith, not even in Israel!'" **Prayer Application:** Father, "say the word" (v. 7) and our church will receive it for the healing of our minds, bodies, and emotions so we can minister to our community with wholeness, authority, and a glowing testimony.

CHURCH ATTENDANCE TODAY

Father, through Your Son, Jesus Christ, you build the Church. According to Your Word, "the gates of hell shall not prevail against it" (Matthew 16:18 KJV). I have a responsibility to attend church, to support the ministries of the church, and to stand against those who hinder church loyalty and attendance by . . .

ACCOMMODATING attendance contentment. Father, all church members are under orders to "redeem the time," "recruit the unchurched," and "restore the fallen." Some believers, however, are content without fulfilling Your orders. I will pray for them and challenge them to embrace Your plan for the mission of the church.

ACCEPTING the ordinary. Master, everything about You, and the manner in which You relate to Your people, is extraordinary. We can never settle for the ordinary, the usual, and the expected. I will be an example and serve as a motivator to expect the unexpected in serving You.

AVOIDING the cost of advancement. Lord, there is a price to be paid for being loyal to the local church—pure-heart worship, expressed confidence in the pastor, and active partnership in ministry with the people. Some members try to avoid paying the price. I will teach, train, and model the qualities of willingness to accept the cost of advancement.

BIBLE READING—LUKE

8. Good Ground—8:8. "But others fell on good ground, sprang up, and yielded a crop a hundredfold. When he had said these things, He cried, 'He who has ears to hear, let him hear.'" **Prayer Application:** Lord, give my pastor a voice to preach Your Word so it will fall on "good ground." Let our church be approved by the Holy Spirit to sponsor ministries that will produce a hundredfold.

CHURCH LOYALTY TODAY

Mighty Master, in Your divine understanding of the crucial needs of believers, You established the Church. The local church is a place of worship, a place to grow in Christlikeness, and a place to prepare for spiritual warfare. In support of the mission of the church, I will pray for, and show . . .

LOVE toward my pastor. My pastor has been called, commissioned, and anointed by You, Father. He is Your messenger, my shepherd, and the leader of the congregation in fulfilling the Great Commission and in making disciples. Father, I ask You to lead me in showing loyalty to my pastor by praying for him, practicing total stewardship, and being involved in the ministries of the church.

LONGSUFFERING toward the lukewarm. Many individuals who attend my church are not involved and seem to be unconcerned about spiritual maturity. I want to be a mentor to them, to motivate them to a new level of experiences and riches in Christ.

LIBERTY toward the unchurched. Father, I will be loyal in supporting the ministries of my church in reaching the unchurched. I will prepare, pray, and participate in outreach activities. I will also demonstrate the joy and benefits of liberty in Christ in my daily lifestyle and relationships.

BIBLE READING — LUKE

9. Groups — 9:14. "For there were about five thousand men. And He said to His disciples, 'Make them sit down in groups of fifty.'" **Prayer Application:** Father of order, miracles are a result of Your divine power, but help our church not be afraid to organize to prepare for them and to maximize the results (v. 17).

CHURCH SUPPORT TODAY

The Church was divinely established on an unmovable foundation, "the gates of Hades shall not prevail against it" (Matthew 16:18). Father, the Church was set in order according to Your plan for fulfilling the Great Commission and guiding believers in maturity and ministry. I will support the purpose of the Church by . . .

INFLUENCING church members. First, Father, I will influence members by my example — consistency in church attendance, commitment, and worship. Second, I will influence members by my consistency in vision, vitality, and action. I will support my influence goals by consistency in prayer, trust, and obedience.

INVITING friends to attend church. First, Lord, I have the privilege and the responsibility to invite friends and neighbors to attend church with me. Second, this privilege is a way of supporting my church — building relationships, sharing faith, showing love, advancing the mission of the church, and serving in love.

INTERCEDING to reach the unchurched. First, I will support my church by praying for effective outreach. Second, I will unite with other church members in praying for the evangelism passion of my pastor, church leaders, and ministry volunteers. I will intercede for outreach impact!

BIBLE READING — LUKE

10. Harvest — 10:2. "Then He said to them, 'The harvest truly is great, but the laborers are few; therefore, pray the Lord of the harvest to send out laborers into His harvest.'" **Prayer Application:** Lord, it is Your harvest; You want Your people to reap it. Grip our church with a sense of "time urgency." Let each of us volunteer for service, and let us recruit and train other volunteers.

CLIMBING MOUNTAINS TODAY

Mountain-moving Master, I do not ask You to move mountains for me; I do ask You for faith and fortitude to climb them. Mountains will loom in the path I walk. I will climb the mountains of . . .

Suppressed AMBITION. Father, You have placed desires in my heart to be unique in following You. Many of these ambitions have been suppressed as a result of difficulties and lack of dedication. Revive my determination. Restore my ambition to excel! Reinvigorate my vision!

Suspended ADVANCEMENT. Contentment has placed me in a hold position. Often I back away from climbing challenging mountains. Father, stir new interest in me to climb and to see what is in store for me in reaching mountain peaks.

Suspect ATTITUDE. Lord, I do not want to suspect the intentions of others by judging, evaluating, or doubting. I want to think the best, offer my best support, and look for the best. Give me insightful wisdom today to do this.

BIBLE READING—LUKE

11. Hear the Word—11:28. "But He said, 'More than that, blessed are those who hear the Word of God and keep it.'" **Prayer Application:** You give out messages from Your Word for us. Help me, help our congregation, to be yielded and receptive to receive Your Word, and then disciplined, determined, and consistent to "keep it."

Affirmation of Vision
FOR CHURCH GROWTH

God has given our church a vision through the Great Commission for aggressive growth—reaching, teaching, baptizing, discipling, and sending out.

THEREFORE, we will make church growth . . .

- A central priority in mission focus.
- A guiding priority in strategic planning.
- A passionate priority in prevailing prayer.
- A transforming priority in harvest thinking.
- A demanding priority in developing leaders.
- A rewarding priority in outreach adventure.
- A God-honoring priority in vision obedience.
- A reality priority in attendance increases.

"The whole city was favorable to them, and each day God added to them all who were being saved" (Acts 2:47 TLB).

BIBLE READING—LUKE

12. Kingdom—12:31. "But seek the kingdom of God, and all these things (food, clothing, prosperity, growth) shall be added to you." **Prayer Application:** Lord, we seek Your total Lordship—Your will, work, and ways (Your kingdom), in every worship service, in every activity of our church, and in our personal lives. This is Your pattern and the path to "all the other things" we might need.

My Journal

FOR THE WEEK

Praise reports, answered prayers, divine provisions, and spiritual plans.

_____

_____

_____

_____

_____

_____

_____

_____

_____

_____

BIBLE READING — LUKE

13. Patience—13:8-9. "Sir, let it alone this year also, until I dig around it and fertilize it. 'And if it bears fruit, well. But if not, after that you can cut it down.'" **Prayer Application:** Father, church work requires patience to love, nurture, wait, develop, and train. Give my pastor patience in dealing with the congregation; give us patience in relating to him; and give all of us patience in planting, watering, and tending the harvest you have set before us.

CLOSENESS WITH YOU TODAY

Affirming and loving Father, You alter situations to accommodate and sustain me in reaching life-goals and in living an anchored life. Closeness to You removes dark clouds, covers me with protective grace, and feeds my faith to achieve. I am extremely thankful. I want to stay close to You through . . .

CONSECRATION—a focused follow-through. What I profess; what I promise in lifestyle behavior; what I do with my time and talents—all of these, Father, indicate the level of my consecration to You and to the ministry You have commissioned me to perform. *I will be trustworthy!*

CONFESSION—heart-emptying honesty. Lord, nothing is hidden from You—nothing, no nothing! I confess the weaknesses in my walk—correct them! I confess the hesitation in my talk—motivate me. I confess backwardness in projecting a radical experience in Christ—empower me. *I will be a transformed witness.*

COMMUNION—worship-centered fellowship. God of great gifts, Your greatest gift to me is close communion with You—talking, sharing, receiving, planning, and becoming. I cherish my time with You, Master. I will anticipate it, protect it, cultivate it, and honor it. *I will be faithful in worshipful communion.*

BIBLE READING—LUKE

14. Compel—14:23. "Then the Master said to the servant, 'Go out into the highways and hedges, and compel them to come in, that my house may be filled.'" **Prayer Application:** Gracious Savior, it is Your will that our church be filled with people. May we use the "compel" strategy—calling, sharing, inviting, loving, and witnessing—to bring them in. Let us also invite "the poor, the maimed, the lame, the blind" (v. 13).

COMMUNITY LIFE TODAY

Lord of faith and fellowship, You have blessed me with a community of believers in my church and a community of families in my neighborhood. I have the honor of being a part of both communities. I also have the responsibility of being a contributor to the health and happiness of both groups. My goal is . . .

To be a LIGHT. According to Your Word, Father, I am not to hide my light (Matthew 5:16). I am to be a light in my church through faithfulness and fruitfulness. I am to be a light in my community through friendship and helpfulness. *I will be a light!*

To show LOVE. Master, Your love never fails (1 Corinthians 13:8). I am to show love in my church through loyalty and load bearing. I am to show love in my community through a Christlike disposition and a caring spirit. *I will show love!*

To be a LEADER. I will be a witness of my commitment to Christ by being a light, by showing love, and by being a leader. I will be a leader in my church through accepting ministry responsibilities and accountability. I will be a light in my community through participation in projects and developing community pride. *I will be a leader, only!*

BIBLE READING — LUKE

15. Sinners — 15:2. "And the Pharisees and scribes complained saying, 'This Man receives [welcomes] sinners and eats with them.'" **Prayer Application:** Loving Father, the parable of the lost sheep (v. 4), the lost coin (v. 8), and the prodigal son (v. 11) are lessons for the church in reaching people in different life situations. Let us welcome sinners and show them Your love.

COMPLETE FAITH TODAY

Father who molds and shapes, You give me faith to live a complete life—fascinating, fulfilling, and fruitful. I marvel at Your mighty acts and provisions. My heart overflows with praise! I thank You for . . .

HOLDING Faith—*persistence*. Trust founded on Your Word, heavenly Father, gives me holding faith whereby I can be persistent and consistent in my testimony and in fulfilling Christian duties. Holding faith will hold me close to Your providing and protecting presence!

HOLINESS Faith—*purity*. Confidence, Father, founded on Your Word gives me holiness faith whereby I can be a model and a motivator in my daily walk with You and in being a Christian influence at home, church, and work. Holiness faith will give me stability and strength to be a glowing witness of Your purifying power!

HEALING Faith—*positiveness*. Wholeness founded on Your Word, Father, gives me healing faith whereby I can be free from wounds of the past, receive health for today, and stand with a positive attitude about the future. Healing faith will give me soundness to minister with might and authority!

BIBLE READING—LUKE

16. Integrity—16:10. "Whoever can be trusted with very little can also be trusted with much, and whoever is dishonest with very little will be dishonest with much" (NIV). **Prayer Application:** Lord God, my pastor depends on me. I want to be faithful in both small and large responsibilities. Let me exercise the discipline, control, and courage to do this.

COMPLIMENTS TODAY

God of endless grace, my heart is filled with praise today for Your gifts of peace, protection, and provisions. I also want to praise others for how they use their gifts to serve. My goal is for my compliments to be . . .

PERSONAL — *sincere expressions from the heart.* I do not want my compliments to be formal, given out of a sense of protocol. I am surrounded by individuals who contribute to my life and to the ministry life of my church. I want to compliment them warmly, sincerely, and thankfully. *Guide me, Master, to do this!*

POLITE — *warm expressions from the heart.* Compliments should be personal and specific, I realize this Father. I will avoid expressions that are general in nature. Compliments denote my Christian character, my commitment to teamwork, and my awareness of ministry contribution. *Anoint me, Lord, to be inspirational in my compliments.*

PURE — *honest expressions from the heart.* I realize I represent You, Lord, in what I say and do — Your holiness, purity, and righteousness. Therefore, I will be both truthful and tactful — sincere, warm, and honest. *Overshadow me, Father, so I can give compliments that compliment You!*

BIBLE READING — LUKE

17. Faith — 17:5. "And the apostles said to the Lord, 'Increase our faith.'" **Prayer Application:** Almighty God, we need to use the faith You have already given us to do Your will in our church. Let us put it to the test. Also, let our faith grow as we trust You and as we testify of Your great grace.

CONFRONTING SATAN TODAY

Unstoppable Commander, I will face hostile forces today directed by Satan. The goal of these evil forces is to battle, block, beat, and bruise Your people and thwart the advance of Your Kingdom. Satan and his army of destruction will . . .

SET traps to kill, steal, and destroy. Satan desires to kill my influence, steal my joy, and destroy my future. He will set traps to do this — temptation to sin, harmful habits, and character defacing relationships. Guide me, Holy Father, around these traps. *Empower me to set up standards against them.*

SABOTAGE God-honoring thinking. Satan desires to fill my mind with negative, unholy, and nonproductive ideas. He will try to invade my thinking — obscene pictures, destructive activities, and compromising conversations. Take control of my thinking, Lord. *Equip me to monitor my thinking with Your Word.*

SWAY Christ-honoring commitment. Satan desires to weaken my commitment, my spiritual convictions, and my lifestyle testimony. He will try to create doubt and confusion about dedication. *Encircle me, Father, with Your power and wisdom to walk and talk as an unmovable soldier of the cross.*

BIBLE READING — LUKE

18. Children — 18:16. "But Jesus called for the children, saying, 'Let the little children come to me. Don't stop them, because the kingdom of God belongs to people who are like these children'" (NCV). **Prayer Application:** God of Compassion, bless the children's ministry of our church — students, teachers, leaders. Let us understand they represent the characteristics of Your kingdom — submissiveness, humility, unpretentiousness, love, openness, and honesty.

PRAYER PATTERN — GOALS

G — GOALS: Master, let us develop and maintain **GOALS** that will glorify You.

O — OFFER: We **OFFER** to You our minds to think through and our hands to work through.

A — ANOINT our pastor to lead us and **ANOINT** us to minister by his side.

L — LOVE: Let Your **LOVE** guide and control our relationship with each other.

S — STRENGTHEN our pastor for harvest work and **SHIELD** him from Satan.

BIBLE READING — LUKE

19. City — 19:41. "Now as He drew near, He saw the city and wept over it." **Prayer Application:** Divine Savior, with our pastor, let us weep over our city and develop a heart burden for the unchurched around us. Then let us go forth "bearing precious seeds" (touching, loving, embracing) and reap a harvest that will bring joy in heaven and in our church.

My Journal

FOR THE WEEK

Praise reports, answered prayers, divine provisions, and
spiritual plans.

BIBLE READING — LUKE

20. Government — 20:25. "And He said to them, 'Render therefore to Caesar the things that are Caesar's, and
to God the things that are God's.'" **Prayer Application:**
Almighty God, You are ruler over all nations and peoples.
May our church support just causes, and may we be examples of respect for political leaders, the laws of the land,
and loyal citizenship.

CONTROL TODAY

Master of every situation, I am thankful You are in control of my life—where I am, what I stand for, and where I am going. I need Your revealing control, Your keeping control, and Your shaping control. I ask You to . . .

Mold My CHARACTER. Father, I know my actions and activities will be dictated by my character—the qualities that constitute my individuality. I want to be known as a person of honor, loyalty, and integrity; mold me to represent You with these qualities.

Motivate Me to CONTRIBUTE. I want to be an influencer—to influence my friends to live open, full, and free; to influence church members to worship, relate and serve; and to influence unchurched friends to think about the future, to evaluate, and to consider a new life in Christ. I want to be known as a contributor to personal growth and church growth.

Manage My CONVICTIONS. Lord, I feel strongly about biblical truths, relationship values, and disciplined conduct! These unique qualities represent my personal convictions. I want You to guide me in managing them in a way that elevates Your majesty and kingdom.

BIBLE READING — LUKE

21. Giving—21:3. "So He said, 'Truly I say to you that this poor widow has put in more than all.'" **Prayer Application:** God of perpetual grace, you have told us to give to You through the church, cheerfully, consistently, and sacrificially. Let our church be covered with a spirit of giving and solid stewardship.

CORRECTION TODAY

Forgiving Father, check my life! Correct me and direct me according to Your master plan. I know You will correct me in love to shape my Christian character and to position me for Kingdom-advancing ministry. I am receptive to correction in my . . .

FAITHFULNESS. Father, check my faithfulness! Faithfulness includes my prayer time, Bible study, participation in church activities, and sharing the message of the gift of salvation. Reveal to me where I need to make adjustments and I will respond.

FORGIVENESS. Father, check my forgiveness! Forgiveness includes self-forgiveness, mistreatment, slander, deception, and unscrupulous deeds. Reveal to me where I need to improve and I will make changes.

FRUITFULNESS. Father, check my fruitfulness! Fruitfulness includes displaying the fruit of the Spirit, serving without hang-ups or hold-outs, maintaining growing relationships, family-life togetherness, and influencing friends and neighbors by living a consistent Christian life. Reveal to me where I am inadequate and need upgrading and I will, by Your holy help and support, accept the challenge.

BIBLE READING—LUKE

22. Attitude—22:26. "But don't be like them. The most important one of you should be like the least important, and your leader should be like a servant" (CEV). **Prayer Application:** Lord of changeless power, it's important to our church that we all have the right attitude about positions, authority, and serving. By Your Spirit let us show an attitude of loving one another, preferring our brothers or sisters in the Lord, and caring for one another.

CREATIVITY TODAY

Creator of heaven and earth, I marvel at Your handi-work; it is excellent in every dimension. Every day there is sunrise, sunlight, and sunset. Every night there are stars, the moon, and constellations. During the day, I enjoy the splendid views of nature — flowers, trees, and streams. You have also invested creative skills in me. Guide me to . . .

BEGIN today creatively. Lord, I want to begin today by recognizing anew the creative forces You have placed in my mind and heart. I will think creatively in my mind and love creatively in my heart.

BUILD on my talents. I am grateful for the talents You have placed in my care. I will value them, creatively develop them, and joyfully use them to honor You, gracious King of glory. I will do this under Your creative anointing.

BLOOM where I am. I will not sit and wait for ideal situations. I will bloom where I am. I will use my skills where I am and with what I have. I will look around for opportunities to create and to make a difference. I will look forward in faith knowing You, Father, have unusual things in store for me. Give me a ready attitude to respond with positive and creative action. I am filled with excitement at the prospects You have placed in my path.

BIBLE READING — LUKE

23. Boldness — 23:3. "So Pilate asked Jesus, 'Are you the King of the Jews?' 'Yes, it is as you say'" (NIV). **Prayer Application:** Lord, our pastor and church must be a bold witness to the community. Anoint our pastor to preach with both fire and compassion. Guide each member in living with confidence and sharing Christ, Your Son, with boldness.

DEMONSTRATE COMPASSION TODAY

Lord of never-failing love, You never give up, give in, or give out. You love the down-and-out, the up-and-out, and the outcast. Your love never fails! Father, I want to demonstrate Your kind of love in my life and in the life of my church. Help me to . . .

UNDERSTAND Mercy. Master, Your mercy is over-whelming—You forgive, forget, and provide a secure foundation for the future. My natural tendency is just the opposition from this. Invest in me Your quality of mercy so I can embrace, forgive, and share shaping faith.

UNTIE Restraining Ropes. Often I am bound by ropes of routine, tradition, and outdated thinking patterns. In order to be an effective witness and an effective worker in my church, I need to be free from restrictive ropes. Father, let Your Spirit free me to think, plan, and approach minis-try differently and creatively.

UNFOLD Grace. Father, Your grace is overflowing and unfolding, it covers all my needs—personal renewal, refreshing spirit, and redirecting priorities to honor You more profoundly, and expand the ministries of my church more widely.

BIBLE READING—LUKE

24. Forgiveness—23:34. Jesus prayed, "Father, forgive them; they don't know what they're doing" (MSG). **Prayer Application:** God of forever forgiveness, Your Son pro-vided the example of ultimate forgiveness. Forgiveness brings people together, binds wounds, and builds a frame-work for teamwork. Let our church, all of us, forgive and forget and bear Kingdom fruit together.

DISCIPLESHIP TODAY

Father, You have called and commissioned me to be a Kingdom disciple—to train, to be a testimony, and to understand the tactical procedures for advancement. I will respond with my heart (compassion), with my head (conviction), and with my hands (commitment) through . . .

DEVOTION. I will check my devotion to You, Father, on a daily basis by being aware and yielded, and with adoration, thanksgiving, intercession, and meditation. Through devotion to You I can reflect the countenance of a devoted disciple.

DEVELOPMENT. I will check my development as a disciple on a regular basis—biblical understanding, spiritual maturity, and reflection of the characteristics of Christ in my lifestyle. Through development I can become a stronger witness and a stronger worker in my church.

DEPENDABILITY. I will check my dependability to You, Master, and to my church, on a consistent basis—sterling integrity, faithful church attendance, and outreach leadership. Through dependability I can be a motivational model in my church.

BIBLE READING—LUKE

25. Remember—24:8. "And they remembered His words." **Prayer Application:** Sovereign Lord, don't let anything block our memory of Your promises of protection, peace, and overcoming power as individual believers and as Your body, the church— "the gates of Hades shall not prevail against it" (Matthew 16:18).

15 HABITS OF A HELPFUL CHURCH MEMBER

A helpful church member . . .

1. Applies common sense in solving church problems.
2. Advocates fun while performing ministry.
3. Disciplined in not criticizing members or methods.
4. Displays a caring spirit in reaching the unchurched.
5. Embraces the mission of the church with zeal.
6. Faithful in systematic financial giving.
7. Firm in making worship a priority.
8. Frugal in giving up on people or projects.
9. Honesty in relationships with other members.
10. Knowledgeable of the pressure of pastoring.
11. Promotes teamwork in all church undertakings.
12. Respects church elders, teachers, and lay workers.
13. Shows concern for the needs of the pastor/family.
14. Strives for effectiveness in church operations.
15. Understands the power of focus and direction.

BIBLE READING — LUKE

26. Burning Hearts — 24:32. "And they said to one another, 'Did not our heart burn within us while He talked with us on the road, and while he opened the Scriptures to us?'" **Prayer Application:** Father, may our church be filled with members who have burning hearts as a result of talking with You (prayer), walking with You (Bible study), and working with You (ministry).

My Journal

FOR THE WEEK

Praise reports, answered prayers, divine provisions, and
spiritual plans.

_____

_____

_____

_____

_____

_____

_____

_____

BIBLE READING — LUKE

27. Understanding — 24:45. "And He opened their understanding, that they might comprehend the scriptures."
Prayer Application: Sovereign Lord, our pastor needs the touch of the Holy Spirit to open the Scriptures to us, and we need the touch of the Holy Spirit to comprehend and to apply them.

DISCIPLING YOUTH TODAY

Father, You invite young people to experience forgiveness, to join You in forming lifestyle values, and in understanding the full meaning of faith. In the future, they will lead families, they will lead in church life, and they will lead in the workplace. I want to be an influence in their journey. Overshadow me to . . .

TOUCH them for MOTIVATION. Father, I want to be a source of motivation for the youth of my church to reach their full potential in Christ and in life by my example, and encouragement, and by highlighting joyful experiences in the Lord. *Let me touch youth today with a caring spirit.*

TEACH them for MATURITY. I will pray for and support the teaching ministry of my church—age-level classes, midweek Bible study, and identity programs. I am open, Lord, if You want me to be a leader in any of these teaching initiatives. *Let me teach youth today with a relationship spirit.*

TRAIN them for MINISTRY. Master, You have a place to serve in ministry for young people now and in the future. *Let me be instrumental in training youth for rewarding involvements in the ministries of my church.*

BIBLE READING—LUKE

28. Church Power—24:49. "Behold, I send the Promise of My Father to you; but tarry in the city of Jerusalem until you are endued with power from on high." **Prayer Application:** Father God, You want our church to be powered by the Holy Spirit. Use all of us—pastor, members, leaders—as instruments for the Holy Spirit to work through to bring renewal, to establish relationships, and to maximize spiritual resources.

DIVINE DELIVERANCE TODAY

Divine Deliverer, You are unstoppable, unmovable, and undeterred in directing the course of my life. You desire the best for me and will provide the best by guiding me to avoid:

DETOURS. Satan's aim is to divert my steps and place detours in my path. These detours consist of sinful side roads, glaring worldly lights that blind spiritual visibility, and eye-catching billboards that advertises deceiving directions. Father, deliver me from detours, and direct my eyes to stay focused on the path You have mapped out for my life.

DISTRACTIONS. There are many people and projects that call for my attention. Father, don't let me be distracted by offers or opportunities that will hinder me from closeness and communication with You. Give me insight and skill to evaluate and to place priority on what will increase my devotion to advancing the mission of Your kingdom.

DIVISIONS. Father, Satan will attempt to create division among fellow church members, in my family, and among my friends. Endow me with wisdom to create and maintain unity by emphasizing the positive, the strength of togetherness in mission, and the scriptural resources You provide.

BIBLE READING — JOHN

1. Witness — 1:7. Your pastor is a man with human limitations and weaknesses. But he is a man sent from God, divinely commissioned to bear witness of the Light, Jesus Christ, that people might believe and be saved. You are a partner with your pastor in helping the ministries of the church bear witness of the Light.

DIVINE LOVE TODAY

Life and liberty flow from Your love, holy Father. Your love was manifested in Christ and released by the Holy Spirit. Your love is active in my life today providing closeness with You and gifts of affection from Your throne. Your love . . .

RENEWS My Spirit. I am renewed daily, Father, as Your love gives me assurance of care, comfort, and courage to achieve Christ-honoring goals. My mind is renewed by Your Word. My heart is renewed through fellowship in prayer. My spirit is renewed as Your will works in my life.

RELEASES for Service. Lord, I am released daily for service as Your love is manifested in my life through kindness, tenderness, and helpfulness. My mind is released for service by adopting the mind-set of Christ. My hands are released for service by accepting the call to stand with the deprived, hurting, and lonely.

REWARDS Me for Faithfulness. Father, as I fulfill Your biblical plans of sharing love, hope, and health; You fulfill Your plans for my personal life by providing holy companionship and a heavenly Comforter.

BIBLE READING—JOHN

2. Obedience—2:5. Following the instructions of Christ resulted in a miracle at the wedding in Cana of Galilee. Working together in ministry, showing obedience to the words of Christ and to each other, the pastor, and the people will solve problems, bring about signs and wonders, and receive strength for service.

DIVINELY DIRECTED TODAY

Father, You know the future and You provide directions for those who trust in You. I trust You and I depend on Your life-path directions. I understand there are things I must do and experience in order to reap divine direction. Therefore, I will be . . .

CRUCIFIED with Christ. Like the apostle Paul, I can say, "I have been crucified with Christ; it is no longer I who live, but Christ lives in me" (Galatians 2:20). Christ in me is the hope of glory—salvation, security, and significance. Father, I am grateful to be crucified with Christ, identified with Christ, and share the love of Christ.

COMMITTED to Good Work. The love of Christ in me inspires me, empowers me, compels me to perform good works which glorify Christ, provide guidance for those searching for meaning in life, and compassion for holding up the needy and suffering. Father, I am grateful for the holy privilege to be crucified with Christ and to represent Christ by advocating and advancing good works.

COMMISSIONED to Proclaim. Lord, You are not willing that any person, old or young, be deprived of fellowship with You now or in heaven. Father, I look to You and to Your Word for direction in proclaiming the message of new life, abundant life, and eternal life in Jesus Christ.

BIBLE READING—JOHN

3. Lifted—3:14-15. Moses lifted up the serpent in the wilderness, and people were healed. Christ was lifted up on the cross, and new life—eternal life—was provided. The mission of the church is to lift up Christ. This is facilitated through UPREACH—worship; INREACH—discipleship; and OUTREACH—evangelism. This requires having all the people together in oneness of purpose.

DIVINE PEACE TODAY

Peace-providing King, thank You that I can begin every day with the assurance of peace—confidence, calmness, and courage. Peace flows from Your throne and meets me where I live and whatever I may face. I receive Your peace with deep respect and devoted appreciation.

PEACE within. Soul peace! Mind peace! Spirit peace! Your peace, Father, gives me joy for the day. This impacts my lifestyle and attitude. In turn, this affects my relationships, my witnessing influence, and my effectiveness at home and work. I will live the peace-centered life today!

PEACE without. Father, I am surrounded by stress, conflict, and strife. These conditions seek to damage my dedication. Even though I am surrounded by these pressures, I am also surrounded by Your peace that issues protection and partnership with You and other believers. I will live a peace-protected life today!

PEACE with a promise. God of guidance, I have Your promise today, "I will never leave you nor forsake you." Your unmovable promise keeps me close to You, orders my steps, and gives me safety for the journey. I will live a peace-grounded life today!

BIBLE READING—JOHN

4. Sowing and Reaping—4: 35-38. The person who reaps the harvest receives wages (gifts, blessings) now; and the sower and the reaper rejoice together (v. 36). There should always be rejoicing in the church by everyone— sowers, reapers, teachers, keepers—as individuals come to the Lord and find peace and security in the family of God.

WHEN YOU PRAY FOR YOUR PASTOR . . .

- YOU become a **PARTNER** in his calling—feel his compassion and see his vision.

- YOU receive **BLESSINGS** from his anointing—feel God's approval and covering.

- YOU accept **OWNERSHIP** of church projects—feel a sense of accountability and adventure.

- YOU serve as a **ROLE MODEL** to others—feel spiritual joy in helping to shape receptive hearts into the likeness of Jesus Christ.

BIBLE READING—JOHN

5. Want To—5:5-9. Jesus looked at the infirm man at the pool of Bethesda and said, "Do you want to be made well (are you sincere about this)?" "Want to," sincere desire to achieve, is a key word in church healing, church health, church holiness, and church happiness. Exhibit a spirit of "want to" in relationship to ministry with your pastor and your church.

My Journal

FOR THE WEEK

Praise reports, answered prayers, divine provisions, and spiritual plans.

BIBLE READING—JOHN

6. God's Will—6:38. The ministry of Christ was wrapped around the will of God; He came to do His Father's business (Luke 2:49). The pastor seeks to guide the congregation in discovering, developing, and deploying God's will through prayer, Bible study, preaching, teaching, and Great Commission ministries. Your part in this is fellowship, discipleship, and stewardship.

EMBRACING GOD'S PLAN TODAY

Creator Lord of form and order, You have a divine plan for fulfilling Your will on earth. The mission of the Church is centered in Your plan—loving the lost, learning God's laws, and leading in Christian maturity. Father, I embrace Your plan, I will . . .

LOVE People. Father, Your love for people led You to sacrifice Your Son to rescue and redeem the fallen. A central plank in Your plan is my involvement to love people like You love people, to sacrifice to support the mission of the Church, and to pay the price that active love requires.

LOVE Learning. Master, I will study and learn how Jesus, His disciples, and early church leaders embraced Your plan of evangelism—witnessing, winning, and working to plant churches and proclaim soul-freedom in Christ. I will love learning, and I will be a student of Your Word.

LOVE Sharing. Christ set the example of sharing—feeding the hungry, healing the afflicted, and setting free the bound. The church has been commissioned to continue His ministry. I will faithfully support my church in fulfilling His commission.

BIBLE READING—JOHN

7. Doctrine—7:16-18. The teaching of church doctrine cannot be based on private belief, group interpretation, or personal authority. Under the leadership of the pastor, the congregation must embrace doctrine as revealed by God's Word. This requires open minds during preaching, receptive hearts during teaching, and Holy Spirit dependence during personal Bible study.

ENJOYING YOUR CREATION TODAY

Matchless Master, Your glorious handiwork greets me every morning — the indescribable wonders of nature. I awake with a new day of adventure before me. I'm thrilled! I'm thankful! Today, I will enjoy the . . .

BEAUTY of Your creation. I will keep my eyes focused on the exquisite, colorful elements of nature, the work of Your hands that engulf me. Father, I am so grateful for the dazzling beauty of Your creation — mountains, fountains, fruit, and flowers. *Yes, I'm grateful!*

BOUNTIFULNESS of Your creation. There are no limits to Your love and creative powers. From sea to shining sea. From mountaintop to mountaintop. From wheat fields to patches of turnip greens, to flourishing cornfields, Your uniqueness is manifested Today, I lift my voice in praise. *Yes, I am thankful!*

BLESSINGS of Your creation. Every day is blessed with beauty, bountifulness, and unlimited blessings. Your gifts, Lord, are marvelous and enriching. I will count my blessings today. I will make a list of my blessings so I will not forget how You keep me, care for me, feed me, and fill me with the divine visitations. *Yes, I am blessed!*

BIBLE READING — JOHN

8. Pleasing God — 8:28-32. Christ bore witness of Himself through His relationship with God the Father; He did the things that pleased Him. When we abide in Christ, we do the things that please Him. As we reflect His likeness, people see our good works, both personally and through the ministries of the church, and God receives glory.

ESTEEM TODAY

Lord who loves, lifts up, and leads in forming high performance values, I am thankful for Your oversight. My strength comes from You and my security is in You. I have self-esteem and self-confidence as a result of Your indwelling, inspiring Spirit. I feel confident as a . . .

WORKER. Father, I have been assigned to be an influence in the ministries of my church, in Your vineyard to harvest fruit, and in my daily conduct. *I will honor Your holiness as my standard!*

WITNESS. I have also been assigned to be a witness — a warning witness, a warring witness, and a winning witness. I will stand tall and be prepared in each of these areas to witness for You, Lord, with Your anointing and Your authority. *I will honor Your power to witness!*

WARRIOR. Included in Your assignments, Master, is that I am to be a warrior — standing up against the attacks of Satan, fighting against spiritual corruption, and marching forward to achieve spiritual victories. *I will honor Your power to defeat the enemies of Your Church!*

BIBLE READING — JOHN

9. Work — 9:4. Performing ministry is work, hard work, tiring work. And it must be done with a sense of urgency, while the sun shines, because night is coming when no one can work. The urgency of God's work places heavy demands and physical strain on your pastor. When you understand this, you are able to feel his burden and help him carry it through prayer, personal participation, and by providing time for him to pause, relax, and regain his strength.

EXCELLENCE TODAY

Master of the universe, creation reveals Your sterling nature; You are excellent in all Your ways. Your excellence is set forth today in restoring the fallen, refreshing the weary, and rewarding the faithful. Your excellence is set forth for the future by providing an eternal home of endless fellowship with You in heaven. I'm elated! I am . . .

APPROVED. I am approved by You, Father, by Your Son, Jesus Christ, the hope of glory living in me. This is a glorious honor! Christ living and working in me gives me trusting power, standing the test power, and security power. I stand approved today!

AFFIRMED. I am affirmed by faith, Father, as Your child, a member of Your family, a representative of Your Kingdom, and an ambassador of Your love and liberty in Your Son, Jesus Christ. I stand affirmed today!

ANCHORED. I am anchored, Father, on Christ the solid rock—unmovable, unshakable, undeterred. I will live a life of excellence today by standing by You, with You, and for You through prayer, trust, and obedience. I stand anchored today!

BIBLE READING—JOHN

10. Abundance—10:10. God's plan for us as individual believers, the church, is to have, and to live, an abundant life—overflowing, extraordinary, surplus. We possess this life as we are faithful to the Great Shepherd, as we follow the leadership of the church shepherd (our pastor), and as we commit to community with each other.

FACING GIANTS TODAY

Lord of love and liberty, I will face evil forces today, giants of destruction that will attempt to cripple my faith and impair my future. You have promised overcoming power, victory! I will face giants that come against me . . .

With the SPIRIT of David. When David faced the giant, Goliath, he said to him, "This day the Lord will deliver you into my hand" (1 Samuel 17:46). Father, I will face the giants of opposition and obstacles today with the spirit of David and believe You will provide me with a pattern and power to achieve victory.

With SPIRITUAL Armor. Today, Master, I am set to put on the full armor You have provided (Ephesians 6:11). Show me how to put on the armor correctly and strengthen me to use the armor to stand bravely and to "fight the good fight of faith."

With SONGS of Victory. After the Israelites had crossed the Red Sea, they raised their voices and sang this song to the Lord, "I will sing to the Lord, for He has triumphed gloriously! The horse and its rider He has thrown into the sea!" (Exodus 15:1). I will sing songs of triumphant today!

BIBLE READING—JOHN

11. Know—11:17-22. When we have a certainty of heart and mind about the words of Christ, His teachings, and His power, we can live with boldness, assurance, and authority. Christ has promised that His church will be victorious. When surrounded by death, both physical and spiritual, let us look to the "I Am," the Resurrection, and the Life, for healing, restoring, and resurrecting manifestations.

My Personal Pledge
TO CONSISTENT BIBLE STUDY

I realize through Bible study I can understand the nature of God, the mission of the church, and His standards for spiritual wholeness. Therefore, I will embrace the value of Bible study!

I pledge to be loyal in consistent Bible study by . . .

1. **SETTING** aside time each day to hear from God through His Word.

2. **SEARCHING** the Scriptures to gain awareness of how God relates, instructs, and blesses.

3. **STANDING** on God's promises and applying them to daily life and Christian service.

4. **SHARING** the good news of saving grace, heavenly security, and Holy Spirit oversight.

5. **SPREADING** God's love, hope, and happiness through the ministries of my church.

BIBLE READING—JOHN

12. Fragrance—12:3. The fragrance of Christ—extravagant devotion and kindness—should come from the church, His body. People are influenced and lives are changed by the fragrance of faith and the acts of mercy that come forth from the teamwork of the pastor and people of the local church.

My Journal

FOR THE WEEK

Praise reports, answered prayers, divine provisions, and spiritual plans.

_____

_____

_____

_____

_____

_____

_____

_____

_____

BIBLE READING—JOHN

13. Servanthood—13:12-17. Jesus washed the disciples' feet to demonstrate the proper concept of serving one another and serving together. Servanthood is commitment of the heart, spirit, and hands that expresses itself in personal relationships, positive action, and productive involvement in church ministry.

FACING LIFE TODAY

Future-knowing Father, I will face life today knowing You have a specific plan and a special purpose outlined for me. Touch my mind to understand and motivate my will to be submissive and obedient. Equip me, clothe me, establish me, and empower me today so I can . . .

EVALUATE my attitude, my disposition, and my plans, Lord. Are they healthy? Do they honor You? Will they push me forward or hold me back? I will be open and honest with You and with myself. Lift me up by your Spirit so I can see clearly, work energetically, and plan wisely.

ELEVATE the solid values, personal skills, and spiritual gifts, Lord, You have endowed me with. You have made me a unique individual. Today, I will elevate my uniqueness by testifying of my relationship with You, by fully developing my skills, and by utilizing my gifts in personal ministry.

ELIMINATE negative thoughts and lifestyle patterns that restrict spiritual growth, progress, and peace of mind, heavenly Father. I will eliminate the baggage of bad memories, unfulfilled dreams, and restricted relationships. I will open my mind to new dreams, accept new challenges, and face the day with a new release of faith.

BIBLE READING — JOHN

14. Disciples — 13:34-35. The true mark, the true test of discipleship, is Christlike love, a binding love toward one another that eliminates schisms and criticisms. It means we are soldiers protecting one another, sacrificing to undergird one another, and serving to build up one another.

FAITHFULNESS TODAY

Today, I will demonstrate faithfulness in my Christian commitment. I will show loyalty to my church, stand with my pastor, and share outreach responsibilities. I ask You, Father, to gird me with grace, guard my devotion, and guide my steps in being an example of faithfulness. Empower and equip me to . . .

SHOW loyalty to my church. When I show loyalty to my church, I show loyalty to Christ who is the head of the church. I will be loyal and consistent in attendance, in worship, and in supporting the ministries of my church. I will also be active and a promoter of evangelism and outreach emphasis.

STAND with my pastor. Heavenly Father, pastors are chosen by You, anointed for ministry by You, and held accountable by You. I will view my pastor as sent by You, and I will stand with him in fulfilling the mission of our church—proclaim good news, provide Word directions for life, and protect members by guiding them to put on the full armor of God.

SHARE outreach responsibilities. Father, I will accept outreach duties as a personal witness, by participating in church evangelism events, and by praying for my unchurched friends and neighbors. I will **SHARE**—Seek, Help, Affirm, Respond, Encourage.

BIBLE READING—JOHN

15. Glorified—14:12-13. The church has been given the responsibility and authority to do the works of Christ—reaching, teaching, healing, and nurturing. Through prayer we are given the gifts and guidance to achieve these goals so the Father may be glorified in Christ and so the church may truly reflect the compassionate nature of Christ.

FAITH TODAY

Wonder working Master, through Christ, Your Son, I am saved, secure, and set apart to serve. I am saved from the consequences of sin. I am secure and safe by Your protective grace. I am under Your calling and anointing to be a witnessing representative of eternal life through Jesus Christ. My foundation is faith (Hebrews 11:1, 2) the . . .

SUBSTANCE of things hoped for. My hope for happiness today and for heaven in the future is secured through faith. My hope is solid because it is based on Christ, my Lord, Savior, and Master. *I will live by faith today!*

SECURITY of things not seen. Father, I cannot see how You will work in my life in the future. By faith, however, I have security in Your promise that You will always be with me and that You will provide for all of my needs according to Your riches in heaven. *I will live a secure life today!*

SOURCE of things framed by Your Word. Master, Your Word is forever settled in heaven. By faith I can embrace Your Word, be guided by Your Word, and receive strength from Your Word. *I will trust Your Word today!*

BIBLE READING — JOHN

16. Helper — 14:20. The Holy Spirit is a Helper — Comforter, Intercessor, Advocate, Counselor — who stands beside us and who enables us to remember the teachings of Christ and to reflect His nature in daily life. As our Helper, the Holy Spirit brings the church together — pastor, people, projects — to do the work of Christ founded on biblical holiness and harmony.

FAMILY DEVELOPMENT TODAY

Father, You have a holy family that reaches around the world—a joyful family, a united family, and a ministering family. I am so happy that I am a member of Your family—adopted, affirmed, anointed, and filled with joyful celebration. I will help my personal family through . . .

Family DEVOTIONS. Father, family togetherness is very important to You. As families develop spiritually, the body of Christ is strengthened and the mission of the church is advanced. Regular family devotions are a mainstay in this process. Guide me in being a part of regular refreshing family devotions.

Family DEDICATION. I am dedicated to families—my family, my church family, and the families in my community. I want to minister to all three of these. My first responsibility, however, is to provide for protection and to prepare my family to love You, Father, Your leadership, and enjoy the bountifulness of Your grace.

Family DELIGHTFULNESS. I praise You, Father, for family happiness. It is a gift from You—a glorious gift that lifts up and binds together. I will hold this gift close and enjoy the richness, fullness, and delightfulness of Your love for family life.

BIBLE READING—JOHN

17. Pruning—15:2. Every person (branch) that produces fruit (godly behavior and good works) God trims and cleans so he/she will bear more fruit. God prunes through the preaching of the pastor, personal Bible study, and insights through prayer. Be open, yielded, and receptive in all three areas.

FAVOR WITH THE UNCHURCHED TODAY

Searching Savior, You continually seek for the lost and wandering and invite them to find life-directions, spiritual-liberty, and purifying-love in You. You are a searching Savior and a caring Comforter. I want Your likeness to be reflected in my life. I want to search for, and embrace the unchurched. I can do this by . . .

FORMING Friendships. It is easy, Lord, to have strong and stable friendships with those who believe like I do, worship like I do, and live the same way I do. I desire to extend my base of friends to those who do not believe, worship, or model the lifestyle that honors You. Give me wisdom and winning ways to connect with these individuals.

FURNISHING Resources. When I follow the admonition of Christ and assist the needy, feed the hungry, and lift up the fallen, I find favor with the unchurched. This erects a structure to show the meaning and changing influence of believing in, and following, Christ.

FULFILLING Expectations. People expect to see the fruit of what I profess. Father, guide me today to influence the unchurched by how I relate to them and show love to them. Let Your caring and compassionate spirit flow impactfully from my life today.

BIBLE READING — JOHN

18. Hate — 15:18-19. Since you don't live by the terms of the world, the system that doesn't embrace Christ, the world hates you — opposes and attacks you. This is why it is so important for the pastor and the people, the church, to stand united so they can defend the faith, build each other up, and live with security, peace, and prosperity.

PERSONAL AFFIRMATION PARTNERSHIP

It is reality that performing God's work calls for partnership—cultivating, sowing, and reaping. There must be agreement and togetherness.

I Will ...

- Partner with my pastor in ministry.

- Unite with church workers in service.

- Encourage children and youth leaders.

- Support city and community officials.

- Pray for the president and national leaders.

- Uphold denominational standards and goals.

- Respect and preserve the rights of citizenship.

BIBLE READING—JOHN

19. Ask—16:24. Like the disciples, we are often perplexed by opposition around us and the opportunities of the future. Christ has invited us to "ask" for insights, information, instructions, and inspiration about today's needs and what will take place tomorrow so that our joy in Him may be full and complete.

My Journal

FOR THE WEEK

Praise reports, answered prayers, divine provisions, and
spiritual plans.

_____

_____

_____

_____

_____

_____

_____

_____

_____

_____

BIBLE READING — JOHN

20. Good Cheer — 16:33. Christ shared with the disciples what they would face from the world after He returned to His Father — crushing, squashing, and squeezing oppression. But Christ stated, "Be of good cheer, I have overcome (conquered, defeated) the world" — take heart, be brave, take courage, cheer up, rally the forces of the church, and live victoriously.

FERVENT LOVE TODAY

Lord, You love beyond measure—unlimited love, unequaled love, and unprecedented love. Your love has given me new life, abundant life, and gift-laden life. I stand in awe, in respect, and in deep, heart-flowing grateful thanksgiving. Your love . . .

EMBRACES. Father, You embrace me with the full scope of Your nature—gentleness, graciousness, holiness, and eternalness. You make me special in Your sight! You are also receptive to every person who will accept Your plan of salvation in Jesus Christ, Your Son. I will be a glowing witness of Your embracing love.

ESTABLISHES. Lord, I am established—molded, founded, structured—by Your love. This empowers me to feel safe and secure because love "bears all things, believes all things, hopes all things, endures all things. Love never fails" (1 Corinthians 13:7, 8). I will live an established life today.

ENCOURAGES. Master, Your love inspires me, upholds me, and provides me with captivating courage to act decisively and to live victoriously. I ask You to direct me in demonstrating my appreciation for Your love by showing a spirit of encouragement, speaking words of encouragement, performing acts of encouragement, and honoring Christ as the source of encouragement.

BIBLE READING—JOHN

21. Follow Through—17:4. Christ brought glory to God the Father on earth by doing everything He told Him to do. God is honored as the pastor, and the people hold hands and devotedly and diligently do the work He gave the church to do—witness, win, nurture, and disciple.

FIRMNESS TODAY

Mighty Master, I know You hold the whole world in Your hands. I also know You hold me firmly in Your hands. In Your hands I feel safe and secure. I feel a flow of holy energy. In honor of divine favor . . .

I will **HOLD Up** high standards of praise, appreciation, and sharing my testimony. I will begin every day with a spirit of praise. I will show appreciation through acts of worship. I will seek ways to introduce the grace of Christ to the wounded and wayward. *I will hold up Jesus as Lord and Savior!*

I will not **HOLD Back** in giving myself in church ministry. I will show biblical respect for my pastor. I will support outreach endeavors. I will seek avenues to create a strong bond among church members. *I will not hold back in supporting my church!*

I will **HOLD On** to the standards of Christlike conduct. I will show determination in pursuing wisdom to witness with love and authority. I will seek an infusion of might to stand strong for the cause of Christ. *I will hold on to treasures You have invested in me!*

BIBLE READING—JOHN

22. One—17:21. People in the community and city will believe that Christ was sent by God the Father as believers become one in purpose and power like the Father and the Son. Oneness with the pastor, harmony among the people, and positive acts of love establish a local church as a true body of Christ exhibiting the true nature of Christ—Forgiver, Leader, and Healer.

FLOWING FAITH TODAY

Father, faith is important to You because faith represents trust in Your Word, Your wisdom, and Your work among the people. My AIM is to be Anchored, Instructed, and Motivated by a flowing faith that is developed and maintained through . . .

SUPPLICATION. Father, talking with You lights a torch of faith that impacts every aspect of my life — family, friends, fulfillment, and future. I honor the time I spend with You in prayer. It is my pathway for pleasing You, for impacting the life of others, and for portraying total-life commitment.

STUDY. As I study the Bible, Your Word, Master, I learn about Your ways and the way You want me to walk with You. This gives me a mixture of faith that molds, motivates, and manages my skills for Kingdom service. I am yielded to the Holy Spirit to continue to illuminate my mind with divine truths.

SHARING. A growing, glowing faith opens doors for me to share my faith — the foundation of my faith, the fruit of my faith, and the fortune of my faith. Father, I ask You for spiritual insight and inspiration to share Your favor and forgiveness and to be a pattern of living a life of faith connected with works.

BIBLE READING — JOHN

23. Sword — 18:10-11. We cannot defend Christ and His message of peace with a sword or with creeds; we must depend upon the Holy Spirit. The work of the church and relationships within the church must be done with spiritual sensitivity and softness, not with hardness or with a dictatorial, legalistic spirit.

FORGIVENESS TODAY

Faithful Father, You never forsake me even though I may be inconsistent in my devotion to You and in my Christian duties. You forgive me, You give me a new grip on grace, You teach me how to go forward in faith, and You show me how to practice forgiveness to . . .

ENTANGLED Friends. When my friends become entangled with deceiving schemes of Satan, Father, let me show forgiveness and assistance in reshaping and renewing their faith. Let me stand with them until their spiritual strength is restored and they are able to once again stand strong and steadfast in Christian commitment.

ENVIOUS Neighbors. Often those around me will become envious of the stream of blessings I receive, Father, from walking with You — material favor, workplace favor, friendship favor, and church life favor. I will convey the source of my blessings and emphasize that God is love to those who will accept His love through a daily relationship with Him.

ESTRANGED Associates. Advancement on the organizational ladder in the office, misunderstanding of assignments, and performance malfunctions can create hurt feelings, hard feelings, and estrangement among associates. Father, give me wisdom to explain, to heal, to come together again as friends.

BIBLE READING — JOHN

24. King — 18:37. Jesus Christ is the King of truth. He came to bring truth to the world and to tell people about the truth. The church will only grow and serve as a lighthouse in the community when truth, in Christ, is defined, proclaimed, applied, and lived out by church members in every avenue of life.

FORWARD TODAY

Your Kingdom, Master of the universe, has always moved forward under Your direction. It is a mighty force providing freedom and declaring peace and spiritual prosperity. Today, I will move forward! I will . . .

BREAK THROUGH Satan's restrictive boundaries. Father, You are aware that Satan desires to box me in, to restrict Your flow of grace in my life, and my growth in Christlikeness. On the authority of Your Word, the Holy Bible, I will break through every barricade, cross every bridge, win every battle to fulfill Your will in my life, and live a fulfilled and fruitful life.

BREAK AWAY from negative influences. "It can't be done!" "You don't have the skills!" I am surrounded by negative influences. Father, I believe Your grace is sufficient, totally sufficient, for every challenge I face and for every opportunity You set before me. I will break away from negative influences and place my trust in You.

BREAK OUT with praise and thanksgiving. Lord of love, I will not be bashful in expressing my appreciation for daily manna from You—physical food and spiritual food. I will break out, break loose, and break free and show my thankfulness with songs of adoration and shouts of praise.

BIBLE READING—JOHN

25. Purpose—19:4. Christ brought glory to God the Father on earth by doing everything He told Him to do. There is no place for politics and power positions in the church. Our key purpose is to exalt Christ, express His love to each other, and experience His gifts in our lives.

PRAYER PATTERN – SURGE

S – Lord, let us **SURGE** forward with the pastor in both personal and outreach evangelism.

U – **USING** our skills, and empowered by Your Spirit, let us represent You with authority.

R – Let **REVIVAL** break out in our church and spread throughout the community and city.

G – **GIVE** us daily bread and fresh manna from heaven to empower us to be effective witnesses.

E – Let us back our pastor in training programs and prayer for **EVANGELISM** and outreach.

BIBLE READING – JOHN

26. Testimony – 19:35. John stated what he had seen and heard, historical certification, so people could know the truth and believe. Our testimony about our spiritual life and our church life should be believable and factual and point to Jesus Christ, Son of God, and Savior of the world.

My Journal

FOR THE WEEK

Praise reports, answered prayers, divine provisions, and spiritual plans.

BIBLE READING—JOHN

27. Sent—20:21-22. Christ sent the disciples. Christ sent your pastor. And Christ sends you to represent Him and to do the works He did. The power force for doing the works of Christ is the empowerment, the enablement, the experince of the baptism of the Holy Spirit, and the operation of spiritual gifts in the church and in the lives of believers.

FREE INDEED TODAY

Freedom-giving Father, You forgive, forget, and forge me into a new creation. I am free, free indeed! I praise You for Your acts of mercy and grace. With freedom comes great opportunities. I will accept opportunities to . . .

BELIEVE. I believe I am a person of value made in Your likeness. Father, You have endowed me with gifts and talents. You have set before me a path that leads to productivity in my career and in my Christian walk. I believe You are all-powerful and will supply whatever I need to succeed.

BECOME. I am a work in progress. Every day, Lord, I am gaining strength and growing in spiritual maturity. Through prayer, You instruct me; through Bible study, You guide me; through worship, You shape me; through being yielded, You direct me in displaying the fruit of the Spirit.

BELONG. I belong to You, Father. I am a member of Your heavenly family. I am a member of my church family. My sense of belonging gives me significance, the power of steadfastness, and binding security. I am free indeed today — I believe, I am becoming, and I belong!

BIBLE READING — JOHN

28. Not Seen — 20:29. Thomas believed Christ had been resurrected from the dead only after he had seen Him and touched Him. A "blessing" is promised to those who believe without seeing and who embrace His resurrection commission to "go with the gospel" without questions or hesitation.

FREEDOM TO LIVE FREE TODAY

Bondage-breaking Master, You give full freedom to live a life of love and liberty, beauty and bountifulness, and grace and giftedness. I marvel at Your mighty acts and magnify Your sustaining presence. Today, I have freedom to . . .

Live without FEAR. Father, You have eliminated fear and replaced it with love, peace, and a sound mind. In times of anxiety and conflict I embrace Your love, claim Your peace, and depend on Your Spirit to think soundly and righteously.

Live without FRUSTRATION. Today, I will encounter disturbing situations and difficult people. My patience will be tested! Lord, don't let me react negatively, coldly, or cruelly. Cover me with Your Spirit of calmness so I can convey a convincing example of Christlikeness.

Live without FAULTFINDING. Every day I need empowerment to stand for truth, make positive decisions, and create unity. I want to see the good in others, not the bad. Anoint me, Father, to avoid finding faults and weaknesses in programs, procedures, and especially in people. I will elevate the good and rejoice in the gifts of others as I look to You for wisdom and to Your Word for guidance.

BIBLE READING—JOHN

29. Feed—21:15-19. To emphasize what He wanted him to do, Christ told Peter three times to tend and feed His sheep. Your pastor has the duty to tend and feed the sheep of the local church. You have the responsibility to follow, to be "feedable," and to be faithful.

FRESHNESS TODAY

Creator, King, Rewarder, every day is a new day with You—one of freshness and aliveness! You give new avenues to explore, new experiences to share, and new opportunities to enjoy the rewards of Kingdom citizenship—freshness and aliveness! Today, I will display . . .

Fresh FAITH—vibrant, super expressive, victorious faith. Today, Father, I will look at what has been, what is, and what is going to be, according to Your acts and promises of mercy, and I will develop fresh faith—great expectations, great God-honoring excitement, and great manifestations of heavenly glory. *Freshness!*

Fresh FELLOWSHIP—uplifting, edifying, and strengthening fellowship. Today, Father, I will look at my circle of friends, their needs, and how they have contributed to my well-being and develop fresh fellowship—highlighting their gifts, supporting their goals, and enhancing their vision. *Freshness!*

Fresh FULFILLMENT—brightness, bigness, and blooming fulfillment. Today, Father, I will look at what You have invested in me and what You have wrought in my life, and I will develop fresh fulfillment—appreciation, affirmation, and a roadmap for advancement. *Freshness!*

BIBLE READING—JOHN

30. Few—21:25. John concluded his Gospel by emphasizing that he recorded only a few of the things Jesus did. We must take the things we know to do, according to the teachings of Christ, and do them, minister them, and mentor others to do them.

FRUITFULNESS TODAY

Father, of all seasons, You make it possible to live a fruitful life throughout the year. Spiritual fruit from Your throne comes in many different forms to cover all areas of daily life. Today, I will harvest fruit to . . .

AVOID fatigue. Master, the fruit You supply is filled with vitamins — Vitamin A — Alertness; Vitamin B — Boldness; Vitamin C — Closeness; Vitamin D — Delightfulness; and Vitamin E — "Excellenceness."

ADVANCE in faith. Your fruit, Father, provides me with a challenging vision — a clear vision of biblical truths; a compelling vision to share God's love; a Christ-exalting vision for pure worship; a convicting vision to safeguard values; and a control vision to live a sanctified life.

ANSWER to follow. Spiritual fruit circulates strength to answer the call to follow You, Holy Father — strength to stand for God-honoring values; strength to lead by modeling the characteristics of Christ; strength to witness in the power of the Holy Spirit; and strength to serve with honor and dignity.

BIBLE READING — ACTS

1. Power Promised — 1:4-5, 8. Lord, guide our pastor as he teaches us about the promise and power of the Holy Spirit, and guide us in utilizing this power in following Christ, in being convincing witnesses, and in living a power-packed, victorious Christian life.

FULL SUPPORT TODAY

Father of faithful support, I am never isolated from Your love—I am insulated by it, inspired by it, and instructed by it. I have full support from You today. I am in Your care. I ask You to . . .

CONFORM me to Your will. Father, You have a divine design for my life. Your will for me is to live a full, free, and fruit-packed life. Move in my mind and heart to conform me to Your will through spiritual development and in setting dedication goals.

COMFORT me by Your Spirit. Your Spirit, Father, comforts me in times of discomfort, forms my aspirations to honor You, and empowers me to be wholly dedicated to dream big dreams, to develop skills, and to be an inspiring and influential witness.

CONTROL me by Your Word. Your Word, Master, is a lamp, a sword, and a shield. A lamp to lead me in paths of righteousness. A sword to defeat the advances of evil. A shield to deflect the fiery darts of Satan. I have full support and complete joy today! I am filled full with gratitude.

BIBLE READING—ACTS

2. Power Received—2:1-4, 40-41. If our church is to truly represent You, Father, our members must receive the power of the Spirit, witness with authority, live with authority, and proclaim with authority. With our pastor, lead us in this authority-based approach to reaching the unchurched.

CHURCH MEMBER'S CREED

— Belief About the Pastor —

I BELIEVE the pastor is called of God, anointed by the Holy Spirit, and commissioned to bear witness of the life, death, and resurrection of Jesus Christ, our Lord and Savior.

I BELIEVE the Church was established by Jesus Christ for the coming together of His people to worship Him and to fulfill the Great Commission, and that the pastor is the spiritual leader who oversees this ministry in the local congregation.

I BELIEVE church membership identifies an individual as a committed follower of Christ and that it provides the spiritual structure to develop and demonstrate the true characteristic of discipleship in daily life.

I BELIEVE it is my responsibility to fully embrace the spiritual authority of the pastor and to support him with respect, consistent stewardship, and to pray regularly for him, his family, and the effectiveness of his ministry.

BIBLE READING — ACTS

3. Steadfastness — 2:42. I understand that doctrine, fellowship, Holy Communion, and prayer represent the framework to build a life of integrity and influence. I will embrace this scriptural pattern.

My Journal

FOR THE WEEK

Praise reports, answered prayers, divine provisions, and spiritual plans.

BIBLE READING — ACTS

4. Power Demonstrated — 3:1-10, 19-20. Lord, as our pastor leads us, let us expect the same power that You exercised through Peter and John. Let us also proclaim the message of Your grace so that people will "repent" and find "restoration" in Jesus Christ Your Son.

GET UP TODAY

Lord of resurrection power, redeeming power, and refreshing power, You are ready to manifest Your power in my life, I realize this. Touch me and transform my thinking. Activate my trust to . . .

GET UP. Father, I want my life to count for You. I want to make a difference in my family, in my church, and in my community. Anoint me to get up and shake off laziness, lukewarmness, and idleness. I will not be content with dullness and sameness. *I will get up!*

STAND UP. I will stand up for the authority of Your Word, Father, for forgiveness in Christ, and for the fortifying ministry of the Holy Spirit to live a life of vibrant faith. I will stand up and hold up the banner of the Church triumphant. I will not be satisfied with a stand-still position. *I will stand up!*

SPEAK UP. I will get up, standup, and speak up. Lord, I will speak about what You have performed in my life—new nature, new disposition, and new goals. I will speak about the mission of the church—worship, win, disciple, and send out. I will speak about spiritual gifts in the ministry of the church. *I will speak up!*

BIBLE READING—ACTS

5. Power Authorized—4:1-4, 13-20. I know, heavenly Father, that evil forces will come against my pastor and oppose him and threaten him "not to speak in the name of Christ" (v. 17). Give him boldness to say, "[I] cannot but speak the things which I have seen (experienced) and heard (revealed to me)" by the Holy Spirit (v. 20).

GLORY LAND TODAY

God of glowing grace, You are my guide as I travel to glory land. You are always with me to show the way—traveling conditions, the contour of the land, and what to expect. I understand there will be varying experiences; I need the guiding influence of Your companionship when I walk on . . .

LOW Land. Father, I know there will be valleys in life, low land—disappointments, draining relationships, and rugged roads. In the low land, I choose to learn three things—Your grace is sufficient; You will guide me; and gifts of glory are ahead. I will stay dedicated and dream without restraint in the low land!

ROUGH Land. I also know, Lord, that I will encounter rough land as I travel in life—construction projects, detours, and unpaved roads. In the rough land, I will focus on three things—Your Word is a proven road map; tough faith will see me through; and rough-land experiences will make me stronger.

HIGH Land. Father, in Your care, I will experience high land—walking on clouds of achievement and harvesting inspirational fruit. I will enjoy three things—spiritual fulfillment, personal success, and impactful Kingdom service.

BIBLE READING—ACTS

6. Power Respected—5:12-16. Our pastor, Lord, has been called by You; Your anointing is upon him to perform Your work. Let our church be in "one accord" (v. 12) with him and "esteem him highly" (v. 13), so that "believers will be added to the church" (v. 14), and people will be healed, delivered, and made free in Christ.

GLOWING VISION TODAY

Vision-casting Master, You reveal future goals for my life and how to achieve them. You give me a vision of what can be by belonging to You, believing in You, and trusting in You. In your undergirding blessings, I have . . .

VALUE in Christ. I am a person of worth and value created in the image of Christ. Father, I live under Your supervision and depend on You to guide me in developing a life that glows with affirmation, adventure, and approval to dream big dreams. *I value my value in Christ!*

VICTORY through commitment. Father, You provide a clear vision of what can be in my life. It is my duty to be committed to embracing and advancing the vision. Vision commitment includes bold steps of action, creative approaches, and strict loyalty to Your leadership. I ask You to direct me in cultivating commitment that keeps me in line with what can be in my life. *I will experience victory through commitment!*

VITALITY in conveying courage. Lord, I must exercise courage in reaching the goals You have set before me. But I cannot be dull or a deadpan in the process. I must, and I will, mix vitality with courage. I will talk with excitement. I will plan with eager anticipation. I will work with glowing enthusiasm. *I will highlight vitality in conveying courage!*

BIBLE READING — ACTS

7. Power Shared — 6:1-7. God of wisdom, I know it is vital for our pastor to "continually give himself to prayer and the ministry of the Word" (v. 4). Help me to be a church member with a "good reputation, full of the Holy Spirit and wisdom(v. 3) so that I might be a team member in doing the business of the church.

GOD'S OVERSIGHT TODAY

All-seeing Father, I depend on Your oversight today. I am ready to follow as You lead. I am ready for your instructions. I am ready for Your enabling energy. I ask You for leadership and instructions to . . .

Overcome VICES. Father, Satan desires to trick, trap, and tempt me to form immoral habits and to engage in practices that soil my soul and lead me away from allegiance to You and the cause of Jesus Christ. I claim Your oversight to overcome the advances and evil action of Satan.

Maintain VALUES. Lord, I want the things that are valuable to You to be valuable to me — pure worship, spiritual maturity, and love for the unchurched. May these things dominant my attitude and my actions to advance Your kingdom. I claim Your oversight to live a life based on values set forth in holy Scripture.

Claim VICTORY. In every battle against the forces of evil I claim victory! In positively influencing my family and friends, I claim victory! In influencing my neighbors and coworkers, I claim victory! Lord, I claim Your oversight to maintain a victory stance that demonstrates Your sufficiency.

BIBLE READING — ACTS

8. Power Resisted — 7:51. Father of truth, I know many people will not accept the truth of Your Word and will fight, persecute, and resist pastors who proclaim it. Give our pastor grace, grit, and glory to stand firm in the faith, and give each member of our congregation gifts to undergird and to stand with him.

GOOD NEWS FOR TODAY

Gift-giving Master, I am surrounded by bad news — discouragement, doubt, destruction, and depression. In the midst of bad news, I will spread good news — encouragement, inspiration, and the liberating grace of Jesus Christ. I will . . .

CARRY good news. Wherever I go today, I want to be an influence by my positive attitude, my positive action, and my positive announcement that God is love and that His love releases from the sting of guilt and blots out the stains of sin.

CONNECT with the unchurched. I want to influence the unchurched by my lifestyle — the way I talk to them and how I treat them. I also want to invite them to have fellowship with me, attend social functions with me, and go to church activities with me.

COMFORT the perplexed. People around me are facing pressure — financial shortfall, family conflict, and employment uncertainty. I want to stand with them in understanding and support. I can only do this, Father, with faith from You. Provide me with words of wisdom, with a spirit of encouragement, and with insights that will provide hope and directions.

BIBLE READING — ACTS

9. Power Explained — 8:14-17. Father, I thank You today for the baptism in the Holy Spirit. Many people do not understand this gift. Be with our pastor as he teaches about the person and work of the Holy Spirit and as he "prays for people to experience the baptism in the Holy Spirit."

My Pledge of Loyalty

TO INFLUENTIAL LIFESTYLE WITNESSING

I am under a spiritual contract with my heavenly Father to be an impactful witness by what I say, what I do, and what I advocate. Therefore, I will closely monitor my actions!

I pledge to develop the spiritual qualities to be a winning witness by . . .

1. **DEDICATING** my skills to touch individuals with the life-giving, liberating love of Jesus Christ.

2. **DEMONSTRATING** compassion for the hurts and wounds of others and offering needed assistance— encouragement, finances, and advice.

3. **DEVELOPING** closeness to share a gospel witness— fellowship with neighbors, relatives, and business contacts.

4. **DEVOTING** time to work in the ministries of my church designed to reach the unchurched.

5. **DELIGHTING** in changed lives as a result of my witness and the outreach witness of my church.

BIBLE READING — ACTS

10. Power Embraced — 9:10-18. Lord, it is sometimes difficult for us to embrace people from a different culture or who have a sordid background. Let us be submissive, like Ananias, and go with our pastor to reach the unloved, the unlovely, and the unconverted so they might receive Christ and be "filled with the Holy Spirit" (v. 17).

My Journal

FOR THE WEEK

Praise reports, answered prayers, divine provisions, and spiritual plans.

_____

_____

_____

_____

_____

_____

_____

_____

_____

_____

BIBLE READING — ACTS

11. Power Distributed — 10:34-48. Father, You are always just and righteous. You never show partiality. Your power is available to all people. They "were astonished . . . because the gift of the Holy Spirit had been poured out on the Gentiles also" (v. 45). Let our church have a spirit of acceptance, reaching people that You have prepared to receive the good news.

GOOD TIDINGS TODAY

Magnificent Master, marvelous blessings surround Your presence. You bring good news, nurturing news, and renewal news. The angel said to the shepherds, "I bring you good tidings of great joy" (Luke 2:10). In Christ, I have . . .

GREAT Joy. Not ordinary joy. No simple joy. Not plain vanilla joy! In Christ, I have super joy! Unsurpassed joy! GREAT Joy! Your joy, Father, is complete, satisfying, and energizing. Your joy keeps me in Your presence and keeps me standing on Your promises. *I will enjoy great joy!*

GREAT Blessings. Yes, Master, blessings flow from Your throne — marvelous blessings, overflowing blessings, abundant blessings. In every area of my life — family, friends, faith — You surround me with unlimited, unrestricted, and unfailing blessings. *I exalt Your majesty!*

GREAT Future. Master, my future is in Your hands, in Your care, and under Your control. My future is secure! I will look within! I will look around! I will look up! I will look up to You because You have unusual and extraordinary plans for me. *I will lift up Your name in praise!*

BIBLE READING — ACTS

12. Power Extended — 11:26. Lord of Hosts, as Christians we symbolize the character and nature of Jesus Christ. The teaching of our pastor guides us along a path of growth and maturity. Let us always be open and receptive to the instructions of Your Word.

GRACE TODAY

Gracious King, whatever challenges or conflicts I face, You give me the assurance that I can apply "Grace to it" (Zechariah 4:7). Your grace is always sufficient, always supplies solutions, and always issues strength for achievement. I will claim Your grace to . . .

Break BONDAGE. When Satan attempts to bind my spirit or block my freedom in Christ, I will say, "grace to it!" Father, to **BREAK** bondage, I will **B**elieve, **R**eceive, **E**xperience, **A**ffirm, and **K**neel in prayer to offer thanksgiving. *"Grace to it" today!*

Build BRIDGES. Your grace, Master, enables me to be a bridge builder—to connect with the perplexed, the persecuted, the poor, and the prosperous. Being certified to **BUILD** bridges requires **B**ravery, **U**nity, **I**nstructions, **L**oad-bearing, and **D**ivine underpinning. *"Grace to it" today!*

Break BREAD. Father, the rising yeast of breaking bread is communion, communication, and close fellowship with You. Breaking bread includes Holy Communion, representing the death, burial, and resurrection of Jesus Christ. **BREAD** includes **B**lessings, **R**everence, **E**ndearment, **A**nointing, and **D**irection. *"Grace to it" today!*

BIBLE READING — ACTS

13. Power Offered — 12:1-10. "Constant prayer was offered to God for [Peter] by the church" (v. 5). This is a powerful statement. When the church prayed for their pastor, the Lord sent an angel and delivered him from prison. As our church prays for our pastor, we believe God will send divine visitation, divine strength, and divine displays of Holy Spirit power.

GREAT EXPECTATIONS TODAY

Miracle-working Master, You always do the unusual, the unique, and the unexpected. You generate excitement and dreams in me for great expectations. I am an inspired dreamer — a great expectations disciple. Today, I will demonstrate and expect . . .

Flowing FAITH. My faith will not be stale or stagnant; it will be swift, fresh, and flowing. Yes, Father, I believe my faith will flow with unrestricted trust in You which will result in great expectations — life-changing worship, dedication-based gifts, and heart-shaping experiences.

Spiritual FIREWORKS. Brightness, color, explosive Scripture-based experiences. Thank You, Master, that life in Christ is full and running over with daily expectations and benefits — peace of mind, purpose in pursuits, and purity in worship.

Personal FULFILLMENT. The most important thing in life, Father, is my life in You. I find it supremely fulfilling — Holy Spirit anointing, advancement in biblical knowledge, and achievements in my career and family life. As a great expectations disciple, I will cherish Your flow of faith in my life and the personal fulfillment You provide.

BIBLE READING — ACTS

14. Power Separated — 13:1-3. Precious Father, You have gifts and callings for people in the church. Our pastor guides us in separating ourselves from clutter to commit to the work to which we have been called (see v. 2). Let us heed His leadership and hearken to the separating work of the Holy Spirit.

GREAT GRACE TODAY

Lord of unlimited love and grace, You are always near, always willing to give a new start, and always ready to respond to earnest petitions. I have experienced Your love and grace, it has been a dynamic force in my life; I depend on it to . . .

GUIDE Me — in claiming Your favor. Father, You want me to claim what You have provided — daily companionship, daily heart cheerfulness, and daily control over pressure to conform. *I cherish Your guidance!*

GIRD Me — with protective garments of righteousness. Father, Your righteousness prepares me to follow the right paths, to make right decisions, and to form right relationships. *I rejoice for Your girding garments!*

GUARD Me — by the surrounding, overcoming power of the Holy Spirit. Father, Your Spirit guards me — against the evil advances of Satan, against temptation traps, against sluggishness in devotional dedication, and against failure to reach my full potential in Christ. *I honor Your guarding oversight!*

BIBLE READING — ACTS

15. Power Preached — 14:21. Your Word, Father, is the force that convicts, converts, and instructs. Let me be attentive and receptive as my pastor preaches, and let me believe with him for new converts and for deeper commitments to the Christian walk among believers.

GREAT JOY TODAY

Giver of joy—great joy, unlimited joy, forever joy—I bow in Your presence with praise and overflowing joy. Your joy issues daily contentment, soul rest, and achievement visibility. My joy is founded on Your . . .

RESURRECTION Power. The resurrection of Christ from the grave signified new life, eternal life, and joy-filled life. Father, Christ broke the chains of death and laid the foundation for eternal life with You. I have great joy today through the resurrection of Christ!

REDEEMING Grace. I'm free in Christ! Father, through Christ You paid the price for my freedom—freedom from the bondage of sin and separation from You. I'm grateful! I have a great joy! Through Your redeeming grace, I enjoy the full benefits of membership in Your family. Amen! Hallelujah! I have experienced redeeming grace!

RENEWING Energy. Every day, Master, You give me winning energy that generates great expectations, spiritual excitement, and great joy. I will worship with enthusiasm; I will walk with biblical assurance; and I will witness about renewing energy today!

BIBLE READING—ACTS

16. Power Contested—15:36-41. Master of mercy, we know there will be differences of opinions in our local church. Don't let this divide us in doing Your work. Give us a spirit of understanding, accommodation, and togetherness with our pastor.

PERSONAL AFFIRMATION — GRACE

By the infinite wisdom, redeeming graces, and compassionate love of God,

I am . . .

- Created in the image of God.

- Privileged to be a child of God.

- Adopted into God's royal family.

- Endowed with value and potential.

- Gifted with Holy Spirit power.

- Established by biblical truths.

- Honored to share Christ's love.

BIBLE READING — ACTS

17.   Power Forbidden — 16:6-9. Father of Light, You close doors and You open doors by Your Spirit. Let us be disciplined in both cases to stand still or to move forward. Our pastor, sensitive to Your Spirit, plays a key role in this process, and we want to partner with him.

My Journal

FOR THE WEEK

Praise reports, answered prayers, divine provisions, and
spiritual plans.

_____

_____

_____

_____

_____

_____

_____

_____

_____

BIBLE READING — ACTS

18. Power Provoked — 17:16-17. There is a time, Father,
to be provoked about sin and evil. Let us "reason" in the
church and daily in the "marketplaces" of life about Your
holiness, Your judgments, and Your invitation to a new
life in Christ.

GREAT THINGS TODAY

Lord of the unexpected and the unusual, You have provided great things for me today. I want to be ready to receive them — open mind, open heart, and open hands. I also want to be prepared to point others in need to You for answers to perplexing situations and for assurance of divine assistance. I will believe in . . .

MIRACLES of Mercy. Lord, I look to You every day for Your mighty hand of mercy to be on my life — compassion, comfort, and control. You work miracles of relief and restoration and keep me safely close to You. I'm grateful!

MOVING of the Holy Spirit. In the beginning of time, the Holy Spirit moved upon the face of the deep and creation was launched (Genesis 1:2). Father, when Your Spirit moves things happen — new life, new paths to follow, and a new flow of energy. I ask for the moving of Your Spirit in and on my life today!

MIGHTY Acts of Goodness. The life of Christ was characterized by mighty acts of goodness — feeding the hungry, healing the afflicted, restoring sight to the blind. I praise You, Father, for the mighty acts of Christ in my life today!

BIBLE READING — ACTS

19. Power Proclaimed — 18:24-26. May our church be a teaching church, helping people to understand Christian doctrine, Christian duties, and Christian devotion. Let us be both teachers and learners under the leadership of our pastor.

GROWING FAITH TODAY

God who establishes and empowers, I am thankful that every day my faith can grow—enlarging my vision, enriching my walk with You, and equipping me for life-changing ministry. I am ready for Your guidance to grow my faith so I can . . .

FOLLOW Your leadership. Father, lead me by a growing faith and I will follow. Your leadership reveals new avenues to reverence, to respond to opportunities to influence, and to receive personal instructions for growth in Christlikeness. *I will grow in faith today!*

FORM strong work habits. Father, Christ set the standard for me to duplicate, "I must be about my Father's business" (Luke 2:49). People will be influenced by my works of righteousness, not by my words. Supervise me in cultivating consistent work habits that advance my effectiveness as a believer, a church member, a neighbor, and a friend. *I will grow in faith today!*

FELLOWSHIP with the unchurched. My unchurched friends will not be churched or led to Christ if I do not connect with them by fellowshiping with them, caring for them, and setting an example of a richer, fuller life. I will fellowship in faith with the unchurched. *I will grow in faith today!*

BIBLE READING—ACTS

20. Power Experienced—19:1-6. Father, I thank You today for the baptism in the Holy Spirit. Many people do not know about this experience (v. 2). Let me be prepared to share the promise and the purpose of the infilling of the Holy Spirit.

GROWING STRONGER TODAY

Vision-giving Author, when You provide a picture of growth possibilities, You anticipate a positive response — excitement, zeal, and an exuberant spirit. I want to display these qualities in my response to growth privileges. Motivate me to grow . . .

MENTALLY sharper. Lord, I want to think bigger, brighter, and better in my walk with You. This will enable me to grow in how to understand Your nature more fully, how to represent You more impactfully, and how to serve You more effectively. *I want to be mentally sharper!*

MOTIVATIONALLY stronger. Yes, Lord, I want to think bigger, brighter, and better, but I also want to be motivated to act faster, wiser, and clearer in my walk with You. This will equip me to be more aggressive in promoting the ministries of my church, to be more involved in reaching the unchurched, and to be more profound in expressing my thanksgiving to You! *I want to be motivationally stronger.*

MANAGERIALLY sensitive. Father, I have the responsibility to manage my life under Your care with keen sensitivity, to think brighter, to act wiser, and to relate openly and honestly. Your grace is my formula to grow in Christlikeness, to grow in applying Scriptural principles, and to grow in expressing overflowing praise in worship. *I want to be managerially sensitive.*

BIBLE READING — ACTS

21. Power Stabilized — 20:24-28, 32. My pastor faces many obstacles and hardships. Let me stand with him so he can say, "None of these things move me" (v. 24), and so we all can be "[commended] to God and to the Word of His grace, which is able to build [us] up, [stabilize us] and give [us] an inheritance among all those who are sanctified" (v. 32).

HAPPINESS PLUS TODAY

Life-giving Lord, my life is filled with joy today because You sent Your Son, Jesus Christ, to redeem me and to provide soul-peace and heart-happiness. This means I have happiness based on the foundation of . . .

HOPE of Heaven. Thank You, Father, for happiness now and for the hope of eternal happiness with You in heaven. This assurance gives me confidence to live life boldly today and to anticipate the beauty of heaven in the future.

HEALTHY Sunshine. Father, Your holy sunshine gives spiritual health, mental health, and physical health. Your sunshine — Your presence, Your promises, Your peace — gives daily happiness, satisfying happiness, and happiness that represents a plus factor in life.

HEART Purity. The happiness You provide, Lord, leads me to maintain heart purity — undivided love, undiluted loyalty, and unrestricted allegiance to Your kingdom. I am so grateful for Your goodness to me. I always want to live in such a way as to bring honor to You, life-giving Lord, and to be a witness of happiness plus in You.

BIBLE READING — ACTS

22. Power Tested — 21:10-13. Father, I thank You for my pastor. He "stands in the gap" and is ready to do whatever is necessary to do Your will and to lead the local flock. Bless him today with Your uplifting Spirit, with spiritual gifts, and with the sunshine of love from church members.

HARVEST TODAY

Lord of the harvest, You are the master of all seasons. You guide in cultivating, sowing, and reaping. I want to join You in harvest action. I will respond to the opportunities You set before me to . . .

TOUCH the Unchurched. The unchurched represent ripe harvest fields — individuals longing for soul rest, a sense of meaning, and foundational security. By Your imparted inspiration, Lord, I will touch them through acts of kindness, supportive service, and a verbal witness of transformation through the touch of Christ.

TUTOR the Young. Father, young people are a harvest field that needs attention, affection, and affirmation. By Your Holy Spirit, I will tutor them by my example, by expressions of appreciation, and by helping shape their faith through scriptural teaching. Touch me to tutor with thanksgiving and deep compassion.

TRACK the Results. Lord of the harvest, I want to proclaim, practice, and be productive. By Your oversight, I will track results — my consistent witness, the impact of my witness, and the follow-up of my witness. Father, I will join You in harvest action today!

BIBLE READING — ACTS

23. Power Defended — 22:1-10. When Paul was confronted about his life and message, he gave a Spirit-directed "defense." Part of his testimony included this statement: "So I said, 'What shall I do, Lord?'" (v. 10). Lord, this statement characterized Paul's submissive attitude. May this statement also depict my yielded attitude.

PRAYER PATTERN — PROVE
Pastoral Support

P — I want to **PROVE** my love to my pastor through loyalty and service.

R — Give me heavenly **RESOURCES** to show my commitment to my pastor.

O — Help me **OUTLINE** goals that will support evangelism, revival, and church growth.

V — May my vision and **VITALITY** in church projects brighten his ministry.

E — In harmony with the pastor, Lord, allow me to **EXPERIENCE** the flow of Your mighty power.

BIBLE READING — ACTS

24. Power Perceived — 23:1-11. My pastor is placed in many different crisis situations. I ask You to give him "perception" during these times about what to say and how to stay calm and balanced. Also Lord, "stand by him" and say to him, "Be of good cheer" (v. 11).

My Journal

FOR THE WEEK

Praise reports, answered prayers, divine provisions, and spiritual plans.

_____

_____

_____

_____

_____

_____

_____

_____

_____

_____

BIBLE READING — ACTS

25. Power Confessed — 24:10-16. Let our church be known as a church with people and a pastor who always cheerfully confess that (v. 10) we worship the true and living God (v. 14), that we have hope in Him (v. 15), and that we have a conscience without offense toward Him and other people (v. 16).

HEALING TODAY

Father of infinite care, loving care, and personal care, I look to You, trust You, and depend on You to oversee the wellness of my life. You provide healing in times of . . .

SICKNESS. Father, I remember the times when I called on You for physical healing and You responded! I also remember the times I called on You for mental, emotional, and relationship healing and You responded. You are the Great Physician that is always present to provide total wellness in my life.

SOCIAL Stress. There will be misunderstanding among friends; conflict in pursuing goals, and different views in fulfilling the mission of the church. I will face difficulty and pain in all of these areas. I will be fair and faithful, but there will be wounds. Lord, I ask You for personal healing and for the wisdom to speak words of healing to others.

SUFFERING. Father, I am surrounded by people who are suffering. There is sorrow as a result of sickness and death. There is loneliness and sacrifice as a result of separation. Father, You provide healing! Guide me in being a messenger of divine healing and of delivering help in Christ.

BIBLE READING — ACTS

26. Power Judged — 25:6-11. Father of fairness, let me never be afraid to be judged according to my works (v. 10). Let me also be fair in judging the methods and moods of my pastor, and let me walk in his shoes through prayer and positive affirmations.

HEART PRAISE TODAY

Heart-changing holy Father, You know the condition and the contents of my heart. You performed a miracle in my heart—cleansed it, transformed it, and filled it with truth. I lift my voice in praise and thank You for a . . .

HOLY Heart. My heart is pure and filled with purpose to please You, Father, to follow a path of character holiness, and to set a pattern of total-life integrity. I ask You to keep Your holy hand on my heart and keep it holy.

HAPPY Heart. My heart is content and filled with joyful praise for the assurance of divine fellowship, for the gifts of the Spirit, and for the Scriptural promise of heaven. Master, I ask You to insulate my heart and keep it pulsating with peace and spiritual prosperity.

HEALTHY Heart. Lord, my heart is sound and in ministry rhythm with You—circulating the good news of abundant life, flowing with creative faith, and beating with valiant courage to achieve God-honoring goals. Lord, I ask You to lead me in maintaining a healthy heart by keeping it pure, filled with throbbing praise, and in love with the things You love.

BIBLE READING—ACTS

27. Power Described—26:12-17. Father, my pastor's call is from You; it is holy and demanding—"to open . . . eyes, and to turn [people] from darkness to light, from the power of Satan to God, that they may receive forgiveness of sins and an inheritance among those who are sanctified" (v. 18). Let me be a "plus" for him in his ministry.

HEAVENLY FIRE TODAY

Fire-providing Father, I am thankful for fire from Your throne. Your fire represents empowerment, evangelism, and enrichment. Your fire protects, reveals, and stimulates. Today, I want Your fire to fall on me, fill me, and ignite me to be a flaming witness. Touch me to . . .

BURN with enthusiasm. Bright, glowing, and contagious—that's the type of enthusiasm I want to display and convey. My enthusiasm, Father, springs from the holy work You have performed in my life—adoption into Your family, heavenly assurance, and the endowment of spiritual skills.

BRISTLE with anticipation. Lord, You have created today and packed it with privileges. I anticipate great and grand things—worship experiences, scriptural revelations, and personal development opportunities. I look forward to the thrills before me today!

BUBBLE with expectation. Father, in Christ, every day is a new day. I will approach today with a new spirit— new creative thoughts, new approaches to responsibilities, new methods of self-motivation, and a new attitude of expecting the best in my home life, church life, and work life. I will work with You today, Master, with exciting expectations.

BIBLE READING—ACTS

28. Power Accepted—27:9-11. Father, Paul gave solid advice from You to the helmsman and owner of the ship about safety and what they should do (v. 10). I know you speak to my pastor, and I always want to be ready to receive from him and to respond to his advice and instructions. Bless him and me together as we walk the path of faith with You.

HIGH CALLING TODAY

Lord of infinite purity, I am not worthy of Your high calling. I am eternally grateful! I will embrace Your calling with sacred trust and turned-on anticipation. Your calling has three special dimensions for me. It is a calling . . .

To be HOLY. Father, You admonish me in Your Word, "Be holy for I am holy" (Leviticus 11:45). I open my heart, mind, and spirit to You. Make my heart pure, my mind clear, and my spirit set on serving. Anoint my walk to be holy and my talk to be holy.

To share HOPE. Many individuals face life without hope; there doesn't seem to be any way to escape the desperate circumstances that binds them. However, there is hope for them—Jesus Christ. I will share His redeeming love and saving grace. I will also provide follow-up nurture and strengthening fellowship.

To HOLD Fast. There will be tricks and traps set by Satan. There will be times of depression, disappointment, and misdirection. During all these situations, I will hold fast—my faith will be firm, my mind focused, and my directions secure. I praise You, Father, for power to hold on and to hold fast.

BIBLE READING—ACTS

29. Power Manifested—28:1-10. People are transformed and influenced by Your unlimited power, heavenly Father. You share this power with us through the gifts and manifestations of Your Holy Spirit. In our church and through our church and in my life and in the life of my pastor, let Your Spirit lead and work; let us share with the sick, sinful, sordid, and scorned.

HOLD FAST TODAY

True and faithful Master, Your promises are unbreakable and Your power never diminishes. Every day You are the same in character, authority, and oversight. I praise and honor You! Empower me today to hold fast to . . .

My CONFESSION of Faith. I confess my faith today in my Lord and Savior, Jesus Christ. I confess my faith in the Bible as God's Holy Word. I confess my faith in the Holy Spirit for holy living. *Empower me to hold fast my confession!*

My CONFIDENCE in Holy Promises. Your promises, Father, are "yes" and "amen." They show forth Your glory and Your guiding hand. I will receive Your promises with humility and a thankful spirit. I will plan and perform spiritual duties based on Your promises. *Empower me to hold fast my confidence in You!*

My COURSE of Commitment. Father, You have outlined a course for me to follow in "serving You in spirit and in truth." I want to be obedient and committed in embracing Your plan and placing my trust in You. *Empower me to hold fast my course of commitment!*

BIBLE READING—ROMANS

1. Bondservant and Apostle—1:1-7. Paul referred to himself as a bondservant, a skilled employee who could not resign or work for anyone else. He was also an apostle, a church leader with absolute authority. What a combination—a servant with authority. **Prayer:** Almighty Father, I pledge to be a bondservant, submissive to You, serving with my pastor, and sowing seeds of grace and peace (v. 7).

HOW TO HELP
MY PASTOR GROW

I WILL . . .

1. **Cultivate** a biblical partnership with him in fulfilling the mission of the local church.

2. **Plant** positive seeds of support for church programs, evangelism, and advancement.

3. **Water** his preaching and leading with responsive action and with changes that make a difference.

4. **Weed** out unproductive areas of church life that disrupt progress by receiving and giving wise counsel and biblical leadership.

5. **Harvest** with him an abundant crop by having a vision of the unreached and a compassion to act.

BIBLE READING — ROMANS

2. Gospel — 1:16, 17. The gospel has the power to bring people to salvation; therefore, we should be "proud of the good news." **Prayer:** Lord of grace, I want my church, my pastor, and myself to proclaim the gospel with dignity, honor, integrity, humility, and boldness, because it is Your power to save everyone who believes (v. 16).

My Journal

FOR THE WEEK

Praise reports, answered prayers, divine provisions, and spiritual plans.

_____

_____

_____

_____

_____

_____

_____

_____

_____

_____

BIBLE READING — ROMANS

3. Teach — 2:17-23. The Jews trusted in the Law and looked upon themselves as teachers (v. 17). Paul said, How can you teach others when you refuse to learn? (see v. 21). **Prayer:** Lord, I want to be a learner, to practice what I teach. Let me learn from Bible study, my pastor's sermons, daily prayer, and participation in ministry.

HOLD ME UP TODAY

King eternal, You hold up the wounded, the weak, and the weary. You also hold me up when I am down as a result of the attacks of the Evil One. You hold me up because I belong to You, a member of Your royal family. I do not fear what may come my way because I know You will be there to hold me up . . .

With divine LOVE. Divine love comes with the full force of the Trinity—holy compassion, holy care, and holy provisions. Your love, Lord, is not based on my goodness but on Your grace. *Lord, I express my love for Your love in my life.*

With spiritual LIBERTY. I am free, free indeed in Christ. Free from controlling influences. Free from growth in Christlikeness restrictions. *Free from success limitations, Lord, I honor You for this.*

With caring LONGSUFFERING. Father, You know my limitations and hesitations and You deal with me with patience and corrective understanding. I praise You for this. *Lord, I will trust You to both direct and develop my life.*

BIBLE READING—ROMANS

4. Justified—3:1-26. It is not what we do; it is what God has done and is doing through His Son, Jesus Christ (v. 24). **Prayer:** In church work, Lord, may we always remember that it is about Your grace, embracing it and sharing it, and not our doctrinal stance or personal opinions.

HOLINESS TODAY

Father of infinite holiness, You are absolutely pure in all Your provisions and requirements. You made it possible by Your example of forgiveness and guidance for me to display . . .

Purity in SPEECH. Speech conveys what is in my soul—thinking, compassion, intentions, values. Father, I want my conversations to be uplifting and laced with inspiration, invitations, and instructions. I can be a more effective witness if people enjoy my communication with them. *Flavor my speech!*

Purity in SEPARATION. Father, You have instructed me to keep my distance from the world—evil influences, activities, and associations. I can do this by putting on the full armor that you outline in Your Word, by a consistent prayer life, and by staying close to my church family. *Keep me pure!*

Purity in SERVICE. I will not perform service to please or to be applauded by the public. I will center my service—giving, supporting, encouraging—on honoring You, Master, and pointing the way to a life of faith and fellowship with You. *Keep me focused in service!*

BIBLE READING—ROMANS

5. Righteousness—4:1-3. God selected Abraham for a special mission because of his faith, not his works (v. 3). **Prayer:** Father, it is easy to get bogged down in church work, using my own strength. I ask You, let everything I do at church be faith-directed, faith-based, and faith-powered. This is the way to do Your work and to honor You.

HOLY FIRE TODAY

God of consuming fire, corrective fire, and compassionate fire, You act with fire to defend Your name, to develop Your followers, and to provide directions for a life of purity and purpose. I honor Your holy fire today and ask for . . .

Fire on the ALTAR of my heart. Father, I want love, sacrifice, and devotion to come from the altar of my heart, ablaze with a glowing fire of reverence and lifestyle worship. I ask that the flame be visible as a testimony to those around me. Guide me to keep the fire burning every hour of every day in every situation.

Fire for ANOINTING for ministry. Your fire, Master, penetrates, softens, and shapes. Anoint me with Your holy fire so I can be persuasive in pointing the unsaved to Jesus Christ, the Lamb of God, who provides hope and the promise of heaven. I am thankful for anointing fire.

Fire for Kingdom ADVANCEMENT and impact. Fire attracts attention. Fire transforms people and situations. Fire creates momentum. Master, let Your fire burn and let me be a part of spreading the flame of evangelism.

BIBLE READING—ROMANS

6. Convinced—4:13-25. God promised Abraham that he would be heir of the world (v. 13), and he was convinced that what He (God) had promised, He was also able to perform (v. 21). **Prayer:** God, You have promised victory for Your church—outpouring of Your Spirit, overcoming obstacles, seizing opportunities. I am convinced; I claim these promises for my church and pastor.

HOLY LAWS TODAY

Gracious and giving Lord, You give life, love, and liberty to those who embrace the laws guiding these gifts. Your nature is characterized by generosity. You want to give — richly, abundantly, regularly. I want to receive Your gifts, and I will observe the laws You have set forth . . .

The law of new LIFE. Old life, new life! It's a choice! I realize this. Master, I choose new life through the new birth — transformed by the redeeming, sanctifying grace of Your Son, Jesus Christ. *I praise You for new life!*

The law of LIBERTY. Freedom! Liberated to think Christ thoughts, to think creative thoughts, and to think uplifting relationship thoughts. Father, I am committed to enjoying the liberty You have provided. I am also committed to prudently protect my unmatchable liberty. *I rejoice in my liberty!*

The law of shared LOVE. Yes Father, I understand I am "to love my neighbor as myself." I need to be anchored in Your love to do this. I love myself — my abilities and my opportunities. In obedience to Your law of love, I will love my neighbors, friends, and associates with the accepting and believing love You have deposited in my heart. *I will share Your love!*

BIBLE READING — ROMANS

7. Problems — 5:1-5. There will be problems (tribulations) in church work. But, we can rejoice (glory), because problems help us learn, endure, build character, and hope (vv. 3, 4). **Prayer:** Your love, Father, gives hope — an undefeatable spirit, a noble trust, and lofty expectations. Let a spirit of hope cover our church.

HOLY STRENGTH TODAY

All-powerful King of glory, nothing is too difficult for You—overcoming obstacles, fulfilling dreams, defeating the destructive forces of evil. Through Your grace, I am a winner in every situation. I lift my hands in holy and reverent praise. I will . . .

STAND for truth. Father, Your Word is truth, and light, and life. I want my actions today to be guided by truth. Therefore, I will read Your Word, respect Your Word, and respond to the instructions in Your Word. It will supply me with spiritual energy and with supportive equipment to both develop and defend my Christian stance.

STATE God is love. Lord, I want to be a witness of Your love today. I realize I witness by comforting the hurting and assisting the needy. I also understand I must share a verbal witness—God's love, care, comfort, and calling. By Your Holy Spirit, I will be an aggressive and effective witness today.

SERVE faithfully. Father, Your Son, Jesus Christ, took on the form of a servant. He set the example for me to follow. Today I want to reflect the disposition and dedication of a servant. I will serve my church, my community, and my country as a committed Christian and loyal citizen.

BIBLE READING—ROMANS

8. Demonstrate—5:8. We were not worth dying for, but God demonstrated His love for us by sending His Son to die for us. **Prayer:** Father of love, our church needs to demonstrate Your love to the unlovely and unreceptive and reveal Your nature of caring, giving, and forgiving. Let us do this!

My Pledge of Loyalty
TO WISE PERSONAL FINANCES

I consider the wise use of my finances a spiritual decision, because the manner in which I spend money denotes what is close to my heart, what I value, and what I want to achieve in life. Therefore, I will seek wisdom on how to spend money!

I pledge to be a wise steward of God's gifts to me by . . .

1. STANDING on God's promises to supply "all [my] needs according" to His riches in glory (Philippians 4:19).
2. SPENDING money wisely in relationship to family needs, physical health, and personal goals.
3. STUDYING financial responsibilities and preparing and maintaining a line-item household budget.
4. SHARING what God has given me to support His plans for discipleship and outreach.
5. SAVING for special needs and special days with consistence and cheerfulness.

BIBLE READING—ROMANS

9. Newness—6:4-5. Look at these two verses; we are "united together" in the likeness of Christ's death and resurrection which produces "newness of life." **Prayer:** Our church influences the community and empowers our pastor as we walk together in unity and reflect "newness" (brightness and blessings) of life. Lord, let me be a person of oneness, thoroughness, and wholeness in my church.

My Journal

FOR THE WEEK

Praise reports, answered prayers, divine provisions, and spiritual plans.

BIBLE READING — ROMANS

10. Slaves — 6:15-19. No longer are we slaves to sin; we have been set free and now we are "slaves" (committed) to righteousness (v. 18). **Prayer:** Merciful Master, I want to show that I am a "slave" (totally belonging to You) in my home life, career pursuits, relationships, and ministry with my pastor and other church members.

HOLY TREASURES TODAY

Unlimited, unrestricted, eternal Creator, I stand in awe of Your holy majesty and Your magnificent works. You give, and give, and keep on giving. I receive, and receive, and keep on receiving. But I receive with gratitude and a gracious attitude of thanksgiving. I view Your gifts as holy treasures.

TEMPLE of the Lord. My body, Father, is a treasure, a temple dedicated to You. I want to treat it reverently and wisely because it is made in Your image. Proper food, proper rest, and proper care; all three are required to please You. *And, I am committed to pleasing You!*

TIME to learn. Every day offers opportunities to learn, grow, relate, and experience. I am thankful for the gift of time, and I desire to use it prudently and productively. Lord, lead me to place a high priority on utilizing my time to please You. *And, I am focused on pleasing You!*

TALENTS to lead. Thank You, Father, for the skills You have given to me—thinking power, relationship abilities, and the fruit of the Spirit. These skills place me in a position to lead in equipping believers in fulfilling the mission of my church. It is vital that my talents be used to please You. *And, I am totally centered on pleasing on You!*

BIBLE READING—ROMANS

11. Death—7:4. Our old selves died, and we became free from the law through Christ to belong to Him, His church, and to do His will. **Prayer:** May my work in the church clearly show that I belong to You in all that I do, say, or attempt.

I AM TODAY

Transforming Father, You have done a complete make-over of my life. You adopted me, affirmed me, and anointed me to follow You in the beauty of purity. I am grateful! I'm super grateful that today . . .

I am a BELIEVER. Father, I believe that You were, that You are, and that You will always be. I believe the Bible is Your Word and a guide for my life. I believe the sacrifices of Christ provide salvation and that the Holy Spirit is my Comforter. *I'm grateful — super grateful!*

I am a BRIDGE-BUILDER. Father, You have commissioned me to build bridges of compassion and care to the outcast, the suffering, and to those searching for hope and healing. Lord, I will trust You today to provide spiritual tools and equipment to excel as a bridge-builder. *I'm grateful — super grateful!*

I am BATTLE-READY. I will face the forces of evil today. Faith in You, Father, has prepared me to be battle-ready. I will take the sword of the Spirit and be victorious in every confrontation and in every area of my life. *I'm grateful — super grateful!*

BIBLE READING — ROMANS

12. Groanings — 8:26, 27. When we don't know how to pray, the Spirit speaks to God for us with feelings that words cannot explain (v. 26). **Prayer:** Father, let Your Spirit pray through me for my pastor because I know he has deep longings to bring the people of our church into a greater, more intimate relationship with You.

IMPACTING CHANGE TODAY

Never-changing Master, You change the lives of those who trust in Your never-changing nature. I want to mirror Your changing nature in my life by my . . .

THINKING. My thinking conveys what I love, my loyalties, and the quality of my lifestyle. Father, Your Word states: "For as he [a person] thinks in his heart, so is he" (Proverbs 23:7). I pray that You would guide the thinking of my heart to bring about changes in my relationships and in renewing my vision to minister to the unchurched.

TALKING. Father, Your Word also admonishes me to "Let the words of my mouth . . . be acceptable in Your sight" (Psalm 19:14). Master, create change in my life, and in the lives of others, by the words I speak. Today, I will speak words that magnify Your majesty, move mountains of misery, and motivate to demonstrate maximum faith.

TRANSACTIONS. I impact change by making sure my "Yes is Yes and my No is No" (Matthew 5:37). This behavioral policy empowers me to establish a reputation of trust which positions me to show how faith in Christ changes a person's value system, and relationships. I am thankful for the change, Lord, You wrought on the inside of my life that brought change on the outside.

BIBLE READING — ROMANS

13. Purpose — 8:28. God has a purpose and plan for your life and the local church. Satan seeks to sabotage God's will and creates roadblocks and detours. **Prayer:** Father, You hold the future in Your hands. When it seems tragedy and trials have the upper hand, let us see You "working together for good" to elevate and encourage Your children.

IMPACT OF THE CHURCH TODAY

All-wise, all-giving, protective Father, I am in Your care today. You have provided a covering for me through my church. I cherish the blessings of my church, and I will support the impact ministries of my church.

PREACHING. Guide my pastor, Lord, to prepare sermons under Your leadership. Anoint him to deliver them as a message from You to instruct in righteousness, to inspire to live victoriously, and to be involved in ministry. *Anoint me to listen, learn, and obey!*

PRAYING. Father, guide me in praying for my church—the pastor, the people, the instructional programs, the preparations for worship, and for outreach productivity. May my church be known as a "house of prayer" where the people are united in believing that consistent communion with You opens the door to Your storehouse of unlimited and uplifting blessings. *Anoint me to bow, believe, and receive!*

PUBLICIZING. Lord, guide me in being a messenger of goodwill for my church—inviting friends to attend, sharing information about character-shaping events, and highlighting captivating activities for children and youth. *Anoint me to practice, proclaim, and promote!*

BIBLE READING—ROMANS

14. Conquerors—8:31-39. Can anything separate us from the love of God? (vv. 38, 39). No! **Prayer:** Faithful Father, Your love cements us to You. Earthly or evil powers cannot separate us. Let this same love cement all the people of our church together with our pastor and with each other to perform Your will.

IN CHRIST TODAY

God of grace and goodness, in Christ I am a new creation (2 Corinthians 5:17)—new liberty, new goals, new lifestyle. I offer praise for Your transforming power and the truths of Your Word to guide me and to affirm that I am . . .

JUSTIFIED. Father, I do not stand guilty before You—charged, condemned, declared unfit, and censured. By faith, grace, and Your love manifested in Christ, my advocate. I have been justified—freed, pardoned, acquitted, and affirmed. I am indebted, gratified, satisfied, and voice life-long, ceaseless praise to You.

SANCTIFIED. Not only have You justified me, Master, You have also sanctified me—secured my position in Christ, separated me for Kingdom service, and set me on a course of a life of holiness and wholeness. I am blessed beyond measure! I bow before Your throne with overflowing thanksgiving.

EDIFIED. Father, I am edified by Your Holy Spirit working in my life—educating me about Your nature, instructing me on how to walk in paths of righteousness, and equipping me with spiritual gifts. I praise, exalt, and magnify you, Lord of grace and goodness.

BIBLE READINGS—ROMANS

15. Control—9:16. God is in control; He acts according to His righteousness and mercy. **Prayer:** Lord, don't let power people or power groups be formed in our church. It is not the person who wills, runs, or leads that brings victory. You are the One who makes things happen.

PERSONAL AFFIRMATION — STUDY

The Word of God instructs me to "study to show myself approved" so I can be prepared to be an effective worker.

I Will . . .

- **Seek** guidance for scriptural understanding.
- **Learn** effective techniques for study.
- **Devote** time for daily Bible reading.
- **Study** commentaries for insights.
- **Read** Christian magazines and journals.
- **Listen** to sermons and Bible lectures.
- **Discuss** Bible subjects with friends.
- **Apply** biblical truth to my life.
- **Rejoice** in God's life-shaping promises.

BIBLE READING — ROMANS

16. Stumble — 9:30-33. Many people stumble at the simplicity of the gospel and question with whom and how God works. **Prayer:** I believe Jesus Christ is my source and the only way to eternal life. In my life, Father, at home and at church, let me exalt Christ, stay close to Him, and share Him with unbelievers.

My Journal

FOR THE WEEK

Praise reports, answered prayers, divine provisions, and spiritual plans.

BIBLE READING — ROMANS

17. Zeal — 10:1-8. There are many people and church groups that have "zeal," but it is not according to "knowledge" (v. 2); this causes confusion and hurts the work of the church. **Prayer:** I ask today that I would be balanced, solid, and consistent in living for You and in working with my pastor and church leaders.

INFLUENCE TODAY

Motivating Master, my goal, under Your guidance, is to be an influence in my church and community — a pure, positive, and progressive influence. I want to radiate a caring and compassionate spirit that reflects Your oversight and ownership. I need Your inspirational touch and instructional training so I can . . .

LISTEN with spiritual ears. Father, I want to listen and hear what Your Spirit is saying to me. I want to listen to hear what people around me are saying — their perplexities, goals, and nurturing needs. Today, Lord of liberty, anoint my ears to listen so I can be an influence for You!

LEARN with an open mind. Every day with You, Father, is a new day — a day to grow, to learn, and to understand Your wonderful will. My mind will be open to learn what my friends and the unchurched are thinking. This will prepare me to meet them and assist them in the zone of their aspirations and needs.

LEAD with a loving heart. People respond to love, not condemnation or rebuke. I will lead people to You, Lord, by showing compassion, care, and true concern. I will influence by a loving heart today — a heart reflecting Your nature of embracing, accepting, and restoring.

BIBLE READING — ROMANS

18. Preacher — 10:14-15. Your pastor is called, sent by God, to preach the "glad tidings of good things" (v. 15). **Prayer:** Father, You said, How beautiful is the person who comes to bring good news (see v. 15). Our pastor is beautiful in spirit, vision, and love. I uphold him today and ask You to bless him as he preaches, teaches, and trains.

INVOLVED TODAY

Father of daily oversight, I honor Your watchful care over me—guiding my steps and enabling me to go "the second mile" in relationships. I will be optimistic! I will seize opportunities! I will be involved! I will be . . .

ENGAGED in forming positive relationships. I will respect my Christian friends by being trustworthy, by respecting their values, and by joining them in both social and spiritual activities. I will also form relationships with the unchurched by showing signs of true friendship, concern for their personal needs, and compassion for their spiritual development.

ENTERPRISING in pursuing personal goals. Each day, Father, is an open door to walk new paths and to address work in new ways. I will not be locked in or locked out. I will be optimistic, creative, and ready to advance.

EXACTING in being responsible. Master, I realize I must accept responsibility and accountability in being exacting in achieving dreams and fulfilling duties. Faith will be my foundation. Your Word will be my guidebook. The Holy Spirit will illuminate my path and generate productivity. I will follow Your leadership today!

BIBLE READING—ROMANS

19. Reserved—11:2-4. We are never alone in serving God. He will always provide for, protect, and reserve for Himself those He has called (v. 4). **Prayer:** Lord, You have reserved us (our church) for Kingdom ministry. Let us not bend or bow but stand boldly for You.

I WILL LISTEN TODAY

Listening Father, You are always ready to communicate with me. You accept my praise! You listen to my requests! You respond to my needs! This provides me with calm assurance and a clear path to follow. I honor You for this, and I will . . .

LEARN to listen. I am surrounded by different voices: "Follow my advice!" "You can trust me!" "Give in, and I will make you a winner!" First, Father, I must, and I will, listen to Your voice. In prayer, I will listen. As I read Your Word, I will listen. In my thoughts and the longings of my heart, I will listen. Speak Lord, I am listening!

LISTEN with reverence. Father, I want to be honest and open. Many times I hear what I want to hear and not what You are saying. Let Your Spirit direct me to listen with an open mind and a yielded heart so I can discern between my way and Your will. Speak Lord, I am listening and I will honor Your voice and instructions.

LIST action steps. Lord, I know I will not be the same if I listen and respond to what You are saying to me. I do not want to forget the instructions You give me. I will write them down and outline methods to make them a part of my plans and practices. Speak Lord, I am listening and I will respond and be accountable.

BIBLE READING—ROMANS

20. Glory—11:35-36. Paul concluded the longest theological dissertation in the New Testament (1:16–11:36) by saying, "For of Him and through Him and to Him are all things, to whom be glory forever. Amen" (v. 36). **Prayer:** Father, may everything we do at church, and may our interacting with our pastor, be doctrinally correct and bring glory to You.

I WILL NOT BE MOVED TODAY

High-and-lifted-up Father, my trust is in Your stabilizing power. I will rely on Your sustaining grace. I will not be moved by . . .

DOUBT. Father, Satan seeks to raise questions about my faith and my future. He seeks to create doubt, to confuse my spiritual concentration, and to break down my resistance to stand firmly in faith. Lift me up on wings of assurance, fortify my faith to proclaim Your Word with boldness, and let my praise be acceptable and honorable unto You. *I will not doubt!*

DISTRACTIONS. There are many things clamoring for my attention and allegiance—time-consuming amusements, social activities, and specialized hobbies. Father, I do not want to be distracted in my walk with You—studying Your Word, lifeline worship, and witnessing of Your love with compassion. Keep me focused by Your instructions and anointing. *I will not be distracted!*

DIVISION. Master, I know division divides unity and fosters discord. Your plan is for believers to be partners in performing Your will—discipleship training, outreach initiatives, and strength-building fellowship. Under Your guidance I will not be a participant in division. I will be a unifier, an encourager, a peacemaker, and a ministry performer. *I will not be moved!*

BIBLE READING—ROMANS

21. Sacrifice—12:1-2. We are told to take our everyday life—work, home, church, goals—and present it as a living sacrifice—the spiritual way to serve and worship. **Prayer:** Today, Lord, I want to serve You, my church, and my pastor by offering myself as a living sacrifice, holy, pleasing, and acceptable to You.

KEEP WATCH TODAY

Watchful and powerful Master, I feel Your comforting and circumstance-controlling presence in my life. I praise You! I will stay close to You and keep a steady watch on the schemes of Satan. Keeping a vigilant watch will equip me to . . .

AVOID Temptation. Father, You desire that I live a pure and purpose-centered life. Satan desires to tempt me to turn from purity and purpose and to follow him in living a life of sinful pleasure. I will keep watch and depend on Your Word and wisdom to avoid and overcome temptation.

ADVANCE in Trust. Master, I face pressure every day — pressure to give up, to give in, to conform, and to compromise. Increase my trust in Your promises to provide strength, angelic protection, and comforting grace. I will keep watch and advance in trust.

ACCEPT Accountability. I cannot let down or turn loose of scriptural standards and life-directing behavioral principles. Father, You instruct me to stay close to You and to receive Your affirming love, Your anointing for maximum effectiveness, and Your anchoring favor. I will accept accountability and stand firm in faith today.

BIBLE READING — ROMANS

22. Affectionate — 12:9-21. In the church, we are to love one another as brothers and sisters and honor others more than ourselves (v. 10). **Prayer:** Father, I want to be what You made me to be — to serve You without envy or pride or comparing myself to other workers. I want to always maintain a spirit of "I will never give up."

PRAYER PATTERN—WORSHIP

W — Witness. Let me be a witness of Your love by the way I worship.

O — Order. Guide us to order our worship services to exalt You in music, praise, and worship.

R — Renew. May a spirit of renewal, prayer, and zeal for outreach rest on church members.

S — Stabilize. Keep me spiritually stable and balanced in the work of the church.

H — Honor. Lead me in honoring my pastor with appreciation testimonies and acts of kindness.

I — Inspire. Inspire us to respect and appreciate one another as we reap the harvest.

P — Propel. Propel us by Your Spirit into a new orbit of greater faith and works in Kingdom ministry.

BIBLE READING—ROMANS

23. Government—13:1-7. Believers and the church, as a light in the community, are to respect and embrace governing authorities as God's ministers for good (v. 4). **Prayer:** You tell us, Lord, there is "no authority except from You" (v. 1). This includes church government, also. Let me be a good citizen, proud and productive; and let our church be an example in rendering "all their dues" (v. 7), thereby creating a base to stabilize our country through spiritual direction and strength.

My Journal

FOR THE WEEK

Praise reports, answered prayers, divine provisions, and spiritual plans.

BIBLE READING—ROMANS

24. Debt—13:8-10. Our only debt should be love, because the person who loves others fulfills the Law (God's standard for representing Him) (v. 8). **Prayer:** Our church—pastor and people—will be recognized and accepted by neighbors if we show love that is supported by tenderness, tears, and triumphant living in daily life.

KINGDOM AWARENESS TODAY

King of all kingdoms, I want to be totally aware of the scope of Your reign. Your kingdom has no geographical limits or language barriers. It includes every person, every culture, and every nation. Your power is unlimited, Your grace is sufficient, and Your love is all-encompassing. Equip me to maintain a . . .

WORLDVIEW. I pray today, mighty King, for Your cause around the world. I want to see and support the ministry of sharing the gospel of Jesus Christ. I ask You to bless pastors, missionaries, Bible schools, orphanages, relief and food efforts, and media outreaches.

WORD view. Father, Your Word trains, teaches, and transforms. I pray for a recommitment among believers to embracing Your Word with new zeal and excitement. May Your Spirit guide me in personal Bible study and in applying scriptural truths and principles to my daily life.

WINNING view. In Christ, I am a winner! Therefore, I want to believe like a winner, act like a winner, and communicate like a winner. By manifesting a winning attitude, I will exalt Christ, influence the unchurched, set an example for young people, and experience radiant communion with You.

BIBLE READING—ROMANS

25. Judging—14:1-8. Judging your pastor and other church members on things that are not commanded in Scripture will cause conflict and division in the church. **Prayer:** Lord of fairness, help me today to take care of my own life and not to do anything that would cause another Christian to stumble.

KINGDOM MINISTRY TODAY

Father of all blessings, in love You give me total support in living successfully—wisdom, watchful care, and spiritual wholeness. In return, I want to give You full support in Kingdom ministry. To do this, I ask You to . . .

Let Your Will CONFORM me. I'm flexible! I'm ready to respond! Father, You have a plan, a holy purpose, a divine will for my life. Lead me and train me to conform to Your will. I will follow Your leadership and accept Your training so I can walk in step with Your will.

Let Your Spirit COMFORT me. Lord, You sent the Holy Spirit, the Comforter, to comfort me, to control my daily pursuits, and to center my focus on pleasing You. I will depend on the Holy Spirit to be my truth guide, my defender against attacks by Satan, and my helper to achieve life dreams.

Let Your Word CONTROL me. Your Word, Master, is a map to guide me in ministry; Your Word is a compass to lead people to Christ; and Your Word is a well to supply life-changing and life-directing wisdom. I will show reverence for Your Word, read Your Word, and respond to the teachings of Your Word. Your Word will make me effective in Kingdom ministry.

BIBLE READING—ROMANS

26. Pursue—14:16-19. In order to be peacemakers, we must "pursue the things which make for peace" (v. 19). **Prayer:** Father, in our church, let us agree and use our strength to create harmony and to edify (build up) one another.

LAST DAYS TODAY

Creator of Time, You know the beginning and the ending of life and everything in between. Not anything is hidden from You. Throughout the New Testament, I am instructed about the conditions of the last days—people will be unthankful, unholy, and unforgiving. In my life, I will reverse these characteristics; I will be . . .

THANKFUL. I will begin every day with an attitude of thanksgiving—for life in Christ, for liberty to grow and achieve, and for love that lifts higher and higher in heavenly experiences. I will express my thanksgiving with high praise and in upholding holy standards.

HOLY. Father, I will begin every day with an open mind and heart to receive—cleansing power from Your throne, keeping grace to live holy, and empowering virtue to be an example of living above shame and reproach. I will express my praise for holiness from a committed and pure heart.

FORGIVING. I will begin every day with a forgiving disposition—for unfounded hard feelings, for critical remarks, for strategies to disrupt unity in fellowship, and for biases that block outreach and growth. I will convey forgiveness through my behavior, through personal conversations, and through prayer.

BIBLE READING—ROMANS

27. Acceptance—15:1-7. Christ accepted each of us so that we might accept each other (v. 7). **Prayer:** Lord of harmony, I believe acceptance is the power of the church. I accept my position in You; I accept my pastor from You; and I accept believers in my church as a part of You.

LAUNCH OUT TODAY

Father, You calm troubled hearts and bring about stillness, peace, and sustaining peace. I am in Your care! I receive Your calmness! Christ told the disciples to "launch out into the deep" (Luke 5:4). They did and a miracle occurred. Today, I will launch out in life under . . .

Divine LEADERSHIP. Father, I will not hesitate to follow You. Psalm 23 says that You will lead me by "still waters" (v. 2); You will "restore my soul" (v. 3); and You will respond to my requests (vv. 4, 5). *Today, where You lead I will follow.*

The Banner of LOVE. Father, You manifested supreme love by sending Jesus Christ, Your Son, into the world to rescue, redeem, and restore—"to set at liberty those who are bound" (Luke 4:18), and to bring faith, freedom, and fullness. *Today, I will follow You under the banner of love!*

A Commitment of LONGEVITY. Lord, I am committed for the complete journey with You. Only You know how long the journey will be, what I will face, and what my needs will be. *Today, I am committed for the journey to see You face to face.*

BIBLE READING—ROMANS

28. Obedience—16:17-20. Obedience requires that we deal with people powers that cause division in the church—faulty doctrine, arrogance, self-centeredness. **Prayer:** Father, our church needs Your grace to confront agitators, to encourage participators, and to honor initiators.

LEADERSHIP TODAY

Lord of glory, You outline the path and direct the steps of those who trust in You. I trust You! I trust Your leadership! I trust You with my future and with oversight of my daily walk. As You lead me, I want to develop the biblical principles of leadership. Teach me how to lead by . . .

LOVING. Father, the ministry of Christ was characterized by love. He loved people and was devoted to fellowshiping with them, caring for them, and providing redemption for them through His self-sacrifice, and death on the cross. I pray today that the love of Christ will flow through my life.

LEARNING. Father, I desire to be a daily learner. I want to continually learn about Your nature and how You want Your will to be developed in my life. I am open to learning through responsive communion with You, by searching the scriptures, and by the guidance of the Holy Spirit.

LEADING. I want to be led by You, Father, and I want to be a leader under Your supervision. I will lead by example, by projecting creative leadership skills, and by accepting responsibility in visionary activities that advances Your kingdom.

BIBLE READING—FIRST CORINTHIANS

1. Unity of Believers—1:10. Four things are set forth in this verse: Paul told the church to have harmony in speaking (testimony), agreeing (unity), thinking (doctrine), and judging (standards). **Prayer:** Lord, let me be a person of unity with my pastor, other church members, and church programs. Let our church be in unity in witnessing, in doctrine, and in standards in living the Christian life.

THE FIVE-WAY TEST

You can help ease the pressure on your pastor and give him positive support by remembering the five-way test before filling key leadership positions, involvement in church programs, taking a position, voicing your opinion, or making a decision.

1. Will it build **TEAMWORK**?

2. Will it nurture **UNDERSTANDING**?

3. Will it undergird **MISSION**?

4. Will it enhance **DISCIPLESHIP**?

5. Will it honor **GOD**?

BIBLE READING — FIRST CORINTHIANS

2. Power of God — 2:1-5. These verses outline the posture of your pastor — commitment to the crucified Christ (v. 2), identifying with the needs of the people (v. 3), dependence on the Holy Spirit (v. 4), and building faith through the power of God (v. 5). **Prayer:** Father, I honor the posture of my pastor and ask You to bless him as he preaches the lordship of Christ, and connects my needs with the Holy Spirit.

My Journal

FOR THE WEEK

Praise reports, answered prayers, divine provisions, and spiritual plans.

_____

_____

_____

_____

_____

_____

_____

_____

_____

_____

_____

_____

BIBLE READING — FIRST CORINTHIANS

3. Planting and Watering — 3:1-10. Some leaders and workers plant, some water, and some supervise or build (v. 6). All are important, and we should honor and respect them "as the Lord gifted each one" (v. 5). **Prayer:** Father, let us recognize that in all we do in church work You are the One "who gives the increase" (v. 7) and "each one will receive his own reward according to his own labor" (v. 8).

LED BY THE SPIRIT TODAY

God of sustaining strength, I will depend on the leadership of Your Holy Spirit today. I will face challenges that include both opposition and opportunities. I will respond to opposition with tough faith and to opportunities with flaming faith. Your Spirit will lead to . . .

RESTORE joy. Both opposition and opportunities can squeeze my strength and joy. I get caught up in designing strategies and in developing an achieving mind-set. Your presence, Lord, brings joy. Restart, review, and restore Your joy in my life today.

REDEEM the time. Time is a gift from You, Father — a valuable, nonreplaceable gift. Today, I will use the gift of time wisely to grow taller in my testimony and stronger in my stand against the vices of Satan.

RECEIVE power. Your Spirit, Master, releases power to be a convincing witness. Lead me today to be a witness of Your grace by my conduct, by my contribution to worthy projects, and by my confession of total commitment to Christ.

BIBLE READING — FIRST CORINTHIANS

4. Imitate Me — 4:1-16. Your pastor is a servant of Christ and a steward of the mysteries (revelations) of God (v. 1). He sacrifices to fulfill these responsibilities (vv. 11-12), and he serves as a model to follow (v. 16). **Prayer:** Today, I ask You to meet my pastor's personal needs. Guide him as he preaches Your Word. Let me reflect on his pattern of behavior.

LIBERATED TODAY

Master of grace and glory, You forgive, set free, and outline plans for my future. I lift my voice in praise and thanksgiving for Your care. Every day Your sufficient grace surrounds me, covers me, and liberates me. Yes, I am liberated to . . .

Follow CHRIST. I am free, free indeed, to follow You, Lord, wherever You lead me. I rejoice in my freedom! I know You will provide extraordinary adventures and enriching spiritual growth experiences. Today, I will follow You closely and obediently!

Think CREATIVELY. Father, You give me building-stone thoughts and out-of-the-box thoughts. You show me new paths to follow in partnership with You. You give me "mind might" to believe, conceive, and release. Today, I will respond to Your creative work in my life!

Act with COURAGE. I will not be hesitant in attempting great things for the cause of Christ. Lord, You give me fortitude, faith, and inspiration to act boldly. Today, my life will be characterized by courage based on the authority of Your Holy Word!

BIBLE READING—FIRST CORINTHIANS

5. Puffed Up—5:1-8. We cannot become arrogant in our Christian walk and fail to mourn when there is disobedience in the church among members (v. 2). **Prayer:** Give my pastor wisdom in dealing with sin problems in the congregation, and guide church members in standing with him, recognizing that "a little leaven leavens the whole lump" (v. 6).

LIFTED HIGHER TODAY

Lord of unlimited provisions, You have provided the resources for me to stand up, speak up, and stand out in difficult situations. Whatever the occasion, You love me and You lift me up. I am grateful for "standing-strong" strength today. I trust You to lift me higher with . . .

Love THAT RELEASES. Father, Your love sent Your Son, Jesus Christ, as a sacrifice to redeem me and to release me into a full life of fellowship with You. Divine love lifts me up to heavenly heights and I am able to walk in newness and wholeness of life.

Spirituality THAT RESTORES. Father, I have liberty today to grow in Christlikeness; to overcome as He overcame; to please You as He pleased You; and to serve as He served. Spiritual liberty lifts me higher to see clearly, act wisely, and love sincerely.

Longsuffering THAT REVITALIZES. I am still learning and growing. I am still in the process of becoming. As a result of inexperience I often slip and slide. Thank You, Lord, for Your understanding nature, Your longsuffering. Thank You for lifting me up, teaching me, and caring for me. I have joy that lifts me higher today!

BIBLE READING—FIRST CORINTHIANS

6. Saints Will Judge—6:1-8. Believers are destined to judge the world (v. 2) and angels (v. 3). Therefore, we must be willing to judge (evaluate and mediate) between believers today (v. 2) and to be wise (v. 5). **Prayer:** Father, there will be problems between church members; don't let our pastor be caught in the middle. Help me, and church leaders, to be sensitive but to judge fairly and scripturally.

LIFTING UP TODAY

Father, who never gives up on people, I am thankful for pursuing, persistent love. I was walking an unholy worthless path; but you pursued me, lifted me up, forgave me, and adopted me. Now I am a joyful contented member of Your family. I want to share You today by . . .

Lifting UP the FALLEN. Father, I will meet people today who have fallen from grace with You; fallen from integrity with their employer; and fallen from fellowship with individuals who had been close to them. I will lift them up in prayer. I will lift them up by showing care and sharing the restoring power of Christ with them.

Lifting Up the FRUITLESS. I have friends at church who feel fruitless in their walk with You, Lord. I will lift them up by modeling a fruitful life, by motivating them with words of encouragement and guidance, and by being a spiritual mentor.

Lifting Up the FATIGUED. I will meet friends today who are tired and fatigued as a result of different pressures of life. I will lift them up by reminding them that every day is a new day in Christ, filled with new beginnings.

BIBLE READING—FIRST CORINTHIANS

7. Principles of Marriage—7:1-40. This chapter outlines proper conduct in marriage. Husbands and wives are to give due affection to each other (v. 3). **Prayer:** Lord of grace, I know strong marriages make strong churches. Bless my pastor's marriage; together, let us build a church of strong marriages by example, teaching, and scriptural guidance.

LIFT ME UP TODAY

King eternal, You lift up the wounded, the weak, and the weary. You also lift me up when I am down as a result of the attacks of the Evil One. You lift me up because I belong to You, a member of Your royal family. I do not fear what may come my way because I know You will be there to lift me up with . . .

Loving GRACE. Divine love comes with the full force of the Trinity—holy compassion, holy care, and holy provisions. Your love, Father, is not based on my goodness but on Your grace. I express my love for Your love in my life.

Liberating GRACE. I am free, free indeed in Christ—free from controlling influences; free from growth in Christlike restriction; free from success limitations. I honor You, Lord, for this.

Longsuffering GRACE. Father, You know my limitations and hesitations and You deal with me with patience and corrective understanding. I praise You for this. I will trust You to both direct and develop my life.

BIBLE READING—FIRST CORINTHIANS

8. Stumbling Block—8:9-13. There are weak Christians and there are strong Christians. Strong believers have a responsibility to set an example and aid weak believers in becoming strong (vv. 10-11). This often requires refraining from certain activities. **Prayer:** Father, help me to be sensitive to things that might tempt, trap, or cause a weak Christian to stumble. Let me be an example and a source of strength.

WHEN YOU PRAY
FOR YOUR PASTOR

1. It gives a **SHIELD** to the pastor and to you to defend against those who would try to divide the unity of the church.

2. It gives **STRENGTH** to the pastor for effective ministry as God honors the teamwork of the shepherd and the sheep.

3. It gives **STRUCTURE** to the congregation for following and supporting the pastor in ministry.

4. It gives **STABILITY** to the pastor, the church, and to you as life and energy flows through each member of the congregation.

5. It given **SECURITY** as the members of the church come together as a unified team.

6. It gives **SATISFACTION** as scriptural gifts are given and the church experiences unity and harmony.

7. It gives **STATISTICAL** results as the mission of the church is undergirded with positive outreach faith and action.

BIBLE READING — FIRST CORINTHIANS

9. A Servant to All — 9:1-19. Your pastor is a servant-leader to all, "that he might win the more [to Christ]" (v. 19). As a servant-leader, give him his "rights" (v. 4), give him "material things" (v. 11), and let him "live from the gospel" (v. 14). **Prayer:** Lord of glory, let me embrace the rights of my pastor to have personal free time, to preach with Your authority, and to prosper financially (not to muzzle an ox while it treads out the grain) (v. 9).

My Journal

FOR THE WEEK

Praise reports, answered prayers, divine provisions, and spiritual plans.

_____

_____

_____

_____

_____

_____

_____

_____

_____

BIBLE READING—FIRST CORINTHIANS

10. Take Heed—10:1-13. Paul talks about Israelites whose bodies were "scattered in the wilderness" (v. 5) because of "lusting" (v. 6), "idolatry" (v. 7), "sexual immorality" (v. 8), and "tempting Christ" (v. 9). He said, "Take heed lest you fall" (v. 12). **Prayer:** May we stay focused on exalting Christ and be accountable to each other and to our pastor for faithfulness in doctrine, purity, and behavior.

LIGHT TODAY

Father of light and liberty, I no longer walk in darkness, I have been delivered. I walk a new path, I have new directions, I have divine oversight. I will bear witness of Your light today by . . .

EXAMPLE. Father, Your light of love has transformed me. I have a new nature, new motivation, and new goals. My prayer is that my lifestyle will bear witness of this remarkable change. Today, I will trust You, Father, for inward grace to be reflected in outward expressions of commitment to Christ.

ENTHUSIASM. "Joy unspeakable and full of glory" conveys my testimony. A new attitude, a new outlook on life, and a new song in my heart. Yes, I am enthusiastic. I am excited. I am eager to share my story of life in Christ with others. I will model the joy of the Lord in my life today!

EXPRESSIONS. I will be a light today by expressing new ways to serve, new ways to share, and new ways to grow in grace. I will speak words of hope and encouragement to others. I will also speak words of gratitude and praise to You, Father of light.

BIBLE READING — FIRST CORINTHIANS

11. Examine Yourself — 11:17-28. It is a wonderful privilege to partake of the Lord's Supper "in remembrance of Christ" (v. 25). It is a time to examine, or evaluate our commitment to Christ and to review His promises to us. **Prayer:** As our pastor administers Holy Communion, let us as a family look into our hearts, lift up Christ, and honor Him with our lives.

LOVING GOD TODAY

Everlasting Lord of love, You are the source of all that is good, holy, and pure. You provide for all my needs — health, hope, and happiness. In return for Your supreme love, You ask me to love You supremely with all my . . .

HEART. Your Word, Father, declares that I am to love You with all my "heart, soul, and mind" (Matthew 22:37). My heart represents purity, passion, and sanctified purpose. I will love You by protecting the love in my heart; to put Your will first and foremost in my daily activities.

SOUL. I will obey Your Word, Father, that instructs me to love You with all my "heart, soul, and mind." My soul represents devotion, dedication, and discipline. I will love You by storing strength from Holy Scripture in my soul that provides me with strength to demonstrate character and spiritual wholeness in my daily Christian walk.

MIND. I am dedicated to Your Word, Father, that directs me to love You with all my "heart, soul, and mind." My mind represents thinking, talking, and training for service. I will love You by observing the mind of Christ that leads me to follow You as a servant with humility and honor.

BIBLE READING — FIRST CORINTHIANS

12. One Body — 12:12-31. The church is one body with many members and "God has set [each] member . . . in the body just as He pleased" (v. 18), and we are to honor and "care for one another" (v. 25). **Prayer:** Father of unity, I want to respect and embrace each member of our local body and do Your work in harmony with them. This is the way to please You, to respect the gifts of my pastor, and to feel compassion for the unreaped harvest fields.

LOVING-KINDNESS TODAY

Lord, of unlimited love, I am free from the restrictive force of sin today as a result of Your love—unfailing love, forgiving love, life transforming love. I am grateful—everyday grateful, lifelong grateful, and eternally grateful. As You have shown me love, I want to show . . .

Love for my FAITH. My faith, Father, is wrapped around Your supreme love, the sacrificial love of Your Son, Jesus Christ, and the empowering love of the Holy Spirit. I am committed to sharing my love for my faith by cultivating it, practicing it, and defending it. Today, I live by faith!

Love for my FAMILY. Lord, You have given me a beautiful family. I cherish the close relationships, the talents, and the uniqueness of each member. I want to contribute to family life by demonstrating a spirit of unity and respect and by the maintenance of Christian values.

Love for my FRIENDS. Friends are a special gift. They make daily life richer, fuller, and more enjoyable. They inspire me to treat them courteously, positively, and fairly. I want to be a steadfast friend and a steadfast follower of You, mighty Master!

BIBLE READING—FIRST CORINTHIANS

13. Love Never Fails—13:1-8. The honorable qualities of love set forth in verses 4-7 should characterize the lives of committed believers and the ministry of the church. Spiritual maturity and ministry are stymied when this is not happening. **Prayer:** Lord, let our church be a First Corinthians, Chapter 13 Church—practicing love in acceptance, forgiveness, and service. Also, let me be a forerunner in this.

MAJESTY TODAY

High, holy, and immortal heavenly Father, You reign and rule with distinguishing majesty, delivering might, and mountain-moving authority. I stand in Your presence with grateful humility, total heart devotion, and heavenly praise. My desire is to view You in all of Your . . .

SPLENDOR and Glory. Lord, gold, silver, diamonds, and rubies cannot compare to Your splendor and glory. You created these valuable properties to reveal the richness of Your nature and what You hold in reserve for Your children. I bow in praise and honor of Your majesty today!

SUPERNATURAL Oversight. Lord and Master, nothing is hidden from you. You know all things and oversee all things — with supernatural, unlimited strength. Your strength is manifested to carry out Your will on earth and to provide for my needs. I'm thankful!

SUPREME Authority. Lord, Master, and divine Ruler, I trust in Your authority to direct my life and to remove any obstacle or barrier that would hinder my closeness with You. I will live and minister under Your majesty and authority today!

BIBLE READING — FIRST CORINTHIANS

14. Let All Things Be Done in Order — 14:26-40. Paul said, "For God is not the author of confusion but of peace" (v. 33), and "be sure that everything is done properly in a good and orderly way" (v. 40 TLB). **Prayer:** Lord of peace, my pastor needs Your wisdom to guide our church in the use of spiritual gifts. Also, we need to be submissive to the working of the Spirit and to the leadership of our pastor in the operation of the gifts of the Holy Spirit in worship services and in the ministries of our church.

MIGHTY GRACE TODAY

Lord of mighty works and unlimited wisdom, I trust in Your grace—grace that rescues, redeems, and restores. Your mighty grace is sufficient to supply whatever I need to fight the good fight of faith and to manifest the fruit of the Spirit in my life. Through mighty grace . . .

I am a PARTAKER of PEACE. Your peace, Father, manifested in the life of Jesus Christ, reveals the essence of Your divine nature. Peace that You provide elevates my spirit, empowers me to be positive in conduct and conversation, and equips me to spread great tidings of great joy.

I have PROSPERITY in PARTNERSHIP. Father, Your peace aligns me with Your will and connects me in partnership with Your mission. Partnership with You gives me priority treatment, and I experience prosperity in all areas of my life.

I will be PRODUCTIVE in PERFORMANCE. I will go forth with mighty grace sowing seeds of success. I will return with rejoicing bringing the fruit of spiritual productivity with me. I will trust You, Lord, for mighty grace to be approved and productive.

BIBLE READING—FIRST CORINTHIANS

15. Evil Company—15:1-12, 33. False doctrine about the Resurrection was being circulated among church members. Paul said, "Evil company corrupts good habits (doctrine)" (v. 33). **Prayer:** Holy Father, let me associate with faith-builders, and let the members of our church stand with the pastor in holding firm to sound doctrine and in constantly searching the Scriptures to receive Your revelation, purposes, and power.

My Pledge of Loyalty

TO CULTIVATE FRUIT OF THE SPIRIT

I have assurance that I can experience and enjoy the fruit of the Spirit in my daily life if I earnestly seek God's will, show a yielded spirit, and sow seeds of righteousness. Therefore, I will direct my performance to ensure a rich harvest yield!

I pledge to cultivate and cherish the fruit of the Spirit by . . .

1. **PLANTING.** I will provide a fertile mind and heart. The Holy Spirit will plant. I will cultivate.

2. **PRUNING.** I will ask the Holy Spirit to guide me in pruning any conditions or conduct that would stymie the optimum growth of spiritual fruit.

3. **PROTECTING.** I will guard the fruit of the Spirit in my life by honoring God with it and expressing daily thanksgiving for it.

4. **PROCLAIMING.** I will give a vibrant testimony on how the fruit of the Spirit refreshes and nourishes with spiritual empowerment.

5. **PROVIDING.** I will share the joy and strengthening force of the fruit of the Spirit with my family and friends.

BIBLE READING — FIRST CORINTHIANS

16. The Collection — 16:1-2, 14. Impulse giving is not the scriptural way to give; inspired giving is the correct method to use — "lay something aside . . . save and give as you prosper" (see v. 2). **Prayer:** Lord, I want to be a faithful, cheerful, and consistent giver. May our church be known as a giving church, loyal to God in tithing and offerings based on Paul's admonition, "Let all that you do be done with love" (v. 14).

My Journal

FOR THE WEEK

Praise reports, answered prayers, divine provisions, and spiritual plans.

_____

_____

_____

_____

_____

_____

_____

_____

_____

_____

BIBLE READING — SECOND CORINTHIANS

1. Fellow Workers — 1:1-11, 24. False teachers stirred the people against Paul. His fellow workers realized God was not pleased with this and joined in helping him through prayer (v. 11). Paul said, "[We] are fellow workers for your joy" (v. 24). **Prayer:** God of harmony, my pastor ministers with me for my joy, my fullness in Christ. Let me pray for him, defend him, and be a "fellow worker" with him.

MINISTER OF MERCY TODAY

Father, mercy flows from Your throne—complete, cleansing, and comforting. I receive it with a blessed heart and heavenly benefits. In my life today, I want to be a minister of mercy and . . .

SEE Without RESTRICTIONS. I do not want to see with a judgmental attitude—flaws, fickle disposition, and fruitless habits. I want to see possibilities and what people can become in Christ. Father, I will be open to Your leadership today to see without restrictions.

SERVE Without RESERVATIONS. I do not want to serve with a selective mentality—biased, belittling, and baseless assumptions. I want to serve faithfully without fanfare to reflect the nature of Christ. Father, I will trust in the guidance of the Holy Spirit to serve without reservations.

SHARE Without REGRETS. I do not want to share with a begrudging disposition—selfish, self-centered, and self-serving spirit. I want to share from a heart of thanksgiving, with hands of respect, and with the compassion of Christ. Father, to honor You and support the ministries of my church, I will share Your love without regrets.

BIBLE READING—SECOND CORINTHIANS

2. Abundant Love—2:1-11, 14. Paul instructed and corrected the people because of his "abundant love for them" (see v. 4); he wanted them to be "obedient in all things" (v. 9). **Prayer:** I want to receive the instructions of my pastor in faith and obedience so I can "triumph in Christ" (v. 14) and "spread the good news like sweet perfume" (v. 15).

MINISTRY CONNECTION TODAY

Lord of the past and the present, You were in control in the past and You are in control of the present. I realize this, and my goal is to be connected to ministry based on what You have done, what You are doing, and what You desire to do. Today, in order to be firmly connected with ministry, I will . . .

REMEMBER how You, Lord, worked in times past — deliverance from bondage, demonstrations of miracle-working power, and devoted care of individuals serving You. When I remember, I am refreshed, my faith flourishes, and I am filled with fresh energy.

REVIVE goals, aspirations, and dreams that have faded or failed. Lord, revive me, renew me, refresh me, so I can have a new start in being connected to ministry that makes a difference in my life and in the impact of my church.

RESOLVE to take giant steps to connect with ministry that You have designed for my life. My resolve, Father, needs Your resources to succeed — spiritual oversight, Holy Spirit enablement, and structured time for study and supplication. By faith, I resolve and accept divine resources.

BIBLE READING — SECOND CORINTHIANS

3. Living Epistles — 3:1-5. The believer is a living epistle (letter), written by the Holy Spirit, ministered to by the pastor (v. 3), and known and read by people in the church and in the community (v. 2). **Prayer:** Lord, I recognize my sufficiency is from You (v. 5), and I lean on You today; I also lean on the instructions (ministry) of my pastor.

MIRACULOUS FAITH TODAY

Miracle-working Master, I have completeness and wholeness in You! I have access to Your throne of grace where I can experience the inconceivable, the unexplainable, and the unexplorable. I praise You for miraculous faith; faith that transforms my thinking, pictures Your unlimited power, and leads me to . . .

Believe the UNBELIEVABLE. With You, Father, all things are possible! I believe! The impossible becomes possible with You. Today I will manifest a faith that has no boundaries.

Anticipate the UNFULFILLED. Father, I know that You have plans, promises, and prophecies about the future. I believe! I stand ready to understand, to adopt, and to adapt to Your will and Your ways for the future. I will exercise miraculous faith.

Honor my UNIQUENESS. Lord of all creation, You have formed me with unique and special skills. I will embrace my uniqueness with a miraculous faith. I will develop and deploy the talents You have invested in me. I will cherish and protect them. I will use them in life-enriching worship, in Christ-exalting service, and Kingdom-expanding vision and witness.

BIBLE READING — SECOND CORINTHIANS

4. Your Bondservant — 4:1-5, 9, 16. Your pastor is a bondservant (v. 5), teaching the truth plainly to show he can be trusted (v. 2). He endures many things, but he stands firmly by the grace of God (vv. 8, 9) to show the dying of Christ in his life. **Prayer:** As a bondservant, my pastor lives in close quarters and is under constant pressure. Lift him up today by Your Spirit and by my understanding and support of his ministry.

MOTIVATED TODAY

High and lifted up Lord, I look to You for the resources to live an overflowing life today. Your resources flow from Your throne of redeeming love and daily watchful care. I am blessed to live an abundant life, an anchored life, and an awarded life under Your care.

ABUNDANT Life. Lord and Master, You are a high and lifted-up King—a gracious King, a glorious King, and a life-giving King. You provide me with an abundant life—sufficient beyond compare, overflowing with richness and fullness, and fulfilling guiding communion. I am motivated to live an abundant life that honors You.

ANCHORED Life. In Christ, I can live an anchored life—solid, secure, satisfying. I can stand up as a testimony of Christ's enriching grace. I can stand out as a model of Your molding influence, Lord. I can stand unwavering, because I am anchored in Christ. I am motivated to live an anchored life of significance and steadfastness.

AWARDED Life. Father, everything I possess are gifts from You—personal skills, material possessions, and energizing peace. I have completeness in Your Son, Jesus Christ. I am motivated to live the awarded life by embracing Your perfect will.

BIBLE READING—SECOND CORINTHIANS

5. Opportunity to be an Ambassador—5:14-21. Pastor Paul said he had been given "the ministry of reconciliation" (v. 18), bringing people to Christ and bringing believers together, and that "the love of Christ compelled him" (v. 14). **Prayer:** It is my privilege to be an "ambassador for Christ" (v. 20) and to work hand-in-hand with my pastor leading people to become "a new creation in Christ" (v. 17). Let me do this with grace, dignity, and joy.

MOVE MOUNTAINS TODAY

Unstoppable, unmovable, and unlimited Master, thank You for the promise of Your presence and the power to move mountains (Mark 11:23). I will face mountains—pressure to conform, power struggles, and personality conflicts. No mountain is high enough or strong enough to block Your mountain-moving intervention. Therefore, I will . . .

Yield COMPLETELY. Master, my life is in Your hands; You are in control! I will not hold out or hold back; I am yielded completely. I am yielded to Your will and to the way You want to move mountains in my path of pleasing You and in my walk of honoring You.

Believe CONVINCINGLY. I believe and I will back my belief with conformity to holy standards—separation from worldly influences, service that impacts Kingdom outreach, and scriptural integrity that denotes rigid steadfastness. Lord, I believe that no mountain can block me from performing Your will for my life.

Act COURAGEOUSLY. Father, Your Spirit equips me to face mountains of emotional distress and evil enticements with courage and boldness and to act with overcoming confidence in Your sustaining and delivering grace. I will be a mountain-mover today!

BIBLE READING—SECOND CORINTHIANS

6. In All Things—6:3-10. Paul presents a vivid picture of Your pastor in these verses. "In all things we commend (give, endure, sacrifice) ourselves as ministers of God: in patience, tribulations, needs . . . labors . . . sincere love, and by the word of truth" (vv. 4-7). **Prayer:** Father, I am thankful for the life of my pastor. I too want to represent You like he does and to act wisely and to be an example in "all things."

PERSONAL AFFIRMATION— PRAYER

Understanding the sacred privilege to commune with my heavenly Father through prayer,

I Will . . .

- Offer praise and thanksgiving.
- Cherish the privilege of prayer.
- Appropriate a daily time for prayer.
- Prepare by examining my devotion.
- Express love, honor, and trust.
- Request wisdom to grow in grace.
- Remember my family and church.
- Pledge Great Commission loyalty.
- Request strength to serve effectively.
- Accept God's revealing leadership.

BIBLE READING—SECOND CORINTHIANS

7. **Confidence in You—7:1-16.** Pastor Paul had to correct his people (vv. 8, 9). They were slow to respond, but they did, and it brought diligence, zeal, and vindication (v. 11). **Prayer:** Lord, let me be open to instructions and correction from my pastor and receive them with an "open heart" (v. 11), thereby bringing us closer together in mission and teamwork.

My Journal

FOR THE WEEK

Praise reports, answered prayers, divine provisions, and spiritual plans.

_____

_____

_____

_____

_____

_____

_____

_____

_____

BIBLE READING — SECOND CORINTHIANS

8. The Gift of Giving — 8:1-24. The congregation actually gave beyond their ability; "they were freely willing" (v. 3). Paul commended and exhorted them to "abound" (excel) in the grace of giving (v. 7). **Prayer:** Father, let me, and our church, "prove our love" (v. 24) through our liberality (v. 2), and by practicing "the grace of giving" — to send the gospel, to help the needy, and to expand helping ministries.

MOVING HIGHER TODAY

High and Holy Creator, walking with You becomes richer, fuller, and higher every day. I increase in knowledge of Your nature and of Your giving spirit every day. I will demonstrate my thanksgiving by . . .

Spreading HOPE. Lord of love, You have given me hope through Jesus Christ. This hope is secure and satisfying. I will spread hope today by a contagious upbeat attitude, by a testimony of God's redeeming grace, and by attesting to the richness of biblical promises.

Providing HELP. I can help friends and family members in many ways—lift them up in prayer to You, Lord, lift them up through expressions of appreciation, and lift them up through support in difficult times. I lift up my voice to You for guidance to fulfill these goals.

Emphasizing HEAVEN. Heaven is a home prepared for Your children, Lord. It is an unbreakable, undeniable promise. In my testimony today, I will emphasize the beauty of heaven and the eternal bliss of Your presence.

BIBLE READING—SECOND CORINTHIANS

9. Sowing Bountifully—9:1-11. God loves a cheerful giver (v. 7) and one who sows "bountifully" (with blessings) (v. 6). He supplies and multiplies the seed and increases the fruit of your righteousness (goodness, generosity) (v. 10). **Prayer:** According to Your Word, Father, sowing bountifully also produces bountiful blessings from You (v. 11). Bless our church to bless the needy, other churches, and social relief work.

MULTIPLIED PEACE TODAY

There is no shortage of peace in You, Holy Father; there is multiplied peace! Your peace covers me, comforts me, and controls my behavior. Your PEACE is Personal, Energizing, Anointing, Creative, and Enriching. I am blessed with a . . .

Calm HEART. Father, Your peace in my heart keeps me calm and settled. I have calmness through purity, and I have security through assurance. I have filled my heart with Your promise of peace. This keeps my heart pure, protected, and loving the things You love.

Clean HANDS. Purified! Sanctified! Modified! My hands have been cleansed, committed to You, Lord, and transformed to hold truth, to perform service, to embrace the sorrowing, and to be lifted up in adoration for Your majesty and acts of mercy.

Clear HEAD. My thinking is clear, my mind is filled with holy thoughts and godly wisdom. I will adopt the mind of Christ outlined in Philippians 2:5-8. Today, Master, I will meditate on Your Word so that it will become the guiding force in my attitude, my convictions, and my actions.

BIBLE READING — SECOND CORINTHIANS

10. Spiritual Authority — 10:7-18. As a congregation's faith and trust in their pastor increases, his sphere of influence and impact is enlarged (v. 15). **Prayer:** Father, as we join with our pastor and glory in You, You commend us, and we recognize the authority that each other has in administering the functions of the church.

MY ACTIONS TODAY

Lord who instructs lovingly, I will follow Your leadership today. I will be surrounded by distraction and I need You to guide and guard my actions. I ask You for both supervision and strength to . . .

Believe STRONGLY. Today, I am determined to believe You, Lord, with all my heart, mind, and spirit. I believe, but like the man in the Bible (Mark 9:24), I ask You to strengthen my belief so that in every situation I will believe strongly without hesitation or reservations.

Behave SCRIPTURALLY. My conduct will identify me as a follower of Jesus Christ. Therefore, my behavior, my walk and my talk, must be scripturally rooted. Father, as I read Your Word open my understanding so I can relate scriptural truths to my life—worship, goals, relationships.

Belong SOCIALLY. I must touch the unchurched if I am to influence them and demonstrate the love of Christ. Guide me, Father, in participating in social projects in a way that reflects the nature of Christ, the nature of the Church, and the nature of the Christian life.

BIBLE READING—SECOND CORINTHIANS

11. Godly Jealousy—11:1-4. The passion of God, godly jealousy, burns inside your pastor because he has the responsibility to present you as a virgin bride to one husband, Christ (v, 2). **Prayer:** Holy Father, let our pastor be "thoroughly manifested (through knowledge and wisdom) in all things among us" (see v. 6). This comes from You. Bless him to guide! Bless us to follow!

MY CHURCH LEADERS TODAY

Lord who calls and leads, I am thankful for the individuals in my church who have responded to Your call to be leaders — to teach, train, guide, and nurture. They are a strong force in the development of my faith and doctrinal integrity.

They LIVE with a sense of spiritual calling. They understand they are accountable to You, Lord, and live a life of obedience — dependability, skill development, and dedication to ministry. I understand the demands on their time, energy, and family life. I will express appreciation for their service to You, to me, and to the church and will hold them in high esteem.

They LOVE me and members of the church family. Lord, I feel a personal connection with them. I sense their love for You and the respect for the calling You have given to them. You have invested a special love in them that is revealed in a caring disposition, a supportive attitude, and a generous spirit.

They LABOR to develop mature disciples. Father, they spend hours in prayer and study to instruct, inspire, and to provide insights about worship, relationships, and service. Give them fruit for their labor! Give them followers who want to grow in purity and maturity.

BIBLE READING — SECOND CORINTHIANS

12. Strength in Weakness — 12:1-11. Paul had "visions and revelations of the Lord" (v. 1). He also had "a thorn in the flesh" (a handicap to keep him from being too proud) (v. 7). God said, "My strength is made perfect in weakness" (v. 9). **Prayer:** Mighty God, You have assured me that Your grace is sufficient for every perplexity or problem (v. 9). I affirm this promise for me, my pastor, and my church. I will live victoriously today!

MY CHURCH TODAY

Loving Lord, who cherishes fellowship with Your people, I honor You for my church where I can sing praises to You, hear promises from Your Word, pray with other believers to You, and pledge loyalty to You. My church deserves . . .

LOVE from me in supporting the mission of the church—to reach, teach, disciple, and send forth. I can reach people through compassion, teach people through biblical instructions, disciple people through mentoring, and help send forth people through the ministries of the church. *I love my church!*

LOYALTY from me in affection and support—faithful attendance, strengthening interaction, steadfast financial commitment, and visionary outreach involvement. I will practice loyalty to my church, promote loyalty, and participate in events that build loyalty. *I love my church!*

LABOR from me in supporting my pastor and church leaders—dependability, devotion, dedication in outreach involvement, and development as a fully engaged, motivated disciple. *I love my church!*

BIBLE READING—SECOND CORINTHIANS

13. Become Complete—13:1-14. In verses 9 and 11 Paul said, "that you may be made [become] complete." The Christian life is a process. But, as you embrace "good comfort . . . one mind . . . live in peace (harmony), God will sustain and uphold you" (see v. 11). **Prayer:** All-sufficient heavenly Father, I strive for "completeness" in Christ. I need the guidance of Your Spirit, the teaching of my pastor, and the support of church leaders and members. I recognize this today and will draw sustaining strength from each one.

PRAYER PATTERN — JOYFUL

This Joyful Prayer Pattern will guide you in becoming a strong church member and a strong supporter of your pastor.

J — Let us reflect overflowing **JOY** in our work in the church.

O — May we **OMIT** negative trends in our thinking, talking, and planning.

Y — Let us maintain a focus on **YOUR** purity and power to perform.

F — Guide us by the Holy Spirit in **FOLLOWING** and respecting our pastor.

U — Our prayer is to be **USED** by You as a partner with the pastor in ministry.

L — Let Your **LOVE** bring us together with the pastor and hold us together.

BIBLE READING — GALATIANS

1. Stance of the Church — 1:6-8. The churches of Galatia were being influenced by Judaizers to switch from the gospel of Christ to the gospel of works; Paul rebuked them. **Prayer:** Eternal Light, shine on our church so that we might ever exalt and proclaim Jesus Christ and not get bogged down with wanting our own way or focusing on our works.

My Journal

FOR THE WEEK

Praise reports, answered prayers, divine provisions, and
spiritual plans.

BIBLE READING — GALATIANS

2. Pastoral Calling — 1:15-17. Paul said he was called by
God to reveal His Son through teaching and preaching.
Prayer: Blessed Lord, may our church fully understand
that our pastor is called by You to preach Jesus Christ that
we might accept Him, follow Him, and strive to reflect His
likeness in our daily lives. Let us accept his messages with
respect and open hearts.

MY CHURCH SUPPORT TODAY

Lord who equips and establishes, I am thankful that Your Church is steady and strong and that "the gates of hell shall not prevail against it" (Matthew 16:18). Your Church is my shelter, my strength, and my source of guidance. Therefore, I will support my church:

By My ATTITUDE. I will exhibit a loving, positive attitude that supports the mission, message, and methods of my church. My positive attitude will be a witness to my love and loyalty to my church and my firm doctrinal stance.

By My ACTIONS. My actions will blend with my attitude. I will be alert to seize opportunities to serve, to support church events and outreach, and to be a guide and guardian for the young people of the church.

By My ACCOUNTABILITY. I will stand up and stand out by being accountable—conistent worship attendance, consistent financial support, and consistent involvement in the ministries of my church. I will show that I am totally commited by my attitude, my actions, and my accountability.

BIBLE READING—GALATIANS

3. Pillars of the Church—2:9. Pillars of the church work together in unity when there are differences of opinion and doctrinal views. **Prayer:** Lord of changeless power, I want to be a pillar of support in my church. Let me respect the leadership of my pastor, the views of other church members, and work in close harmony with them.

MY EXAMPLE TODAY

Great and awesome Lord, Your Word sets forth portraits of men and women who were electrifying examples of closeness with You; an unwillingness to compromise convictions, and courage to relate to non-Christians on their territory. I want to follow their example and be a . . .

BIBLE-believing example — applying Your Word, Lord, to everyday life. If Your Word says it, I will believe it, claim it, and cherish it. If Your Word says it, I will live by it, defend it, and share it. *I will be a Bible-believing example!*

BATTLE-ready example — putting on Your complete armor. Father, You have promised to supply everything I need to be fully prepared to defeat the advances of the Enemy. Therefore, I will not let go of Your promises, let down on upholding the flag of victorious faith, or let anything separate me from the empowerment of the Spirit to advance. *I will be a battle-ready example!*

BRIDGE-building example — reaching those who are not followers of Christ. Father, You have equipped me to build bridges across chasms that separate individuals from You — skeptics, those held in Satan's grip, and those with self-serving interests. I will erect a bridge to reach them based on love, acceptance, compassion, and care. *I will be a bridge-building example!*

BIBLE READING — GALATIANS

4. Crucified with Christ — 2:20. What does it mean to you to be crucified with Christ, and how does your answer relate to sharing Christ and serving in the church? **Prayer:** Help me today to see myself on the cross with Christ and to feel and see like Him in performing Your will, Holy Father.

MY PASTOR TODAY

Father, You are the Great Shepherd and the keeper of my soul. You watch over me and protect me from evil influences and invasions. You have appointed my pastor to be a shepherd-leader to serve under Your guidance. I will stand with him, for him, and by him because of his . . .

CALLING. Father, my pastor has been called by You, anointed by You, and empowered by You to be a leader, an instructor, a protector, and a comforter. I recognize, and will depend upon, his spiritual oversight and his instructions from Your Word.

COMMISSION. My pastor has been commissioned to guide the church family and me in fulfilling the Great Commission—to reach, teach, train, and live the life of a mature disciple. He is also commissioned to guide me in observing the Great Commandment—to love, embrace, and care for those in need.

COMMITMENT. Father, my pastor maintains biblical convictions about Your call on his life—total commitment to proclaiming Your Word, caring for the local flock, and modeling fruitful steadfastness. I will stand with him, for him, and by him.

BIBLE READING—GALATIANS

5. Hearing of Faith—3:5. Our works, or following a rigid routine, does not bring about the ministry of the Spirit or the working of miracles. These things come from God by "the hearing of faith," and the expression of faith in prayer. **Prayer:** Lord, may You "hear faith" from our church through our prayers, our verbal witness, and our firm stand on Your promises so we can experience the moving of the Spirit and mighty miracles.

MY TESTIMONY TODAY

Lord of life-directing wisdom, I thank You for the inspiring testimonies of men and women in the Bible. Their testimonies are motivating and proof-positive that Your wisdom guides believers in living high influential and holy lives. I ask You to endow me with wisdom so I can share a scriptural testimony that proclaims . . .

God LOVES the world. The world represents people You love. Father, You love people. As a result of Your love, You sent Your Son, Jesus Christ, into the world to seek, save, and restore. *I will testify about Your love today!*

Christ LIBERATES from the Fall. Adam's disobedience in the Garden of Eden caused a fall from guiltless to guilty. Father, Your Son, through His death and resurrection, broke the bondage created by the Fall and provided liberty and new life connection and closeness with You. *I will rejoice in holy liberty today!*

The Holy Spirit LEADS in revealing truth. Your truth, Father, is the dynamic force for living a balanced and overcoming life. The Holy Spirit reveals and guides in understanding Your truth—doctrine, Christian duties, daily devotion, and directions for sanctified service. *I will depend on the leadership of the Holy Spirit today!*

BIBLE READING—GALATIANS

6. Sons of God—3:26-28. We are all sons and daughters of God, one in Christ. There is no separation as a result of family, position, skills, or age. **Prayer:** God, Your Son was the Lamb of Calvary. He gave His life for all peoples. Guide our church in embracing all peoples—rich and poor, high and low, strong and weak, and the mature and the struggling.

NEW AVENUES TODAY

Master, You move me forward every day. I experience new avenues of learning, loving, and leading. You make life exciting and filled with possibilities. I am thankful, and I will respond by asking for . . .

UNITY in Mission. Father, unity among members is essential in fulfilling the mission of the local church. I will be a unifier by recognizing the talents of other believers, by praying for them, and by joining them in embracing the responsibilities of ministry. I will stand in unity with You to achieve these goals.

UNDERSTANDING in Outreach. I understand, Master, that sharing my faith in Christ with others requires understanding—their ripeness to receive and their readiness for renewal. Lead me by Your Spirit in understanding ripeness, readiness, and the right witnessing approach to take.

UNCTION to Achieve. I ask for your favor and anointing, Lord, to move forward in achieving goals that honor you. Guide me in building bridges of goodwill, of Christian fellowship, and of outreach service. Thank You for fortifying grace to embrace new avenues today.

BIBLE READING—GALATIANS

7. Christ Formed in You—4:19. The ministry of the pastor and church is to embrace , love, and teach people so that "Christ can be formed in [them]"—His characteristics, conduct, and commitment. **Prayer:** Blessed Lord, bless me with a leadable, teachable, agreeable, and peaceable spirit as my pastor, church leaders, and members guide me and support me in maturing and developing in Christlikeness.

EXCELLENCE IN MINISTRY PERSONAL PLEDGE

I am committed to excellence . . .

- In purity of worship and witness.
- In prayer and diligent study.
- In praise and daily thanksgiving.
- In purpose and ministry objectives.
- In personal conduct and relationships.
- In positive role-modeling and mentoring.
- In performance goals and lifestyle.
- In productivity and consistent vision.
- In partnership and teamwork loyalty.
- In promoting and honoring excellence.

Signed _____

BIBLE READING—GALATIANS

8. Serve One Another—5:13-14. We have liberty in Christ to be, to become, and to belong. This liberty is two-fold: (1) to serve one another in love; and (2) to "love your neighbor as yourself." **Prayer:** Lord, through the richness of Your mercy, let the members of our church serve one another—respect, relate, and respond to the needs for attention, affirmation, and affection.

My Journal

FOR THE WEEK

Praise reports, answered prayers, divine provisions, and spiritual plans.

_____

_____

_____

_____

_____

_____

_____

_____

_____

_____

BIBLE READING — GALATIANS

9. Fruit of the Spirit — 5:22-23. The fruit of the Spirit is to be grown in our lives and shown in our activities — this is a call to character. **Prayer:** Father, You are the giver of grace and gifts. Let my association with my pastor and other church members be controlled by the production and practice of the fruit of the Holy Spirit.

NEW VIEW TODAY

My spiritual view can be dimmed by discouragement and limited devotional time in prayer, Bible reading, and worship. I realize this! I ask You to anoint my eyes and mind with a new view of spiritual qualities that will keep me strong, balanced, and focused on . . .

MAXIMUM Potential. Father, You have invested skills, talents, and abilities in me. Guide me in maximizing my potential through devotion to You, by developing avenues of impact, and by demonstrating determination to achieve and succeed. A new view generates new values!

MINISTRY Possibilities. Lord, I am surrounded by possibilities to share Your love, to serve those in need, and to reflect the glory of Christ in my work ethic and Christian etiquette. Give me courage to stand up and step out and seize growth privileges. A new view opens new doors to minister!

MOTIVATION for Productivity. Master, today I want to be excited, energetic, and motivated for "good works." Let Your Spirit cover me, clothe me, and commission me with authority to be alert and aggressive in living an uncluttered and visionary life. A new view generates new power for excellence in performance!

BIBLE READING — GALATIANS

10. Share in All Good Things — 6:6. The pastor is a leader and teacher. His life is driven by telling you about the "good things" of God and how to enjoy spiritual prosperity and pleasure in Him. **Prayer:** Father of goodness, let me practice the law of sowing and reaping with my pastor. Let me do all within my power to help my pastor receive the "good things" he teaches me about.

NO CRISIS OF CONFIDENCE TODAY

Never-failing Father, I rejoice today because You know and control my life. You know my steps and thoughts and You control my future. I have complete confidence in Your care. I have no crisis of confidence—I stand steady, secure, and satisfied in You. On this foundation, I will . . .

CONFESS my faith. My faith is firm! I believe, Lord, because I have received Your glorious gifts. I have received unlimited grace. I have received Your anointing to shine spiritually and to serve effectively. I confess my faith in the solid Rock, Jesus Christ.

CONTROL my actions. The way I behave reveals what I believe and where I place my confidence. Father, my confidence is in You! I want my actions to demonstrate this and to create confidence in Christ among my friends and associates.

COUNT my blessings. Lord of love, I have confidence in Your promises—daily watchful care, devoted guidance, and deliverance from evil attacks. Today, I will count my blessings from You—all of them! I will express thanksgiving and convey confidence in You, never-failing Father.

BIBLE READING—GALATIANS

11. Refuse to Grow Weary—6:9. Church work is work! It requires diligent, determined, and dedicated labor rooted in love. It is a constant ministry of "giving." **Prayer:** Giver of rest, I ask You to refresh my pastor and church workers today. Give them a harvest of strength, a harvest of support, and a harvest of souls.

NO EMPTY FAITH TODAY

Lord of high-level living, Your will for me is to live an abundant life through faith that is clear, uncluttered, and without fog. Faith that is clouded by fog, a lack of understanding and adaptation, limits a full release of Your provisions. Direct me and develop me by . . .

REVIEWING faith promises. Father, Your Word is filled with faith promises that support holy living, healthy living, and heaven-bound living. I will constantly review faith promises by daily Bible reading, memorizing promise scriptures, and rejoicing in fulfilled promises.

RESTRICTING negative-thinking patterns. Satan seeks to restrict my faith by entertaining negative conclusions, a negative atmosphere, and negative behavior. Master, I will fight the good fight of faith against Satan and stand on a platform of positive faith, productive faith, and partnership faith with You. I will exhibit a positive faith in all aspects of my life.

REFOCUSING on personal skills. Father, You have invested in me skills and abilities to earn a living, to engage in Christ-exalting evangelism, and to exercise faith to achieve life-enriching goals. I will concentrate on the positive, eliminate the negative, and cultivate a clear and growing faith.

BIBLE READING—EPHESIANS

1. Every Spiritual Blessing—1:3-4. God has given the church divine privileges and resources that are available right now. The gifts of the Holy Spirit are included among the "spiritual blessings." **Prayer:** Lord of abundance, may our church be an "every blessing" church. Fully trusting You, may we affirm Your blessings, appropriate Your blessings, and be an ambassador to share Your blessings.

NO FEAR TODAY

Mighty Master, You have replaced fear in my life with faith in Your restoring power, supplying power, and sustaining power. This gives me freedom to think clearly, plan wisely, and to live victoriously. I will live a fear-free life today.

No fear of FAILURE. In Christ, I am a winner. Father, You have invested in me the characteristics of a spiritual winner—trust, obedience, endurance, and the energizing principles of righteousness. I will be successful today in worship, in witnessing, and in walking a positive, God-pleasing path.

No fear of FULFILLMENT. In Christ, I am a winner! Father, You have given me the resources for fulfillment—vision, energy, talents, and the initiative to take action. I will be successful today in achieving goals, in developing skills, and in capitalizing on opportunities.

No fear of the FUTURE. In Christ, I am a winner! Father, You have provided assurance for me—the unshakable promise of heaven, daily provisions, and protection against the assaults of Satan. I will be successful today by validating Your promises of victory now and in the future.

BIBLE READING—EPHESIANS

2. Giving Thanks for You—1:16-19. Pastor Paul told the Ephesians that he was thankful for them and that he prayed consistently that God would equip them with wisdom, understanding, and awareness of His great power toward them. **Prayer:** Lord, I know my pastor prays for me and my spiritual development in Christ. I thank You for him and ask that his prayers for me and the church family will be answered.

NO STRAYING TODAY

Safe and secure! In Your hands, under Your watchful care, and directed by Your wisdom, I am safe and secure. Safe from destructive forces that would lead me astray and secure in the expansive wealth of heavenly grace. I will not stray today by . . .

Standing on Scriptural PROMISES. Your Word, Father, is forever settled in heaven. All the promises of personal peace, day-by-day provisions, and protection from the storms of life are secure, settled, steadfast. I will not stray from following You. I will stand on Your unmovable and unshakable promises!

Standing on Holy PRINCIPLES. Father, You have set forth principles and practices to guide me in living a daily life that would reflect Your character, my response to challenges around me, and to reap scriptural fruit that would attest to my biblical convictions and commitment.

Standing on Assurance of PARADISE. Master, all of Your promises are "yes" and "amen." They are unchangeable! They never fail! I live with the assurance of heaven, paradise, my eternal home with You. This future assurance ignites my faith for today to live in the fullness of Your promises and to safeguard holy principles.

BIBLE READING—EPHESIANS

3. Prepared for Good Works—2:10. "We are His workmanship" is a beautiful statement. Through the new birth, we are living possibilities of "good works" in Christ by the enablement of the Holy Spirit. **Prayer:** By grace, heavenly Father, we can point the unchurched to You through good works. May our church be known by our faith, our reaching out in love, and our "good works."

PLEDGE TO DEVELOP FRUITFUL FAITH

I am aware of the components of faith outlined in Hebrews 11:1, and will earnestly strive to cultivate a pleasing disposition, maintain a positive mind-set, and develop a spiritual work ethic for faith to germinate and grow in my life. I am ready for God-pleasing action!

I pledge to follow a path of fruitful faith by . . .

1. **CULTIVATING** a disposition of openness and readiness for fruitful faith to develop.

2. **CONDITIONING** my mind to comprehend the scope of boundless blessings when scriptural faith is released.

3. **CONTROLLING** negative thoughts that would detour positive faith and personal stability.

4. **COMMUNICATING** with language that inspires family members and friends to exercise faith to achieve honorable goals.

5. **COMMENDING** my pastors and church workers for faith in developing devoted and fruit-bearing disciples.

BIBLE READING — EPHESIANS

4. Being Built Together — 2:20-22. As we surrender to Christ and seek to please Him as a body of believers, He brings the church together as a holy temple for a dwelling place of God in the Spirit. **Prayer:** Father, we are "fitted together" as we recognize the mission of our church, the ministry of our pastor, and the responsibility of church members. Let us "grow into a holy temple" where we exalt You and equip Your people to live the abundant life in Christ.

My Journal

FOR THE WEEK

Praise reports, answered prayers, divine provisions, and spiritual plans.

BIBLE READING — EPHESIANS

5. Prisoner of Jesus Christ — 3:1. Pastor Paul told the people he was a "prisoner" for them. This indicated self-imposed restrictions in order to teach them about God's promises and their position in Christ. **Prayer:** Lord, my pastor is a "prisoner" for our church. He willingly endures confinement and faces stressful circumstances to lead, feed, and tend the church flock. Bless him today. Bind our people together in love to support him.

OBEDIENCE TODAY

Unchangeable Lord, Your vision for my life never varies. You want me to prosper and be in good health, to pray and to receive, and to proclaim and reap the harvest. I will be obedient to Your vision for my life by manifesting . . .

A Willing WILL. Father, my will is to embrace Your will! I will be obedient and follow Your plans for my growth in Christlikeness, for my daily communion with You, and for connection with other believers in worship and outreach ministry.

A Winning WALK. I will show a positive attitude today that reveals strength of character and spiritual stability. I will walk with steady steps by trusting, obeying, and reaching goals that honor You and that reflect a winning walk in daily life.

A Wise WATCH. Your Word, mighty Master, denotes that I am to "watch and pray." I will do this with wisdom from the Bible and from revelation in my prayer life. I will be on watch today to achieve and to advance the cause of Christ.

BIBLE READING—EPHESIANS

6. Glory in the Church—3:17-21. God is honored in the church, and through the ministries of the church, as believers are "rooted" (deep faith) and "grounded" (firm foundation) in love (v. 17), and reach for His fullness through scriptural resources and spiritual wisdom (v. 19). **Prayer:** Lord of glory, may our church be "rooted and grounded," balanced, through strong and consistent programs of discipleship, stewardship, and fellowship.

OPEN DOORS TODAY

Every day is a gracious gift from You, life-giving Master. It is Your desire that I experience new adventure, learn new ways to receive and relate, and to grow daily in wisdom, grace, and understanding. I have open doors to . . .

Great OPPORTUNITIES. Holy Creator, I have opportunities to read, understand, and apply the principles of Your Word; to grow stronger in my Christian walk, and to be more proficient in living my standards and in pursuing life goals. I will walk through open doors today!

Overcome OPPOSITION. Lord, Satan will try to block my communion with You through conflict and confusion. He will oppose my testimony, my prayer time, and my ability to walk in truth and love. I will walk through open doors of overcoming strength, problem-solving instructions, and victory-ensuring grace.

Promote OUTREACH. Father, I will promote and participate in outreach—touching the unchurched, the distraught, and those suffering under the weight of sin. I will walk through every open door You set before me to stress the beauty of Your kingdom.

BIBLE READING—EPHESIANS

7. **Equipping the Saints—4:11-13.** God has set leaders in the church to equip church members—train, perfect, and make fully qualified for service. **Prayer:** Father, I know it is the responsibility of my pastor to equip me for "the work of ministry." I ask You to give me grace to love him, listen to him, lean on him, and labor faithfully and fruitfully with him.

OPEN EYES TODAY

Watchful Master, Your eyes are always open to protect Your people, to provide for them, and to steady their steps on the path of life. I'm thankful; I offer praise to You! I ask You today that my eyes would always be open to . . .

Expect MIRACLES. Father, miracles flow from Your throne — daily, freely, abundantly. This is supported by biblical promises and by the life experiences of believers down through the ages. Thank You that I have experienced miracles and that I can expect miracles. Keep my eyes open to love, grace, and gifts.

Explore MAJESTY. Heavenly Father, with open spiritual eyes, I can explore Your majesty, sovereignty, supremacy, and splendor. When I think about Your throne, I see unlimited authority. When I think about heaven, I see unmatched, unrestricted beauty. When I think about Your nature, I see pure holiness. Keep my eyes open to explore Your nobility, magnificence, and perfection.

Experience MANNA. Master, I will look up and look around to experience Your manna — holy visitations, faith food, and power provisions. In every area of my life, You send heavenly manna. Keep my eyes open to experience Your strength, sufficiency, and amazing support.

BIBLE READING — EPHESIANS

8. Be Kind to One Another — 4:32. How can a church impact its community and city? By following the example of Christ — kindness, tenderheartedness, and forgiveness. **Prayer:** Lord of Light, we live in a dark, damp, and divided world. Let our church, through motivated members, provide light for darkness, warmth for dampness, and togetherness for division.

OPENING DOORS TODAY

Problem-solving Master, You open closed doors and close opened doors. You do this to guide me in following Your ideal will for my life and to fulfill Your eternal purposes on earth. Today, I look to You to open doors for me to . . .

WITNESS in Love. Judgment Day is a reality! There will be a day of judgment for me and for every person—deeds, devotion, and destructive habits. Today, I want to witness about Christ in love. I do not want to emphasize judgment; I want to emphasize the joy of the Lord. Inspire me, Lord, to do this!

WORK in the Community. My words will be extremely weak if I do not back them up with a visible Christian work ethic—social projects, assisting the suffering, and solving community problems. May my unselfish work lead to winning the lost.

WORSHIP With Influence. Master, I worship to exalt and honor You. I pray that my worship will always be sincere and a penetrating, visible, and influential sign of my all-out commitment to You, my family, and my church. Today, I will pray with passion, sing "soul-music," and interact with others with an open, Spirit-filled heart.

BIBLE READING—EPHESIANS

9. Walk in Love and Light—5:1-2, 8-10. How does a church love the community and city? It begins with the love of church members, demonstrated through living clean and convincing lives and "walking as children of light." **Prayer:** Light that never fades, may our church walk our talk by walking in love and light. Let us live sermons that show we are genuine, that Your grace is sufficient, and that Your love never fails.

OPPORTUNITY TODAY

Lord of new beginnings, You have set open doors of opportunity before me to learn, lead, and labor in Your vineyard. I will learn through being yielded! I will lead by example! I will labor to expand Your kingdom. I will also respond to opportunities to . . .

Stretch Mind MUSCLES. Lord, I will trust You today to grow more intense in developing mind muscles — thinking holy thoughts, memorizing holy scriptures, and planning holy discipleship activities. I will do this, Father, by asking You to develop the mind of Christ in me.

Stretch Motivational MESSAGES. You, Lord, have placed a message of love in my heart for others. I want to stay motivated to share the message — preparing for opportunities, capitalizing on opportunities, and praising You for the fruit of opportunities. I will depend on You, Master, for an upbeat, infectious attitude.

Stretch Ministry METHODS. Father, stretch my thinking to employ methods of ministry that reach people of different age groups, different backgrounds, and different needs. Let Your Holy Spirit guide me in impactful ministry approaches that bear fruit, much fruit, and more fruit.

BIBLE READING — EPHESIANS

10. Stand Therefore — 6:13-20. Your pastor cannot lead you in successful warfare against evil unless you are equipped with the "whole armor of God." He preaches, teaches, and guides. You must receive, develop, and follow. **Prayer:** Almighty Lord, with my pastor, make us mighty in battle through Your anointing, Your armor, and the leadership of the Holy Spirit.

PERSONAL AFFIRMATION — IMPACT

By supporting ministries that make an **IMPACT**, I can "come rejoicing bringing the results with me." This is God's will for me and for every believer.

I Will . . .

- Cast a vision for reaching the unchurched.
- Set goals for Kingdom performance.
- Outline ethical standards for relationships.
- Reach out daily with positive news.
- Maintain optimism and endurance.
- Monitor transformation results and rewards.
- Highlight achievements and share glory.
- Rejoice and sing worship songs.

BIBLE READING — PHILIPPIANS

1. Being Confident — 1:3-6. God always finishes what He starts. He will complete the work He started in your life, the life of the church, and the pastor's life. **Prayer:** God, I know You are faithful. Do not let circumstances or conflict influence Your plans for my life or the leadership of my pastor. Let me walk, run, and work in Christian ministry with full confidence in Your presence, power, and provisions.

My Journal

FOR THE WEEK

Praise reports, answered prayers, divine provisions, and spiritual plans.

_____

_____

_____

_____

_____

_____

_____

_____

BIBLE READING—PHILIPPIANS

2. Stand Fast—1:27. Look at the word **TEAM**—**T**ogether **E**veryone **A**chieves **M**ore. The church must stand fast as a team in spirit, mind, and faith. This is "striving together" to impact the city for Christ. **Prayer:** Father of unity, striving together means carrying the same burden, seeing the same vision, and depending on the same source for victory. May our church be knit together in love, following the leadership of our pastor.

OVERCOMING ADVERSITY TODAY

Life is filled with adversity and obstacles, I realize this, Father. I also realize You are in control and will guide me along a path of partnership with You to overcome and achieve success. You will direct me to . . .

SEE beyond the present. Very often, Father, I am blinded by present conditions, challenges, and conflicts. Open my eyes! Open my eyes to see beyond the present, to see You at work in my life to fulfill Your will, and accomplish Your holy purposes.

SIZE the situation spiritually. When David faced the giant, Goliath (1 Samuel 17), he sized up the situation spiritually. He did not look at the size of Goliath or the circumstances. David looked at the size of his faith in God and the bold courage He formed in his heart.

SEIZE foundational strength. Father, I will not be timid or backward in seizing (gripping) my foundational strength — Your Holy Word, Your hand of safety, and spiritual healing through the healing virtue of Jesus Christ.

BIBLE READING — PHILIPPIANS

3. Esteem Others — 2:2-4. The church functions as a team as each church member looks out for "the interests of others" — to help others grow in Christ, to get ahead, and to find fulfillment in ministry. **Prayer:** Giver of grace, it begins with me. Let me put aside "selfish ambition and conceit" and give a helping hand to others so we can stretch forth as a team to achieve the goals of the local church.

OVERCOMING GUIDANCE TODAY

Strengthening Savior, You give guidance to be an over-comer—to overcome the faith-draining acts of the Evil One. I embrace Your love-based guidance today. I will go about my routine with heaven-sent confidence and spirit-inspired courage to . . .

Face OBSTACLES. I will face obstacles today by living a surrendered, separated life. I ask You, Father, to increase my level of endurance. Let me face every obstacle with penetrating faith and power-packed fortitude.

Confront OPPOSITION. I understand, Father, that opposition will surface in different ways. Even among believers there will be opposing sides related to projects and patterns. Empower me to project concepts of agreement and of coming together to focus on unity in discovering Your will.

Embrace OPPORTUNITIES. Lord, let me face open doors of opportunities with an open mind and an open heart. Let me think of what can be. Let me exhibit passion on what can be. Let me be dedicated to achieve what can be. Let Your sufficient strength surround me, support me, and propel me.

BIBLE READING—PHILIPPIANS

4. Blameless and Harmless—2:12-16. Paul told the members of the church at Philippi they would "shine as lights in the world" if they would join their pastor in ministry—readily, cheerfully, and "without complaining and disputing" (without murmuring, arguing, or grumbling). **Prayer:** I want to be a ready and willing worker in my church. I don't want to complain, pout, or fume. I want to respond cheerfully, loyally, and lovingly. Teach me and touch me to do this!

OVERCOMING SPIRIT TODAY

Lord that lifts up and sends forth, I rejoice that You instill in me an overcoming spirit—a spirit that binds, blesses, and blossoms with optimism. Father, I am supremely thankful that You give me . . .

Power that MASTERS Difficulties. Father, You give me power to overcome, to stand up, and to master difficulties—faith challenges, financial conflicts, and frontal attacks against my convictions. I will use this power discreetly and honestly to testify of Your power to master difficulties.

Love that MOTIVATES to Act. Lord, Your love is unlimited and unfailing. Your love was active—in creation, in providing a Savior, and in preparing heaven for me and the worldwide members of Your family. I want Your love in my life to motivate me to serve You with positive action.

Soundness that MOLDS Steadfastness. Through prayer, Master, I find soundness that molds steadfastness. Reading Holy Scripture gives me soundness. In worship with other believers I receive soundness that molds steadfastness. Father, I want to be molded in the likeness of Your Son—the heart of a servant, helping hands, and a holy willingness to embrace Your will.

BIBLE READING—PHILIPPIANS

5. Forgetting Things Behind—3:13-16. Every individual, every church, has things in the past that are not pleasant—failures, fusses, family friction. "[Forget] those things" and "reach forward to those things which are ahead" (v. 13). This shows maturity; this focuses on the prize (mission and reward) "of the [heavenly] call of God in Christ Jesus" (v. 14). **Prayer:** Lord of the future, let our church and pastor forget the problems of the past and elevate the goal to win the prize and obtain everything You have for us.

PARTNERSHIP TODAY

God of eternal glory, thank You for the honor to walk daily with You and to experiences partnership in the work of ministry. You supply all I need to be aggressive and accountable in advancing Your precise plan for my life. Through a willing and yielded spirit, I will know the . . .

FULLNESS of PARTNERSHIP. Father, You do not place me on the sidelines; You permit me to partner with You and to be on active duty in ministry — to share and serve, to teach and train, and to enlist and equip. I praise You!

FRUIT of PEACE. Peace flows from Your presence, Master. Your peace gives confidence, courage, and competence. Your peace leads, liberates, and liquidates. I honor You!

FORTRESS of PROTECTION. I am safe and secure in You, Almighty Master. You protect me! Your protection defends and delivers. Your protection demonstrates Your authority and power. Your protection reenforces Your oversight of Your unstoppable plan for my life. I praise You, honor You, and trust You!

BIBLE READING — PHILIPPIANS

6. Follow My Example — 3:17-21. Your pastor is a pattern. Paul told his people to follow his example (his love, care, and concern) and to note other church members who did so. This speaks of harmony, goodwill, and singleness of purpose in the church family. **Prayer:** Heavenly Shepherd, I know I'm in Your care. I know You appointed my pastor to be my earthly shepherd and my pattern for commitment, godly character, and righteous conduct. Let me "follow his example," accept his instructions from Your Word, and embrace his leadership.

PAUL'S PRAYER TODAY

Father, You do not screen or put my prayers on hold. You are always available to receive my prayers and to respond according to Your divine wisdom and my walk with You! Today, I will follow the pattern of Paul in praying for other believers (2 Thessalonians 1:11).

GOD'S Calling. Father, every believer has responded to Your call to accept Christ as Lord and Savior, to be separated from sin and evil, and to serve You with a life of passion and purpose. I pray for all believers to be faithful to Your holy calling.

GOOD Pleasure. Your goodness gives me flowing peace, abiding pleasure, and a productive positive disposition. Father, You show goodness to all believers regardless — yes, regardless! I pray for all believers to live in expectation of Your good pleasure!

GREAT Words of Faith. Father, I want to perform great works of faith by Your Spirit that reveals Your desire to prosper, protect, and provide for believers. You are ready to respond with acts of grace and glorious demonstrations of Your power. I pray for all believers to perform great works of faith.

BIBLE READING — PHILIPPIANS

7. Don't Fret or Worry — 4:5-7. Instead of being anxious, pray. And while you pray, thank and praise God for what He has already done. **Prayer:** Most merciful Father, You have told me not to worry about anything but in everything to talk with You, offer praise, and to expect results. Today, I am looking to You for my needs, the needs of my church, and the needs of my pastor. I believe!

PRAYER PATTERN
CHERISH GOD'S WORD

When we cherish God's Word, it becomes part of our daily lives and we reap the benefits it proclaims. Lord . . .

C — **CONFIDENCE**: I have confidence in Your Word.

H — **HOLD** me close to it by Your Holy Spirit.

E — **ENTRUST** me with insight to understand it.

R — **RESPOND**: Let me respond to its teachings.

I — **INFUSE** my pastor and me with unity from it.

S — **SHOW** us how to share it convincingly.

H — **HELP** me support my pastor in defending it.

BIBLE READING—PHILIPPIANS

8. Meditate on These Things—4:8-9. Paul outlines a list of things on which to meditate. Fill your minds with things that are noble, holy, honorable, excellent, friendly, gracious, compelling, and lovely. These thoughts will lead to a solid foun¬dation upon which to live and minister. **Prayer:** Lord, I want Christ to be at the center of my life. I want to put into practice His teachings so I can be a part of His church—a body of believers that nothing can stand up against, divide loyalties, or reduce progress.

My Journal

FOR THE WEEK

Praise reports, answered prayers, divine provisions, and
spiritual plans.

_____

_____

_____

_____

_____

_____

_____

_____

_____

_____

BIBLE READING—PHILIPPIANS

9. God Shall Supply—4:19. Paul wanted the church to
know that God would supply the resources for what He had
commissioned them to do. God's work is always backed by
His promise to "supply." **Prayer:** God of unlimited supply,
may our church trust You to meet every need for evangelism and expansion. Let us also act on Your promises that if
we will give, You will return in a manifold way.

PEACE TODAY

Peace that surpasses explanation comes from You, Father. You are the peacemaker, peace-provider, and peace-restorer. My peace comes from You! My church is an agent of Your peace! Together, we will spread Your peace that is . . .

PURE. Father, Your peace is pure—no strings attached, no straining demands, and no performance standards. Your purity flows from Your nature of love, acceptance, and forgiveness. This is also the nature of Your church.

PROTECTIVE. Your peace, Master, generates assurance and protects from low self-esteem, sluggish faith, and inconsistent conduct and commitment. I will testify of Your protective faith. I will join other church members as a witnessing team of Your peace that pardons, provides, and protects.

PRODUCTIVE. Peace from You, Father, gives me courage to try new things, convictions to stand strong, and calmness in achieving goals. Together, in harmony with my church, we will be productive in touching our city with the peace of Christ.

BIBLE READING—COLOSSIANS

1. Pastor and Apostle—1:1, 3. God our Father, I recognize that my pastor is an apostle (minister) by Your will, and that he shares Your grace and peace with me. I give You thanks for him and commit to always pray for him.

PERFORMANCE POWER TODAY

Father of supernatural strength, I will stay close to You today to receive power to perform ministry with a full flow of energy, excitement, and efficiency. I will stay close to You by . . .

Embracing Your HOLY Word. Your Word, Master, is my guide to understanding Your will to walking side-by-side with You, and to receiving wisdom to represent You with balance and integrity. Your Word also equips me to be successful in my Christian testimony and in my career.

Depending on the HOLY Spirit. Master, the Holy Spirit was sent to empower me, equip me, and energize me to live a bold, overcoming, and performance-driven life. The Holy Spirit also reveals truth to me, reveals traps of Satan, and reveals patterns of triumph in Christian service.

Practicing a HOLY Walk. In the Bible, Enoch pleased You, Lord, by a holy walk. His life was one of direction, devotion, and demonstration of Your power. I want to observe the pattern of Enoch in my life. I ask for Your directions. I will be devoted in worshipping You. I will demonstrate loyalty and overcoming faith to perform with authority and Your anointing.

BIBLE READING—COLOSSIANS

2. Love for the Saints—1:4, 6. Father, thank You that my pastor has built my faith in Jesus Christ and my love for all the saints. He preaches Your Word and this brings forth fruit in my life. Continue to anoint him as he preaches and teaches.

PERSONAL GAIN TODAY

Creator and Caregiver, in Your divine design for my life, You set forth a pattern for personal gain. Every day I have the privilege to gain respect by my commitments, by my conduct, and by demonstrating an attitude of care for others. Look on my life today and tutor me in understanding the . . .

PATH of Gain. Father, I am aware that Your **PATH** for my life includes **P**urpose and **P**urity, **A**ttitude and **A**ctions, **T**ruth and **T**orchbearing, and **H**ope and **H**eaven. When I stay on this path, I am rewarded with personal gain — achievements, accolades, and advancements. I ask You to be my pathway guide today.

PAIN of Gain. Father, everything of value calls for sacrifice and personal service. If I want to be served, I must serve. If I want respect and honor, I must give respect and honor. If I want the benefits of the cross of Christ, I must take up the cross of Christ and follow His example. I will!

PROVISIONS for Gain. Faith is the foundation for gain. Master, I believe You are all-powerful, all-sufficient, and always present to meet every challenge, every conflict, and to control every situation. I receive Your provisions today with great expectations and great appreciation.

BIBLE READING — COLOSSIANS

3. Filled with Knowledge — 1:9-11. Lord, help me to pray for my pastor as he proclaims the truths of Your Word so I can be filled with the knowledge of Your will in all wisdom and spiritual understanding. I want to fully please You and be fruitful in every good work according to Your glorious power.

PERSONAL STANCE TODAY

God of great grace, thank You for the privilege to stand in Your presence through being yielded, open, and thankful. I am yielded to Your will for my life. I am open to Your guidance. I am thankful for new life, new hope, and new experiences. Today, I will be . . .

DEDICATED. In response to Your call on my life, Father, I will exhibit the characteristics of dedication — singleness of purpose, scriptural purity, and sustained Christ-honoring service. My dedication will be a testimony of my stance in Christ.

DETERMINED. I will face opposition in my walk with You, Lord. Satan will set traps to ensnare and weaken my allegiance. I will depend on You for a Spirit-supported determination — to walk worthy, to work energetically, and to witness boldly.

DEPENDABLE. Through Your equipping grace, Master, I will show forth the fruit of dependability — consistent Christian conduct, church attendance, and honest conversation. I will show You are faithful in all Your ways by the way I depend on You and by the way I show I am a dependable witness of the message of Christ.

BIBLE READING — COLOSSIANS

4. Delivered from Darkness — 1:13, 18. May I always remember that I have been delivered from the power of darkness, and that I must work with my pastor in reaching those still in darkness, and in giving Christ the preeminence in all things.

PERSONAL WORSHIP TODAY

God of daily compassion and care, You are worthy of glory, praise, and honor. You are worthy as a result of Your majesty, might, and miracles. You are worthy of my allegiance because You found me, delivered me, adopted me, and provide daily care for me. I will worship You with my . . .

TIME in Devotion. Father, time is a gift from You. It is precious and packed with potential. Guide me in the allotment of my time for daily devotions—expressing worshipful praise, experiencing Your voice of guidance, and finding faith enlightenment through Bible study.

THOUGHTS of Thanksgiving. I will experience different categories of thoughts today. My goal is to manage my thought journey and focus on thanksgiving—loving-kindnesses, saving and sustaining grace, and surplus supplies for daily life. I will strive for my thoughts to be anointed with the "mind of Christ."

TONGUE of Praise. You have told me in Your Word, Father, that the tongue is an "unruly" member of my body. I do not want my tongue to act independently from my devotion to You. I ask that my tongue be tamed by Your Spirit and that I would speak words of praise for pardon of sins, promise of paradise, peace of inward purity, and divine protection from the assaults of Satan.

BIBLE READING—COLOSSIANS

5. Steadfast Faith—1:23. As a congregation, let us support our pastor and follow his leadership so we can continue in the faith—grounded and steadfast.

MY COVENANT COMMITMENT WITH MY PASTOR

Understanding that it is God's plan for the pastor and the people to come together as partners and coworkers in the mission and ministries of the local church, I covenant to . . .

- SUPPORT him with an attitude of congeniality, openness, and cooperation.

- STRENGTHEN him with a caring spirit of trust, loyalty, and dependability.

- STAND with him in confidence for visionary planning and consistent performance.

- SAFEGUARD him with authority against pastoral fatigue and unfounded criticism.

- SALUTE him in honor for compassionate leadership and Kingdom achievements.

Signed _____

BIBLE READING — COLOSSIANS

6. Perfect in Christ — 1:27-28. Lord, guide my pastor as he continually reminds the church family that it is Christ in us that is the Hope of Glory. Give him wisdom as he teaches so he may present us perfect in Christ Jesus.

My Journal

FOR THE WEEK

Praise reports, answered prayers, divine provisions, and spiritual plans.

_____

_____

_____

_____

_____

_____

_____

_____

_____

BIBLE READING — COLOSSIANS

7. Partners in Ministry — 2:2-3. My pastor and I are partners in ministry. Father, let us knit together in love, and let this same spirit be present throughout the congregation so we might know all the treasures of wisdom and knowledge in You.

PLANTING SEEDS TODAY

Master of the harvest, You have proclaimed that the harvest is ripe and ready, but the planters are sluggish and stay at home. I do not want to be a stay-at-home saint, I have a vision to go into the harvest and plant seeds of . . .

INFLUENCE. Father, I desire to plant seeds that influence the values of those around me. My attitude will play a major role in this goal. I ask You to anoint my attitude so I can be an influence by my upbeat spirit, by forming rich relationships, and by a glowing lifestyle of total commitment to Christ.

INSTRUCTIONS. I am thankful for the instructional seeds planted in my life by mature leaders and teachers in the church. They were a strong force in shaping my Christian walk. I want to follow their example and share insights with young believers about successfully walking the Christian walk.

INSPIRATION. Master, I receive inspiration by hearing life-changing testimonies, victory reports, and physical healings. I will plant seeds of inspiration by recognizing quality service, praising steadfastness, and standing with my pastor in visionary ministry.

BIBLE READING — COLOSSIANS

8. Good Order — 2:5-7. When I have "good order" in my life and I am steadfast in faith, I am strengthened, my pastor is strengthened, and my church is strengthened. Order is achieved by walking in Christ Jesus our Lord.

PLEASING YOU TODAY

Divine Instructor, I desire to be an open-minded, eager, and receptive student. I will begin today with a ready spirit to learn, understand, and grow. Work in my mind to comprehend and commit to Your will. Work in my heart to receive and release "good tidings of great joy." I will please You by . . .

My PETITIONS — Prayer. Thank You, Father, that I can come into Your presence through prayer and open my soul to receive and open my mouth to offer praise and petitions. I desire to please You by being humble, honest, and heart-praising with thanksgiving.

My PERFORMANCE — Ministry. Today, Lord, I will be involved in ministry that honors You — speaking in love, sharing my faith, and serving unselfishly. I will perform with spiritual pride that reveals respect for Your holy nature.

My PROFESSION — Witness. Lord of glory, I will walk and talk today in a manner that honors Your call on my life and my commission to represent You with dignity and honor. I will profess my love for You and the abundant life You provide in Christ.

BIBLE READING — COLOSSIANS

9. Attentive to Doctrine — 2:8. May I be attentive to the doctrinal instructions of my pastor so I will not be taken captive through philosophy, empty deceit, tradition of men, or the basic principles of the world.

POSSESSIONS TODAY

Father of majesty and might, it is Your will that I grow, prosper, and receive Your gifts. I will embrace Your will today. I will grow in grace, prosper in understanding my possessions, and become enriched by abounding in Your gifts. I possess . . .

PARDON from Bondage. I possess liberty today! I am not in captivity. The chains of bondage have been broken. I have been pardoned, freed, and forgiven. I possess new life in Christ! I am thankful! I rejoice! I will share my story of Your liberating love today.

PEACE of Mind. I possess restful peace today! I can think clearly, soberly, and righteously. I can think peacefully, productively, and positively. By Your Spirit, Father, I can follow the thinking pattern of Christ—giving honor to You, loving the lost, and fellowshiping with other believers. I will share my story of peace in Christ today!

PRIZE of High Calling. I possess a vision of the goal and the "prize of the upward call of God in Christ Jesus" (Philippians 3:14). I will stay focused on possessing the prize. I will keep the vision clear and compelling. I'm committed! Lord, I will live under the glow of Your majesty and might!

BIBLE READING—COLOSSIANS

10. Performing Ministry—2:9-10. In Christ dwells all the fullness of the Godhead bodily, and I am complete in Him. May this completeness and maturity lead me in walking hand in hand with my pastor and church volunteers in performing ministry.

POSSIBILITIES TODAY

God of the present, You are at work today fulfilling Your plans in the world. I know that You are, that You always have been, and that You will always be. This sets unlimited possibilities before me. These possibilities are based on . . .

My POSITION in Christ. I am a child of the King, a member of Your family, Holy Father—accepted, adopted, and anointed. All of the benefits of belonging to You are before me. I will praise and honor You today for my position in Christ!

My POTENTIAL in Christ. In Christ, I can be, do, and become! You, Lord, have set open doors before me to cultivate mind skills, spiritual skills, and physical skills. You have promised to walk beside me through open doors and to supply whatever I need to excel and to honor You.

MY POWER from Christ. Thank You, Father, for the gift of the Holy Spirit. Father, through Christ You sent the Comforter to guide, empower, and establish. The Holy Spirit is my source to succeed in life, to be a winning witness, and to fully develop my possibilities.

BIBLE READING—COLOSSIANS

11. Alive in Christ—2:13. I have been made alive together with Christ, having all my trespasses forgiven. Let this aliveness be demonstrated in my witness and through a spirit of love, acceptance, and forgiveness.

POWER GRACE TODAY

Father of peace and partnership, Your grace empowers me to be bold in exercising faith, equips me with swift momentum to advance Your message, and energies me to engage in victorious battle against the forces of evil. I am grace blessed!

Partaker in PEACE. Through grace, I have peace — peace with You, Father, peace of mind, and peace in my relationships. Peace with You gives assurance! Peace of mind gives me calmness! Peace in relationships gives me stability! Your power grace provides me with a complete life.

Prosperity in PARTNERSHIP. Thank You, Master, for permitting me to be a partner in fulfilling Your will — reaching the unredeemed, the misdirected, the unfulfilled, and the misinformed. Through partnership prosperity, spiritual gains that honor You are realized.

Productivity in PERFORMANCE. Measurable progress, marvelous Kingdom-building productivity, influential scriptural performance, Holy Father, these achievements are Your will for all believers and for my life. I confess them; I claim them; and I accept them. Power grace is sufficient for all my circumstances. I PRAISE YOU!

BIBLE READING — COLOSSIANS

12. Exalt Christ — 2:16-17. Guard me from becoming legalistic and judging others regarding food, festivals, or tradition. Let me always exalt Christ and what He is doing through the pastor and the people in my church.

WHEN YOU PRAY CONSISTENTLY FOR YOUR PASTOR

1. It **SHOWERS** him with heavenly peace that gives contentment.

2. It **SHOWERS** him with spiritual manna that gives energy.

3. It **SHOWERS** him with divine insight that gives purpose and courage.

4. It **SHOWERS** him with majestic splendor that gives beauty.

5. It **SHOWERS** him with God-awareness that gives authority.

6. It **SHOWERS** him with divine abilities that give vision to act.

7. It **SHOWERS** him with mission unity among church members.

BIBLE READING — COLOSSIANS

13. Honor Christ — 2:20, 23.   Let me remain dead to the basic principles of the world and the doctrine of men so that I can honor Christ in all I do and not neglect the body — the church.

My Journal

FOR THE WEEK

Praise reports, answered prayers, divine provisions, and spiritual plans.

_____

_____

_____

_____

_____

_____

_____

_____

_____

_____

_____

BIBLE READING — COLOSSIANS

14. Mind of Christ — 3:1-2. Lord, give me wisdom to always seek those things which are above; set my mind on things that pertain to You, Your Son, and the operation of the Holy Spirit in my life, the life of my pastor, and the lives of the people of my church.

POWER LIVING TODAY

Energy-supplying eternal Master, You are all-powerful. Nothing is too hard or difficult for You. Power flows from Your throne—power to dream, power to perform, and power to achieve. Today, I want Your transforming power to work in my life and to guide me to . . .

TRUST Completely. Power for impactful living comes through "complete trust" in You, Holy Father. Complete trust means I will give all of my life to You—totally, unreservedly, without holdouts or hesitation. I trust You that in all circumstances You will work out the best for me in relationship to Your will.

THINK Creatively. Power for new life living comes through having "the mind of Christ"—dependence on Christ to think new beginnings, new processes, and new outreach actions. Father, let me think like Christ. Fill my mind with Christ-centered creativity today.

TOIL Committedly. Power for productive living is derived from toiling and being "instant in season and out of season"—working wisely, witnessing intently, and winning victoriously. Lord of love, by holy grace, I will experience power living that demonstrates Your kingdom authority.

BIBLE READING—COLOSSIANS

15. Christ's Return—3:4. I want to be ready when Christ appears so that I can be ready to appear with Him in glory. To do this, I must be in harmony with You, Lord, with my pastor, and with others in the body of Christ.

PRAISE EXPRESSIONS TODAY

Lord of music and mercy, in Your presence today I will praise You. I will praise You for peace of mind, purity of heart, and the promise of paradise. I will . . .

SHOUT Words of Praise. I will not be timid! I will not be bashful! I will not be backwards! I will shout words of praise so all can hear and understand that my life has been transformed by Your mercy and mighty power, Lord. I will shout words of praise today!

SING Songs of Thanksgiving. Father, I will sing songs of thanksgiving in my soul — daily, perpetually. I will sing songs of thanksgiving with the choir. I will sing songs of thanksgiving with the congregation. I will sing songs of thanksgiving with my family. I will go about my duties today with thanksgiving and "thanksliving." I will sing songs of thanksgiving today!

STAND Up With Uplifted Hands. Father, You are worthy of all praise. I will not sit down with folded hands in Your presence. I will stand up in respect and honor. I will stand up with uplifted hands in reverence, rejoicing, and in anticipation of Your return to establish Your kingdom. I will stand up with uplifted hands today!

BIBLE READING — COLOSSIANS

16. Image of Christ — 3:9-10. Lord, I know I must "put off" some things, such as anger, wrath, and malice, in order to grow spiritually. I also know that I must "put on" the new man, renewed in knowledge, to realize the full image of Christ in me and to represent You, my pastor, and my church with a positive image and scriptural authority.

PRAISE TODAY

Father, You are worthy of praise, glory, and honor. I want my daily life to reflect these three expressions—in worship, in witness, and in working effectively. My heart is filled with thanksgiving.

I Praise You for FAITH. Lord, I could not live a life of fullness without faith—faith in Your promises, faith in Your superior power, and faith to be spiritually productive. Faith has given me stability to stand firmly and to serve effectively.

I Praise You for FULFILLMENT. Father, You meet all my needs—my spiritual needs, my social needs, and my financial needs. I am complete in You! I am content! I am fulfilled, and I praise You and lift high the banner of Your glory and honor.

I Praise You for My FUTURE. Lord, You never leave me; You are always present to supply, to strengthen, and to set forth new visionary goals. I praise You for the assurance of heaven—an eternal home of joyful praise in Your presence.

BIBLE READING—COLOSSIANS

17. Labor in Church—3:12. As I labor in the church and with my pastor, let me always display tender mercies, kindness, humility, meekness, and longsuffering. This will stimulate both compassion and cooperation.

PRAYING CONSISTENTLY TODAY

Father, You hear and answer prayer. I have a tendency to be self-centered in my prayer time with you—my needs, my nurture, and new gifts for my life. Let me see and understand the mission of my church and pray for . . .

Outreach ACTION. Father, may my church have a vision for outreach action—mobilizing, ministering, and managing. I want to be an example of outreach action. Touch me, teach me, and train me to do this.

Outreach ACTIVITIES. Father, bless the ministries of my church designed to touch the sick and shut-ins, the confined and addicted, the lost and lonely, the bewildered and those in bondage, and the searching and stranded. Bless and empower the church members who give themselves to these ministries. May they be fruitful and faithful.

Outreach ADVANCEMENT. Father, effective outreach advancement honors You—Your name is elevated, Your love is demonstrated, Your power is activated, and Your plan for the local church is illustrated. I will pray consistently for church growth!

BIBLE READING—COLOSSIANS

18. Bear Burdens—3:13-14. Bearing burdens is not just the responsibility of my pastor. You, God of love, tell us to bear one another's burdens, to forgive one another, and to do this in the bond of perfection which is love.

PREPARED FOR TODAY

Father of new beginnings, a new day is before me. I can start fresh with new thoughts, new releases of energy, and new methods for meeting new challenges. My petition today is for You to prepare me to respond to new beginnings by staying . . .

AWAKE for heavenly leadership. Lord, where You lead me I will follow! But I must be awake—wide awake—fully prepared for the journey—equipped, empowered, and excited. I will look to You for leadership to overcome spiritual drowsiness and sluggishness, and help me to stay awake to new beginnings today.

ARMED for spiritual warfare. New beginnings will birth new tactics and threats by the army of the Evil One—Satan. I will be prepared for his assaults by putting on the full spiritual armor that You, Lord, provide (Ephesians 6:13). I will stand strong, advance aggressively, and achieve victory in Your name and under Your conquering banner.

ANOINTED for breakthrough ministry. Your anointing, Master, will gird, encircle, and guide me in performing breakthrough ministry—ministry that makes a difference in my personal growth, the growth of my church, and the growth of Your kingdom. Thank You for preparing me for new beginnings today!

BIBLE READING—COLOSSIANS

19. Church Unity—3:15. Unity is so vital to the health of my church and the effectiveness of my pastor. I ask that Your peace rule in my heart in all church business, relationships, and activities. Also, let me be an example of thankfulness. All of these requests will help establish church unity.

My Pledge of Loyalty

TO DEVELOP FRUITFUL FAITH

I am aware of the components of faith outlined in Hebrews 11:1, and will earnestly strive to cultivate a pleasing disposition, maintain a positive mind-set, and develop a spiritual work ethic for faith to germinate and grow in my life. I am ready for God-pleasing action!

I pledge to follow a path of fruitful faith by . . .

1. **CULTIVATING** a disposition of openness and readiness for fruitful faith to develop.
2. **CONDITIONING** my mind to comprehend the scope of boundless blessings when scriptural faith is released.
3. **CONTROLLING** negative thoughts that would detour positive faith and personal stability.
4. **COMMUNICATING** with language that inspires family members and friends to exercise faith to achieve honorable goals.
5. **COMMENDING** my pastors and church workers for faith in developing devoted and fruit-bearing disciples.

BIBLE READING—COLOSSIANS

20. Receive the Word—3:16. Father, may your love and mercy prompt me to receive Your Word from my pastor as he preaches and teaches and to show forth this receptive spirit in psalms, hymns, and spiritual songs, singing with grace in my heart to You.

My Journal

FOR THE WEEK

Praise reports, answered prayers, divine provisions, and spiritual plans.

_____

_____

_____

_____

_____

_____

_____

_____

_____

_____

BIBLE READING — COLOSSIANS

21. Trust in the Lord — 3:17. It is easy to do things for self, even in church work, and to trust in money and management principles. But Lord, whatever I do, in attitude or action, let me do it in the name of Your Son, Jesus Christ, always giving honor and thanks to You.

PROGRESS TODAY

Master of progress and productivity, You reveal Your power through many different avenues—mending, molding, and motivating. I want to be receptive in all three of these avenues. I depend on You to supply strength not to . . .

HOLD Back. Father, I am in contact with people every day who have a sour outlook on life—hostile attitude, angry disposition, antagonistic spirit. I have a tendency to hold back from being around them. Turn me around and let me find ways to change their outlook, directions, and values about life.

HOLD Up. I also find it convenient to hold up where I am in life and not to set new goals, see new opportunities, and try new approaches. Touch me, Lord, to be visionary! Open my eyes to see You at work in different, unique, and creative ways.

HOLD Out. Father, I do not want to hold out in using the skills You have placed in me. Give me an urgent spirit! I will honor You by utilizing them to witness of Your mercy and the magnitude of Your Kingdom.

BIBLE READING—COLOSSIANS

22. Learn Trust and Respect—3:18-20. Bless my pastor's companion today. There are pressures in their home created by the demands of church life—telephone calls, meetings, problems, and spiritual challenges. May both of them, by Your Spirit, learn patience, trust, and respect for each other's feelings and situations.

PROMOTING VISION TODAY

Father who births vision, I need a clear and compelling vision to unite with my church family in reaching the unchurched. A clear vision will let me visualize Your strategy for church growth. A compelling vision will prompt immediate and consistent action. I will . . .

SET an EXAMPLE of pure interest and involvement in church growth. Supporting plans to influence the unchurched is my responsibility. It is also the responsibility of every church member. I will be a leader in casting a vision and in taking part in making the vision a reality.

SHINE with ENTHUSIASM in seeing the possibilities of attendance increase in my church. Father, You are the Lord of the harvest. I will join You with shining enthusiasm in reaping the unlimited harvest of the untouched, the uninvolved, and the unconverted.

STAY FOCUSED on the mission of the church and my vision and commission to be an active participant. Today, Master, equip me, energize me, and encircle me with Holy Spirit power so I can be an enthusiastic example of commitment to Kingdom enlargement.

BIBLE READING — COLOSSIANS

23. Encourage Children — 3:20-21. As my pastor works with children and their parents, may he know the right steps to take, the right advice to give, and the right programs to implement so our children will always be encouraged in the Lord.

PROTECTING VALUES TODAY

Powerful Protector, thank You for watching over me and keeping me from physical danger and destructive enemy forces. I also thank You for the values the Holy Spirit has developed in me through prayer, Bible study, and life-shaping sermons. My life is built on these values. They form the core of my commitment. I ask You to protect my values.

FAITH Values guide me in walking daily with You, Lord, and in worshiping You. Faith values are vital in living a victorious Christian life. My faith values hold me, mold me, and control me. They are my power line for a rich, full life in Your care.

FAMILY Values give me a structure in which I learn, grow, share, and feel secure and significant. I ask You, Father, to protect each member of my family—protect their values, their loyalty to You, and their growth in the nature of Christ. I also ask You to let me be a model for my family in daily goals, work habits, and relationships.

FUTURE Values shape who I am, where I am going, and what I will be able to contribute to the cause of Christ, my church, and community life. I will build my life on the solid Rock, Christ Jesus, and the values He has placed in my mind and heart.

BIBLE READING—COLOSSIANS

24. Build up the Church—3:23-24. I pray that I would always honor You, heavenly Father, in all that I do and that my participation in Kingdom ministry would be from my heart and show that I am truly serving You, supporting my pastor, and "building up the church."

RAIN TODAY

Father of all seasons, in the Bible rain is often used to symbolize blessings from Your throne—abundant, rich, flowing blessings. Believers need Your rain! The church needs Your rain! I need Your rain! I ask You, let it rain! Your rain will bring . . .

RESOURCES for Renewal. Lord of new beginnings, I sometimes get dry in my spirit and in serving You with a full throttle of power. When I am dry, I do not inspire or influence. I claim resources from You today to cultivate a growing faith, to reverse inferior zeal, and to renew a high level of spiritual enthusiasm.

RIPENESS for Nourishment. Lord of the harvest, Your rain brings harvest ripeness. This ripeness is for my nourishment and growth—spiritual strength, stamina, and "stickability." The harvest ripeness also represents the ripeness and openness to minister to the lost and lead them in becoming a member of Your family.

RESPONSIVENESS to Grow. Lord of refreshing rain, You respond to my needs with refreshing rain and manna from heaven. My duty and privilege is to respond to Your rain and manna wholeheartedly with open arms to receive and with a raised voice of praise and thanksgiving.

BIBLE READING—COLOSSIANS

25. Watchful in Prayer—4:2. Father, You tell me to be vigilant, watchful in prayer, and to continue earnestly in prayer with thanksgiving. I want to obey Your will and to talk with You daily about my life, the life of my pastor, and the life of my church. I commit myself anew to You this today.

REACHING FORWARD TODAY

Master of the universe, every day with You is a new day brimming with open opportunities and fantastic possibilities. In Your Word, You admonish me not to be stuck in the past but to reach forward and experience new guidance, goals, and growth. I will reach forward today!

New GUIDANCE. As I reach forward, I am open to a new flow of divine motivation, new methods of performing ministry, and new ways to mix faith and works. Lord of liberty, guide me in reaching a higher relationship with You and in guiding others into a fruitful relationship with You.

New GOALS. As I reach forward, I want to form new goals of personal development, of spiritual performance, and of influencing the happiness of family members and friends. Lord of love, guide me in reaching new heights of achievement by setting new scripturally sound goals.

New GROWTH. As I reach forward, I will experience new growth in Christlikeness, in compassion for the unchurched, and in effectiveness in sharing the good news. Lord of longsuffering, renew me and watch over me with heavenly wisdom.

BIBLE READING—COLOSSIANS

26. Open Doors—4:3. I ask You Father, to open doors for my pastor and my church to reach people with Your Word, to minister to the dejected and destitute, and to reap the ripe harvest with intensity and joy.

PERSONAL AFFIRMATION — SHARE

A willingness to share with others reveals a spirit of love, acceptance, and loyalty. It also pictures the nature of God the Father who gives openly, freely, and continually.

I Will . . .

- Set an example of obedience by sharing.

- Share my testimony of abundance in Christ.

- Assist in projects of sharing food/clothing.

- Give support to friends in need.

- Participate in church relief projects.

- Communicate with local service groups.

- Ask God to open sharing opportunities.

- Rejoice in the rewards of sharing.

BIBLE READING — COLOSSIANS

27. Communicate Effectively — 4:6. It is very important to the life of my church that I communicate effectively with my pastor and volunteer church leaders. Touch my heart and tongue so that my conversations will always be saturated with grace, seasoned with salt, and supported by trust and respect.

My Journal

FOR THE WEEK

Praise reports, answered prayers, divine provisions, and
spiritual plans.

BIBLE READING — COLOSSIANS

28. Share Good News — 4:7-8. My pastor is a faithful
minister and fellow servant; he faces many difficult circumstances that I am not aware of. Help me to share good
news with him and words of encouragement that will lift
him up and strengthen him.

REACHING NEIGHBORS TODAY

Lord of the harvest, You taught us who our neighbors are—the wounded, the weary, and the wayward. I have the honor and the responsibility to reach them with the redeeming love of Jesus Christ. This requires alertness and attention that includes . . .

AWARENESS. Yes, I must be aware, Father, of the spiritual condition of those close to me—those who are weary, weak, and without hope. This includes people across the street, up the street, and down the street. They are my neighbors! You want me to be a messenger and a minister to them.

AFFINITY. I realize that to minister to my neighbors I must create affinity with them—trustworthy, likeable, serving relationship. Father, guide me in establishing friendships based on mutual interests, care, and enrichments.

ANOINTING. The work of the Holy Spirit is to prepare the hearts and minds of my neighbors to be receptive. Anoint me, Father, to know when the time is right to present the invitation to accept Christ and to follow Him as Lord and Savior. I yield to Your leadership!

BIBLE READING—COLOSSIANS

29. Spiritual Maturity—4:11. I pray that I will be a comfort to my pastor and to fellow workers in the church. Let me prove this by kind acts, cheerful encouragement, steady assistance, and spiritual maturity.

REACH TODAY

Lord of unlimited vision and strength, You see me where I am with my dreams and drawbacks; I ask that You supply the strength to achieve and overcome. This sets me on the path of spiritual maturity and personal motivation. I will . . .

REACH In to develop full allegiance to carrying the cross of Christ. I will stay in touch with my faith, keeping it strong and active. I will stay in touch with my feelings, keeping them focused and spiritually balanced. Through prayer, Father, I will reach in and stay in touch with Your will for my life.

REACH Out to discover the deep truths of Your Word, Lord. I will stay alert to new avenues to advance my spiritual skills. I will keep my eyes open to see how You are working in the church world. I will stay receptive, eager, and aggressive. Through Bible study, Father, I will reach out and grow in grace.

REACH Over and connect with the unchurched. I will stay aware of the destiny of those who are not followers of Christ. I will look for opportunities to share, serve, and encourage. Through alertness, Father, I will reach over and minister to outsiders.

BIBLE READING—COLOSSIANS

30. Labor Fervently—4:12. My pastor is my leader and model, and he must stand perfect and complete in all of Your will. Help me to labor (completely give myself) fervently (with consistent intensity) in prayer for him so that together we can please You and honor You.

REJOICE IN CHRIST TODAY

Inspiring Master, I rejoice today because You have supplied everything I need to live an upbeat, overcoming, and heaven-focused life. Your provisions include adoption into Your family, affirmation of divine guidance, and assurance of eternity in heaven. All of these provisions are based on . . .

RESURRECTION of Christ. "Up from the grave He arose!" Christ arose to break the cords of death, to establish a lasting Kingdom, and to make provisions for turnaround, transformed living. I rejoice in the resurrection of Christ—it guarantees my resurrection and a new body and a new life.

REDEMPTION in Christ. Father, the sacrificial death of Your Son redeemed me and returned me to You. I am free! I am free from the pain of separation from You, free from the guilt of transgressions, and free from the restrictions imposed by sinful bondage! I rejoice in the redemption provided by Christ—it guarantees my freedom from the control of sin.

RETURN of Christ. Master, the return of Christ to rapture Your people is a blessed hope, a secure hope, a personal hope. I rejoice in the promise of Christ to return and to establish a new heaven and a new earth—it guarantees my future.

BIBLE READING—COLOSSIANS

31. Holy Privilege—4:17. Lord, it is a holy privilege and a sacred responsibility to receive a call to the ministry from You. I want to use the gifts You have given to me to help my pastor fulfill his ministry. In so doing, we will become partners in Kingdom service according to Your master plan for the pastor and the people in the church.

REMEMBER TODAY

God of yesterday and today, You are faithful in all Your ways and works. You do not want me to live in the past, but You do want me to remember those things that keep me and those things to be on guard against. Today I will remember my . . .

FOUNDATION. I will remember that I stand on a sure foundation, the solid rock Christ Jesus. My foundation is faith in His completed work—redemption, restoration, and eternal rewards. *I will live a fruitful life on this foundation!*

FRIENDS. I will remember my friends—family friends, faith friends, and church friends. They are a joyful, strengthening aspect of my life. I will pray for them, support them, and cherish their nurturing fellowship. *I will live a fulfilling life with my friends!*

FOES. I will remember Satan, the enemy of my soul, and those who oppose my faith and the work of Your church, Lord. I will use Your Word to stand against them and to advance Your message of truth. *I will live an overcoming life against my foes!*

BIBLE READING—FIRST THESSALONIANS

1. Give Thanks—1:3. The church members at Thessalonica were characterized by three outstanding virtues—their "work of faith," "labor of love," and "patience of hope." **Prayer:** Master of mercy, I ask that our church would be distinguished by the attributes of faith, love, and hope, and that we would blend into their work (ministry), labor (service), and patience (commitment and consistency).

REQUIREMENTS FOR TODAY

God of infinite wisdom, You have set before me a clear path to follow to please You. It is described in Your Word: "And what [do I] require of you . . . to do justly . . . love mercy . . . walk humbly" (Micah 6:8). Steady my steps today so I can . . .

PERFORM Justly. Father, I want my daily performance—uprightness, honesty, fairness—to honor You and be an example of a committed follower of Christ. You are just and holy in all Your actions and I want to embrace Your model in my lifestyle.

PRACTICE Mercy. People will judge me by what I profess and by my actions. They must blend together, complement each other, and reflect Kingdom standards. I need You, Father, to steady my steps so I can demonstrate the fruit of mercy—forgiveness, kindness, and soft heartedness.

PURPOSE to Walk Humbly. Humility in my daily walk—gentleness and unpretentious peacefulness—demonstrate my Christian character and my calling to live a life of influence for the cause of Christ. Lord, I will walk with steady steps by Your guidance and the anointing of the Holy Spirit. I will perform justly, practice mercy, and walk humbly.

BIBLE READING—FIRST THESSALONIANS

2. Entrusted With the Gospel—2:4-12. Your pastor has been entrusted by God with His Word—to preach it, teach it, defend it, and guard it. He "imparts" it to you and shares his "own life" (v. 8) with you so that you can "walk worthy" (v. 12) of God's kingdom and glory. **Prayer:** Lord, I want to receive Your Word from my pastor. Let me respond to his preaching, be refreshed by it, and reflect the message and meaning in my daily life.

PRAYER PATTERN — ENERGY

Your pastor needs ENERGY to perform ministry that guides you in enjoying God's fullness.

E — **Eventfulness**. Lord, bring **EVENTS** into my pastor's life that will expand his perspective and lift up his spirit.

N — **Newness**. Give him **NEWNESS** of vision in leading our church into a deeper understanding of Your love.

E — **Emptiness**. **EMPTY** my pastor of pressures that sap his strength and turn him from priority tasks.

R — **Restfulness**. Let my pastor find **REST** from the strain of ministry through my commitment to support him.

G — **Giftedness**. Our pastor has **GIFTS** to speak and to serve; may the church recognize his **GIFTEDNESS**.

Y — **Youthfulness**. My pastor is not a **YOUTH**, but give him a **YOUTHFUL** spirit to lead us with excitement.

BIBLE READING — FIRST THESSALONIANS

3. Glory and Joy — 2:19-20. Look at the words "crown of rejoicing." The crown represents authority, leadership significance, and fulfillment in the life of your pastor. You are his "glory and joy" as you partner with him in ministry and develop in Christian maturity. **Prayer:** Father, I want to be a "joy maker." Let me stand by my pastor, stand with him, and stand up for him by being a dedicated, diligent, and dependable disciple.

My Journal

FOR THE WEEK

Praise reports, answered prayers, divine provisions, and
spiritual plans.

_____

_____

_____

_____

_____

_____

_____

_____

_____

_____

BIBLE READING—FIRST THESSALONIANS

4. Good News—3:6-8. The "life" of your pastor is the
"good news" of your faith, love, and steadfastness in the
Lord. **Prayer:** Shepherd of my soul, I want to be "life"
and "light" to my pastor. Let me join him in faith for our
church to go forward in love, and to lift up the fallen, and
to be steadfast in ministry.

RESPONSIBILITIES TODAY

Refreshing Redeemer, You have transformed my life and turned me around. I have new directions and new dreams, I walk a different path and I have new responsibilities. I will . . .

Show RESPECT. Father, I respect Your Word and all the promises it contains. I respect my church and all the members that lead me and stand with me. I respect my pastor and all the ways he guides me in living a Christ-centered life.

Accept RESPONSIBILITY. Your gifts, Master—atonement, adoption, affirmation—are given freely, openly, and without hesitation. I respect these gifts. I also accept responsibility to protect them, to share them with others, and to offer daily praise for them.

Stir RENEWAL. Lord, You have given me new directions and new dreams. You lead me and stand with me. You have given me precious gifts. I will not be selfish with blessings. I will keep my faith fresh, and I will stir renewal in my own life and in the body of Christ, my local church.

BIBLE READING—FIRST THESSALONIANS

5. Lack Nothing—4:9-12. Paul wanted the church to have an "abundance mentality"—to "lack nothing" (v. 12). He outlined the formula in verses 9 and 11: (1) increase love for one another; (2) learn the art of quietness, and (3) work with your own hands. **Prayer:** Our church can be complete, and a certain part of the completeness is up to me. Let me lead the way in love and in alertness to know when to talk and when to listen, and to form proactive work habits.

REVEAL YOURSELF TODAY

Lord of everlasting love, reveal Yourself to me in illuminating ways today. Let brightness break through darkness. Let understanding cover misunderstanding. Let heavenly empowerment surface over human weakness. I want to know You in a fuller measure today. I ask You to reveal Yourself . . .

In Your Holy WORD. As I read Your Word today, Father, let the Holy Spirit give me revealing insights, instructions to live an impactful life, an inspiration to stand firmly and to shine with convincing convictions. Today, I will receive light, liberty, and love from Your Word.

With Helpful WORKS. I ask You, Father, to reveal Yourself in my life with works of righteousness, holiness, and fruitfulness today. I will look up, not down, and witness Your mighty acts of restoration and renewal.

With Heavenly WISDOM. Master, you know all things. Give me Your guidance today. Lead me by Your grace. Let me abide in Your goodness. Let me be prudent in my transactions, positive in my testimony, and productive as a model of a Christlike life.

BIBLE READING—FIRST THESSALONIANS

6. Esteem Highly—5:12-13. These two verses set forth recognition, appreciation, and commendation for pastors, church leaders, and workers. The framework for doing this is to "be at peace among yourselves" (harmony, love, and unity in the church). **Prayer:** Father, let our church practice holy behavior, worship in an atmosphere of harmony, and hold hands in aggressive Christian service.

RIPE HARVEST TODAY

Lord of the harvest, through Your Son, Jesus Christ, You demonstrated Your love to rescue, redeem, restore, and provide everlasting life (John 3:16). I am secure in You today, and forevermore! I rejoice in this nonnegotiable assurance. I will go forth into the harvest with a . . .

SHARP Sickle. Father, Your Word is a sharp sickle that defends and delivers. It represents life, hope, and peace. I realize the laborers are few in the harvest fields (Matthew 9:37; Luke 10:2); I will respond to the harvest challenge and I will recruit others in my church to join me.

SANCTIFIED Lifestyle. I understand to be an effective worker in the harvest fields, I must live a sanctified life—a set apart, steadfast, and serving life. I will reflect the nature of Christ in my life by showing love for the lost, the outcast, and the hurting.

SCRIPTURAL Balance. In my attitude, approach, and actions in reaping the harvest, I am committed to maintaining a scriptural balance. I will stand on Your Word, Lord, for wisdom, instructions, and empowerment to be effective in reaping a harvest that honors You.

BIBLE READING—SECOND THESSALONIANS

1. Growing Faith—1:2-8. The church was facing persecutions and tribulations, but their faith was growing; they had love for each other, and they were patient in enduring hardship. **Prayer:** God of sustaining grace, may our church follow the model of the Thessalonica congregation. As we face conflicts and challenges, let us be patient in trusting You, express caring love to each other, and release our faith to overcome and achieve.

SALT TODAY

Father of salt and sanctification, You season my life daily and sanction me for noble service. Your Spirit radiates Your nature in my life whereby I become an agent of salt and seasoning to . . .

INFLUENCE my family. Master, I have the privilege to influence members of my family by my lifestyle, my love, and my language. Today, I will show my commitment to You, convey my love for You, and focus my conversations to honor You.

INSPIRE my friends. I desire to be salt in the lives of my friends today by example, by encouragement, and by embracing them in time of need. Father, I request Your overshadowing grace to do this. I will look to You, I will listen to Your instructions, and I will learn from gifted believers around me.

IMPACT my church. Father, You have called me to be a seasoned servant in my church—to welcome visitors, to be a witness by consistent attendance, and to win the confidence of other members by being dependable and accountable. "Please pass the salt!" Yes, I will!

BIBLE READING—SECOND THESSALONIANS

2. Stand Fast—2:1-17. Paul talked about the "falling away" (v. 3) that will occur before the day Christ returns. He told the congregation not to be "shaken" or "troubled" (v. 2), but to "stand fast" and to "hold firmly" the "traditions" (truths, doctrine) (v. 15) they had been taught. **Prayer:** May the thoughts of "the coming of our Lord Jesus Christ" (v. 1), Your Son, be a rallying point for our church to be doctrinally strong and to be spiritually motivated to proclaim the good news with power and passion.

SCHOOL LIFE TODAY

Teaching Master, I am thankful for the privilege to learn and grow. Over the years dedicated teachers have guided, nurtured, and tutored me. I pray for the effectiveness of teachers in their ministry to . . .

SHAPE Values. Father, under Your leadership, teachers guide in shaping lifelong values in relationship to character, church loyalty, commitments, and career objectives. Surround them with Your guidance so their instructions will be practical and motivational, and scripturally founded. May they follow the example of the master Teacher who taught to change lives.

STRENTHEN Study Habits. Teachers are in a position to influence lifelong study habits that will result in foundational knowledge, decision-making wisdom, and pathways to serve and please You, Father. Bless them so their teaching ministry will incite a desire to study consistently and devotedly. May they follow the example of the master Teacher who taught to learn and grow.

SHARE Experiences. Teachers are models! Lord, inspire them to share experiences of Your oversight in career development, building relationships, and reaching goals that provide spiritual and financial stability. May they follow the example of the master Teacher who taught from His position of unity with You, Holy Father.

BIBLE READING—SECOND THESSALONIANS

3. Pray for Us—3:1-5. Paul asked the people of the church to pray for him and his staff that the Word of God may "run swiftly" (spread rapidly) and be "glorified" (honored). **Prayer:** Father, You have entrusted our pastor to share Your Word with us. Anoint him to preach with authority. Anoint our hearts and minds to receive so that Your Word will spread with speed and be received and honored.

FIVE WAYS A CHURCH CAN
Cultivate a Positive Image

1. Join other churches in sponsoring citywide events — Thanksgiving services, civic projects, educational programs, and care for the poor.

2. Promote ministries that touch the community and that build respect and trust for the church.

3. Maintain church property in such a way that it denotes pride and a commitment to quality. A "windshield tour" by neighbors can create a spirit of friendliness and welcome.

4. Develop attractive signage and advertise the church. Place directional signs at strategic locations, feature ads in the local newspaper, and periodically do a citywide mailing.

5. Sponsor big events that gain the attention and the attendance of people from different areas of the city — seasonal plays, singing groups, crusades, special speakers, school projects (homework helpers), food functions, and honor programs for public servants.

BIBLE READING — FIRST TIMOTHY

1. Goal of Instruction — 1:1-5. The church at Ephesus was facing false doctrine and false teachers. Paul told them the goal of his instructions was "love from a pure heart, from a good conscience, and from true faith" (v. 5). **Prayer:** May our church be known as a church of love, embracing sound doctrine and demonstrating closeness with Christ through acts of compassion and kindness.

My Journal

FOR THE WEEK

Praise reports, answered prayers, divine provisions, and spiritual plans.

BIBLE READING—FIRST TIMOTHY

2. Pray for Everyone—2:1-4. Paul said to pray for everyone you know and in every way you know how. **Prayer:** Lord, I pray for family and friends today. I especially pray for those in authority in our church and in our country. Bless my pastor, church leaders, and officials in local, state, and national government positions.

SEIZE TODAY

Faithful Father, today is a gift from You — a glorious gift, a gracious gift, a magnificent gift. I cherish Your gift and will guard it and use it wisely. Today offers opportunities to . . .

EXPLORE. Life is beautiful! I am surrounded by opportunities to explore — the intriguing marvels of nature, the beckoning call to discover biblical wonders, and the invitation to grow in the amazing art of communication. *I am thankful for the glorious gift of today!*

EXPERIENCE. Life is marvelous! I have the privilege to experience — a deeper relationship with You, Master, creative ways to learn and grow, and different territories that offer captivating scenery that gives a foretaste of Your plans for the future. *I praise You for the gracious gift of today!*

ENJOY. Life is magnificent! I have unmatched benefits to enjoy — open and personal communion with You, Holy Father, enriching fellowship with believers and open roads to reach new destinations of joyful praise and enriched relationships. *I honor You for the magnificent gift of today!*

BIBLE READING — FIRST TIMOTHY

3. Appointed a Preacher — 2:3-7. It was important for the people to know that God appointed and ordained Paul to preach the good news. It is important today to recognize that the pastor is sent by God and sealed by God to preach and teach about faith and truth. **Prayer:** God who calls and separates, touch the people as our pastor teaches; let us receive Your Word from him with open hearts, a thankful spirit, and scriptural respect.

SELF-EVALUATION TODAY

Lord of total understanding, You know the beginning of my life as well as the ending. Nothing is hidden from You—my thoughts, my dreams, and what I cherish in my heart. You have instructed me to examine myself in order to follow Your precepts and plans for my life (1 Corinthians 11:28). Today, I will examine my . . .

MOTIVES. Father, it is easy to get sidetracked in running the Christian race—selfish motives, self-serving priorities, and self-centered behavior. Instruct me, illuminate my thinking so my motives will be Christ-centered, scripture-based, and others-centered. *I will examine my motives today!*

MESSAGE. Father, do the words I speak send a positive message of the forgiving and freeing love of Your Son, Jesus Christ? Is my message clear and supported with sincere compassion, unselfish guidance, and life-changing directions? *I will examine my message today!*

MOTIVATION. Lord, I want to stay motivated in serving You and influencing those around me—sowing seeds of goodwill, of vision for the harvest, and of enjoying the gifts that flow from Your throne of grace. *I will examine my motivation today!*

BIBLE READING—FIRST TIMOTHY

4. Qualifications for Church Leadership—3:1-13. Your pastor and church officials must meet high standards of personal commitment and professional conduct. They must be respectable, hospitable, and faithful. They must be temperate, prudent, and sensible. **Prayer:** My pastor has heavy responsibilities. I uphold him in prayer. Keep his heart pure, anoint his preaching, and let peace surround him.

SERVE TODAY

Serving Savior, You were sent by God the Father to serve—heal the sick, feed the hungry, set free the captive, and give the promise of the Comforter. You fulfilled the will of the Father, and now You have assigned believers to carry on Your ministry. I will be obedient in following in Your steps. I will . . .

SHOW Love Openly. Jesus, You loved the multitudes, the children, individuals, and showed Your love openly—inspiring words, delivering works, and empowering wisdom. I will embrace Your pattern and show love openly—visibly, colorfully, unselfishly, and actively.

SHARE Willingly. Father, You shared Your love willingly with the world by sending Christ to redeem the fallen. Christ shared His love willingly by paying the supreme price, death on the cross. Empowered by Your Spirit I will willingly share Your love—relating to the lost, releasing the love of Christ that rescues and sets free, and refreshing the weak and weary.

STAND Steadfastly. I will show love! I will share willingly! I will stand steadfastly! I will serve faithfully, fervently, and forcefully! Lord of the harvest, I will honor You by being a servant who reflects the servant characteristics of Christ!

BIBLE READING—FIRST TIMOTHY

5. A Good Minister—4:1-6. What makes your pastor a "good minister"? Paul gives several points in verses 1-6; warn about false doctrines and leaders, instruct in the goodness of God, and emphasize living a thankful life. **Prayer:** Master of mercy, I thank You for my pastor; bless him and bless me as we join You in expanding Your kingdom through the ministries of the local church.

SERVING IN LOVE TODAY

Loving and liberating Lord, it is Your will for me to live a life of love and freedom. You sent Your Son into the world to save, restore, and serve. He had a servant's heart! I will follow His pattern! I will be . . .

ACTIVE. My love will be visible, open, and active. I will love with words and works. I will be a loving friend in the time of need, a loving friend in the time of crisis, and a loving friend in supporting a grace-filled life. My love will be unconditional, authentic, and unselfish.

ALERT. Christ shared love with a spirit of generosity with individuals on all levels of life—the rich, the poor, the sick, the social outcasts, and the religious outcasts. His love was for everyone, everywhere, and for whatever circumstances existed.

ACCOUNTABLE. "Love never fails" (1 Corinthians 13:8). I will demonstrate the serving love of Christ at all times—in times of difficulty, physical danger, and depressing encounters. Father, I will trust in Your Spirit to empower me and to fortify me to stand steadfastly and victoriously.

BIBLE READING—FIRST TIMOTHY

6. Take Heed—4:12-16. A pastor must "take heed" to himself—his conduct, faith, purity, gifts, study, and teaching—so that his example will be a "guiding force" for the congregation. **Prayer:** My pastor needs Your grace to gird him, Your strength to sustain him, and Your wisdom to mold him. Bless him abundantly today!

SERVING STEADFASTLY TODAY

Sanctifying and strengthening Lord, by Your Holy Spirit, You teach me how to serve You with whole-life integrity and how to serve in my church with steadfast commitment. I want to consistently practice what You have taught me. I will serve today with . . .

PURE Conscience. I will not serve with a hidden agenda or with the intentions of getting something in return. Father, I will serve with purity of purpose—to highlight Your holiness, Your healing virtues, and Your helping hands to deliver. *I believe You!*

POWER of the Holy Spirit. Father, You sent the Holy Spirit as a Comforter, a Guide, and as an Equipper for service. The Spirit comforts in troubling situations, guides in developing uncontested character, and issues undeterred power to serve You with authority and impactful influence. *I praise You for this!*

PURSUIT of Holiness. My desire, heavenly Master, is to follow You and embrace Your ordinances with trust, transparency, and devotional dignity. I will strive, under Your care, to be holy in my thinking patterns, in my togetherness spirit with other believers, and in my devotional practices. *I trust You for this!*

BIBLE READING—FIRST TIMOTHY

7. Honor Each Other—5:1-25. Specific instructions are given by Paul on how to treat each other—older and younger men, older and younger women, widows, and elders. He also says to give "double honor" (v. 17) to your pastor because he works hard to minister to you and he deserves his pay. **Prayer:** Bless my pastor with Your favor and the favor of the people. May he receive the gift of cooperation and of compensation.

My Personal Pledge

TO CONSISTENT BIBLE STUDY

I realize through Bible study I can understand the nature of God, the mission of the church, and His standards for spiritual wholeness. Therefore, I will embrace the value of Bible study!

I pledge to be loyal in consistent Bible study by . . .

1. **SETTING** aside time each day to hear from God through His Word.

2. **SEARCHING** the Scriptures to gain awareness of how God relates, instructs, and blesses.

3. **STANDING** on God's promises and applying them to daily life and Christian service.

4. **SHARING** the good news of saving grace, heavenly security, and Holy Spirit oversight.

5. **SPREADING** God's love, hope, and happiness through the ministries of my church.

BIBLE READING — FIRST TIMOTHY

8. Godliness with Contentment — 6:1-9. Being a Christian makes your life rich by making you content with what you have. There is peace of mind and daily provisions. This eliminates worry, tension, frustration with issues, and calmness and contentment. **Prayer:** God, You are good and generous. You have blessed me, made me rich in You. Let me exhibit calmness and contentment in my home life and church life.

My Journal

FOR THE WEEK

Praise reports, answered prayers, divine provisions, and spiritual plans.

_____

_____

_____

_____

_____

_____

_____

_____

_____

BIBLE READING — SECOND TIMOTHY

1. A Holy Calling — 1:8-11. Like Paul, your pastor's life belongs to the people because of his "holy calling" to be a preacher, emissary, and teacher. **Prayer:** God of perpetual grace, our pastor lives a restricted life. He must do Your will and work, and guide our congregation in Your paths. This is a tough assignment! Cover him with Your grace. Cover us with grace to be obedient and to follow his leadership.

SHARING CHRIST TODAY

Father of all goodness, I want to represent You with both humility and authority. I want to be a tender witness, bearing the truth in love, but I also want to be an aggressive witness. Today, I ask You to guide me in . . .

SEEKING Opportunities. Many times in my daily routine, the privilege to witness comes easy and natural, opportunities are abundant. At other times, however, I must seek opportunities to share my love for Jesus Christ. Father, guide me in the seeking process!

SHOWING Compassion. I understand, Master, that a powerful witnessing vehicle is to show compassion—sympathy, support, and sharing scriptural promises. Only by the leadership of Your Spirit can I do this. Therefore, I will be submissive, alert, and aggressive in showing genuine compassion as a committed Christ-exalting witness.

SHARING Good News. I realize there are numerous ways to share "good tidings of great joy"—modeling, witnessing, and serving. However, a major effective model is for me to invite friends, neighbors, associates, and relatives to attend a church worship service or event with me. I want to stay motivated to do this. Lord, keep Your prompting and empowering hand upon me!

BIBLE READING—SECOND TIMOTHY

2. Process of Refreshing—1:16-18. Onesiphorous supported his pastor. He refreshed him through encouragement by standing with him during difficult times, by helping to meet his needs, and by working side by side with him. **Prayer:** Lord of glory, I want to follow the example of Onesiphorous. I want to cheer up, refresh, and encourage my pastor. Let me take definite steps of action today.

SHARING TODAY

Compassionate Lord, You shared Your Son, Jesus Christ, with the world (John 3:16). You shared the indwelling of the Holy Spirit with believers. You provide miracles, promises, and demonstrations of divine power. I want to obediently follow Your pattern by . . .

SEEING Needs. Father, people are in need all around me and my church. Being busy often blinds me from seeing these needs—the hurting, hopeless, spiritually handicapped. I ask You to open my eyes so I can see these needs clearly and with understanding.

SHOWING Compassion. Christ showed compassion to the weak, weary, and wayward. He expressed His feelings through prayer, weeping, and personal intervention. Father, teach me, train me, tutor me in showing intense concern for those in need. Let my concern reflect the love and compassion of Christ.

SUPPLYING Support. Guide me, heavenly Father, in showing personal support—witnessing, sharing, working, and encouraging. I will show how the ministries of the church supply support through relationships, worship, counseling, biblical instructions, relief programs, and life-sustaining peace.

BIBLE READING—SECOND TIMOTHY

3. Endure All Things—2:10-13. As a leader and a pastor, Paul said, "I endure all things" so I can protect, prepare, and provide for God's people. **Prayer:** God of eternal wisdom, You "know all things" about our congregation—our attitudes, affections, activities—and how they relate to our pastor shepherding us. Make us leadable, likeable, and loveable. Let us help lift our pastor up and not load him down with our quirks, smirks, and flirts with the world.

SHELTER DURING STORMS TODAY

Protecting Father, You provide shelter during times of storm in my life—peaceful security, calming protection, and satisfying provisions. I find rest in Your care! I honor the attributes of Your nature—righteousness, holiness, eternalness, forgiveness, and "longsufferingness." You keep me during the storms of . . .

Negative SURROUNDINGS. Satan sees to it that I am surrounded by negative circumstances. Father, You see to it that I am surrounded by a heavenly host that dissolves the negatives and magnifies the positives—guarded by grace, grounded by faith, and gifted to serve.

Temptations to SIN. Satan seeks to lead me to ignore and to disobey Your laws and precepts, Father. You lead me in paths of righteousness and You walk by my side to steady my steps, to give resistance strength, and to show Your power to overcome.

Desire to Take SHORTCUTS. Satan tries to influence me to cut short my prayer time, my worship time, and my Bible-study time. Father, You influence and inspire me to be committed and consistent—in communion with You, in honoring You in praise, and in demonstrating a winning lifestyle.

BIBLE READING—SECOND TIMOTHY

4. Be Diligent—2:15. Consistent, responsible Bible study is the only way a believer can know God, join Him in His plans for the church, merit His approval, and honor Him. Bible study is both personal and congregational. **Prayer:** Truth Divine, I want to study Your Word at home, study Your Word with other believers, and study Your Word as my pastor preaches.

SHINE TODAY

Illuminating Father, You break through darkness with the light of Your love. You deliver from difficulties with the dissolving flow of Your grace. I'm thrilled. I'm an overcomer and will shine as a light today (Philippians 2:15) by my . . .

REVERENCE—respecting Your holiness. Father, Your kingdom is founded on Your Word, the functions of Your church, and the dedication of Your people. I will show daily reverence by studying Your Word, supporting Your church, and sharing blessings with Your people.

REPUTATION—representing Your kingdom. I realize my actions form an unquestionable reputation or a questionable reputation. By Your leadership, Lord, I will live a life of integrity, inspiration, and involvement in ministry that reflects the love, nature, and actions of Jesus Christ.

RESPONSIBILITIES—responding to Your commands. Master, people will know that I belong to You if I advance Your commands—love You with my heart, soul, and mind; love my neighbors as myself; and love those searching for meaning in life. Love will guide my life today!

BIBLE READING—SECOND TIMOTHY

5. Follow Doctrine—3:10-11. Paul said that doctrine was a source of deliverance. Doctrine is what we believe about God, His Son, the church, Satan, heaven, and hell. Bible doctrine defends, develops, and delivers. **Prayer:** Lord, I want to stand on the Scriptures, to be prepared to worship, witness, and claim every "good work" in serving with You.

SHOWING HOSPITALITY TODAY

Father of acceptance and hospitality, You invite every person to be part of Your kingdom. The doors into Your presence are always open—You receive, redeem, and richly reward. I must reflect this same spirit. The doors of my church must be open to invite people in to experience fellowship, saving faith, and family. My responsibility is to show . . .

A Welcome SPIRIT. Father, You welcomed me into Your family—graciously, forgivingly, and lovingly. I will be part of the spirit of my church that welcomes newcomers warmly, openly, and lovingly. I will follow Your example!

A Broad SMILE. A broad, holy smile indicates a joyful heart of welcome, compassion, and concern. I want to smile every day. I will also smile at church to show a kindred spirit with church members, a caring spirit for children, and a belonging spirit to guests.

A Focus on SIGNIFICANCE. Lord, I thank You that I am a person of worth and value in Your sight—accepted, adopted, and affirmed. I want to be a champion in pointing individuals to Jesus Christ to find salvation, significance, and security.

BIBLE READING—SECOND TIMOTHY

6. Embrace All Scripture—3:16. God wants us to be equipped, thoroughly prepared, to carry out His will in our lives and in the church. His Word is our source, resource, and force. **Prayer:** Divine Truth, Your Word is for reproof, correction, and instruction in relating properly to You, to fellow believers, and to those in the world. Let us believe it, obey it, and cherish it.

PERSONAL AFFIRMATION— SERVE

Jesus Christ set the example for me, "He came to serve, not to be served." My goal is to follow His example and to be a Christ-honoring, God-pleasing, and Spirit-led servant.

I Will . . .

- Prepare to be an effective servant.
- Find a place to serve in the church.
- Go into available harvest fields.
- Serve in community activities/events.
- Pray for God to send forth workers.
- Touch others to serve by example.
- Be accountable as a faithful servant.
- Experience the fruit of serving.

BIBLE READING—SECOND TIMOTHY

7. Be Watchful—4:1-5. Watchfulness is the responsibility of the entire church—pastor, leaders, workers, and members. Watch for false teachers and doctrine, lukewarmness, inattention to outreach, frictions, and wavering faith. **Prayer:** Lord, let our church stand together in total unity in holding to sound doctrine, in being ready in season and out of season, and in being burning evangelists (witnesses).

My Journal

FOR THE WEEK

Praise reports, answered prayers, divine provisions, and spiritual plans.

BIBLE READING — SECOND TIMOTHY

8. Present World — 4:10. The "present world," the temporary glow of sin, is one of Satan's main weapons. The glow is attractive, enticing, misleading. **Prayer:** Almighty Lord, we know Satan is mighty, but You are almighty. In our church, may we encourage one another — stand with, hold close, lift up, and support. May we be a true family of faith.

SHOW ME YOUR GLORY TODAY

God of wonder and wisdom, I want to see You clearly today. I want to see You up close in all Your majesty and glory. I seek these insightful experiences with deep humility and with a heart full and running over with expressions of praise and adoration. Your glory represents who You are and what I can become in You. Your glory . . .

Reveals Your NATURE. Father, You are ever-present. You are all-powerful. You know all things. You are not restricted in any way—form or fashion. Today, I will dwell on Your glory as revealed in Your nature and will live in the full dimensions of all the benefits it offers.

Provides NURTURE. Every day, God of wonder, You set new avenues before me to walk on, new projects to undertake, and new relationships to form. This equals excitement plus! But, I need divine nurture to clothe me, guide me, and sustain me. I trust You to provide nurturing care.

Creates NEWNESS. I am a new creation in Jesus Christ. This means I can do things in new, exciting ways. I will not be blocked or bogged down by outdated, limited practices. I will walk new paths of trust, share my faith, and live victoriously.

BIBLE READING—TITUS

1. Purpose of Preaching—1:1-3. The plan of God, the path He wants believers to follow, and the promises He has given, are set forth through preaching. Your pastor is a bondservant to God, commissioned to preach His Word. **Prayer:** Father, bless my pastor in his preaching responsibilities—study, prayer, anointing, delivery, and connecting with the congregation. Prepare the church to be receptive and to respond with positive action.

SINGING IN MY SOUL TODAY

God of miracles and melody, I am singing in my soul today. This singing is generated by Your presence in my life that gives assurance, calmness, and value. The singing produces a sunshine attitude, a contagious smile, and a sparkling disposition. Today, I will sing . . .

JEHOVAH songs — songs that reflect Your majesty and mighty acts, Lord. Throughout the Bible, Your people sang songs about Your creative power, delivering power, sustaining power, and promise-keeping power. They sang Jehovah songs. *Today, I will sing Jehovah songs in my soul!*

JUBILEE songs — songs that denote milestones of ministry achievements. Jubilee songs remind me of past miracles and mighty spiritual moves in Your Church and among Your people, Lord. They keep my faith fresh, flourishing, and active. *Today, I will sing jubilee songs in my soul!*

JOYFUL songs — songs that declare my love, loyalty, and liberty. I have joyful songs in my soul as a result of sins forgiven and security in Christ. A joy-filled life attracts attention and is a vibrant testimony of contentment in Christ. *Today, I will sing joyful songs in my soul!*

BIBLE READING — TITUS

2. Pattern of Good Works — 2:1-10. The impact and advancement of Your church will be determined by the "pattern of good works" of the members. This means consistent, daily Christian living — doing good deeds, reflecting purity in doctrine, and practicing soundness of speech. **Prayer:** Kind Father, today let me do good deeds, thereby demonstrating Your love and my commitment to You. Let our church always practice what we believe, teach, and preach.

SINGING TODAY

Creator of music, You receive songs of praise and petition from Your people. They represent happiness, joy, and thanksgiving. Through singing, I worship You with my voice and with expressions that originate in my heart. Today, I will sing songs of . . .

DEVOTION. I will sing songs that convey my dedication to You, Lord—a lifestyle of holiness, wholeness, and spiritual wellness. I will sing songs that exalt Your name, that express Your majesty, and that extol the beauty of Your nature. "I will sing joyful songs unto the Lord."

DELIVERANCE. Lord, the psalms are highlighted with songs of deliverance; how you delivered Your people from the traps of Satan, evil temptations, and tormenting trials. Songs express praise and thanksgiving. I will sing joyful songs today about Your acts of deliverance in my life.

DELIGHT. My heart is filled with songs of delight—victory in Christ, victory over the vices of Satan, and victory over vile and vicious attacks. I will manifest a spirit of delight. I will sing songs today about how You, Lord, fill my life with love, joy, and peace.

BIBLE READING—TITUS

3. Ready for Good Works—3:1-2. With an eagerness to do "what is good" there comes the responsibility to be "subject" (obedient, cooperative) to civil authorities, church leaders, family members, and employers. **Prayer:** Father, You have told me to be at peace with everyone and to be considerate of them. I want to do this because this is the only way my Christian witness can be effective. Give me a sensitive, supportive spirit.

SKILL TO UNDERSTAND TODAY

Skill-investing Creator, I cherish the talents You have deposited in my life. I honor them! I respect them! I will develop them! Today, I ask You to lead me in the process of understanding how to utilize them in cooperation with Your master plan. Reveal to me the . . .

SCOPE of my duties. I understand, Father, my first duty is to love You with all my heart, mind, and strength. Fortify my faith to do this! Equip me with skill to do this! Empower me with spiritual energy to do this! I will accept my duties with Spirit-powered dedication.

STRENGTH for my dedication. I want my life to be marked by dedication to You, Master, and to the ministry You have called me to be part of. Strength is needed for the task—heavenly strength, health strength, and home strength. I confess openly and honestly that my strength comes from You, wonder-working Master.

SUPPLIES for my journey. Thank You, Father, for supplying all the resources needed for my Christian journey: water—the water of life; bread—manna from heaven; fruit—the fruit of the Spirit; my church—a supportive family of believers! I will use these resources with preserving reverence, binding trust, and honorable appreciation.

BIBLE READING—PHILEMON

1. A Beloved Brother/Sister—1:10-16. When a person accepts Christ, he or she becomes a brother or sister. He or she is to be forgiven for wrongs committed, accepted into the family, and shown love and kindness. **Prayer:** Our church is a family; we are to forgive, forget, and form a loving, binding family relationship with each other. Soften my spirit Lord. Let me be a reconcilor, a catalyst to help church members communicate, cooperate, and celebrate together.

SOLID FOUNDATION TODAY

Father, You provide a solid foundation on which to build a life that is accepted by You, anointed by the Holy Spirit, and that advances the mission of Your Son, Jesus Christ. In Your love I am stable, secure, and steadfast. I live on a solid foundation by . . .

GRACE—sufficient grace. Father, Your grace is sufficient—for every condition, for every circumstance, and for every challenge. You extend it to everyone who will receive it by exercising faith in You and Your plan for salvation in Christ and security in the Holy Spirit.

GODLY Character—guiding character. Standards, values, mind and heart aspirations, and spiritual commitments form my character. Character directs my attitude, my actions, and my activities. Godly character enables me to live a life of influence and to invite others to walk a path of purity in Christ.

GOOD Works—Christ-exalting good works. The life of Christ was characterized by good work—feeding the hungry, healing the sick, restoring sight to the blind, and freeing the oppressed. Master, equip me, and my church, to advocate and advance the model of Christ.

BIBLE READING—PHILEMON

2. Prepare a Guest Room—1:22. Paul had faith that Philemon would pray for him and that God would permit him to make a visit in the near future, "so get a guest room ready." **Prayer:** God, You are my dearest friend. I want to pray for my pastor today, every day, and to help provide for his physical needs—a "guest room." I pray for the boldness of his faith, the happiness of his family, and the sufficiency of his finances. Bless him richly, abundantly, daily!

PRAYER PATTERN — INTEGRITY

I will pray for my pastor today and support him in being an integrity-based leader.

I — My pastor needs the daily **INFLUENCE** of Your Spirit.

N — Teach him to **NUMBER** his days and use them wisely.

T — **TAKE** him to new heights in his relationship with You.

E — **ENCOURAGE** his heart as he encourages and lifts up others.

G — Help my pastor show a spirit of **GENTLENESS** in all aspects of his ministry.

R — Let him set an example of **RELIABILITY** and scriptural stability.

I — **INSTILL** grace to be a man of Your Word, and his word.

T — **TEACH** him to walk the path of love, forgiveness, and service.

Y — May he always **YEARN** to know You more and more in the fullness of his calling.

BIBLE READING — HEBREWS

1. Ministers a Flame of Fire — 1:7. In Chapter 1, Christ is exalted above angels — "Let all the angels of God worship Him: (v. 6). He rules with righteousness, and God has anointed Him with the oil of gladness. He makes pastors "a flame of fire" to witness of the superiority of His Son, Jesus Christ. **Pray** for witnessing opportunities and the effectiveness of your pastor.

My Journal

FOR THE WEEK

Praise reports, answered prayers, divine provisions, and spiritual plans.

_____

_____

_____

_____

_____

_____

_____

_____

_____

_____

BIBLE READING — HEBREWS

2. Merciful and Faithful High Priest — 2:17. Christ became one with the people through His physical birth in order to represent them to God the Father — their salvation, happiness, and future. The pastor is commissioned to be one with the people in leading them to surrender to Christ and to serve Him. **Pray** for the pastor and the people to be connected in love, worship, and mission.

SONGS IN MY SOUL TODAY

Master of Music, I have songs in my soul today—songs with lyrics of love, of liberty, and of lasting fellowship with You. I'm privileged! I'm blessed beyond measure! I will raise my voice in songs of . . .

THANKSGIVING. My soul is filled with thanksgiving! I'm thankful for my family, my faith, my friends, and for my secure future in Christ. I will express my thanksgiving today by singing praise to the Father, Son, and Holy Spirit.

TRIUMPH. Father, in Christ I am a champion! He has empowered me to triumph over the forces of evil, to raise the flag of victory, to stand in the winner's circle, and to sing songs of success. I will express my triumphant posture today by singing songs that magnify Your supreme strength and generous grace.

TESTIMONY. Master, the songs in my soul will come forth as a testimony of Your purifying power, the healing power of Christ, and the energizing power of the Holy Spirit. I will share songs of thanksgiving and triumph with others today!

BIBLE READING—HEBREWS

3. Partakers of Christ—3:14. As a partaker of Christ, you are His associate, partner, and companion. This calls for a continuance in faith and a growing, binding relationship. **Pray** for the discipleship training programs of your church and the expository preaching of your pastor.

SOURCE OF STRENGTH TODAY

Lord that lifts up, You lift me up daily and empower me to stand up, and stand out, and stand with You in total trust and obedience. You are my source of strength! By the guiding force of Your strength, I will . . .

Look UP. I will look up, Father, and visualize Your storehouse of endless blessings, Your sufficient strength to overcome, and Your superior gifts to live the super abundant life. *I will look up today!*

Shake UP. I realize on many occasions I need to shake up the way I see and perform ministry—direction, development duties. Today, Lord, I am open and ready to respond to Your propelling spirit to advance in effective Christ-centered behavior. *I will shake up conformity today!*

Go UP. I will, Master, accept Your strength and supplies to go up to a higher level of representing You, of responding to opportunities to share Good News, and of refining my skills to serve with greater influence. I will study Scripture and form a sturdy structure to advance in closer harmony with You. *I will go up in fellowship with You today!*

BIBLE READING—HEBREWS

4. Mixed with Faith—4:2-16. The Word of God must be heard, believed, and "mixed with faith" in order to merit results. God's Word is "living and powerful" (v. 12) and provides "rest" (v. 11) and "boldness" (v. 16). **Pray** for open ears and hearts in the congregation while the pastor preaches so that the message will be "mixed with faith" and produce positive action.

SOWING SEEDS TODAY

What a magnificent privilege, holy Father, to sow scriptural seeds and then to stand back and experience the amazing results with rejoicing. When I sow seeds five things take place: (1) Salvation; (2) Expansion of Your Kingdom; (3) Experiences of graces; (4) Dedication; and (5) Super joy. I will sow seeds by . . .

GODLY Principles. Father, I will sow seeds by developing and demonstrating principles that reflect Your nature — purity, kindness, compassion, total forgiveness, and a steadfast willingness to stand alongside in support. *I will sow godly seeds!*

GENEROUS Practices. I will sow seeds by showing a spirit of generosity in my relationships and responsibilities. I will be generous in sharing my faith, my love, my finances, and my support for my family. *I will sow generous seeds!*

GLORIOUS Praise. I will sow seeds by lifting my voice in glorious praise! I will sow seeds by lifting my hands in glorious reverence! I will sow seeds by showing glorious praise in worship services — singing, attention to the sermon, and financial support. *I will sow glorious seeds!*

BIBLE READING — HEBREWS

5. Solid Food — 5:12. It is God's will for believers to grow from drinking milk to eating solid food; from being taught, to teaching other; from being led, to developing leadership skills. **Pray** for the church body to mature spiritually under the godly guidance of your pastor, seasoned mentors, and visionary leaders.

SPEAK TODAY

Father of openness and fruitfulness, I stand in Your presence to receive Your anointing and advice. Speak to me! I will listen! I will follow Your instructions! The doors into Your presence are always open and Your supply of life-enriching fruit is always available. Today, I will check my . . .

SANCTIFICATION. Lord, You have told me to separate myself from the world that does not recognize Your sovereignty and Holy Scriptures. I will do this by the indwelling guidance of Your Spirit. *Today, I will live a separated and sanctified life!*

SPIRITUALITY. Through sanctification, I can be a shining example of Your transforming grace. Touch me, Father, to be spiritual and Bible-based in manifesting the characteristics of a fully devoted follower of Jesus Christ. *Today, I will live a pure and purpose-driven life!*

SPONTANEITY. Yes, I am ready to respond to Your leadership, Father, with both faith and flair — bold energy, stirring excitement, and adventure-based expectations. I desire to walk with You every day with a flow of Your creative power working in my mind, heart, and hands. *Today, I will live an action-centered, no-limits life.*

BIBLE READING — HEBREWS

6. Inherit the Promises — 6:9-12. God does not forget the "work and labor of love" of His people (v. 10). He wants them to be active, not sluggish; to show "faith and patience" (v. 12); and to receive what He has promised in full measure. **Pray** for both personal and congregational steadfastness in performing Kingdom ministry and in claiming the divine provisions God has promised.

SPIRITUAL BALANCE TODAY

High and holy Helper, You provide directions and balance for my life. Balance enables me to be disciplined in my conduct, testimony, and ministry ethics. However, You require me to cultivate spiritual balance in my life. I will do this by demonstrating . . .

HOLY Standards. Father, You are the essence of holiness. You are exact, definite, and precise in Your standards to live a holy life. Clothe me with divine grace so I can comply with, and live out, Your standards of holy and impactful living.

HEALTHY Vocabulary. I want to speak healthy words every day — positive words, encouraging words, supportive words. People around me will be influenced by my words, either positively or negatively. I will speak words of health, healing, and hope today.

HIGH Expectations. Thank You, Master, that I can live with high and holy expectations every day — new horizons, new experiences, new opportunities, and new phases of personal growth! Give me a clear, compelling vision to go forward with vitality to achieve faith-stretching goals. I will face work and worship with high and holy expectations.

BIBLE READING — HEBREWS

7. Make Intercession — 7:25. Christ is presented as our changeless, perfect High Priest and the perfect sacrifice for sins. He "lives to make intercession" to God the Father on behalf of the needs and welfare of people. **Pray** for your pastor as he serves under Christ to constantly pray (intercede) for church families, for the faith of the congregation, and for fruitfulness in reaping the harvest of unchurched seekers.

FIVE WAYS TO PERSONALLY STRENGTHEN THE IMAGE OF YOUR CHURCH

1. **Show** respect for the position of your pastor. Embrace him as God's person to lead the church in fulfilling His will and divine purposes.

2. **Show** authentic Christian commitment in the way you conduct business, relate to neighbors, and guide your children.

3. **Show** that you are a fully surrendered steward by your faithful giving to the church, in keeping your finances in order, and the way you view and value money.

4. **Show** respect for other churches and believers by sharing with them, praying for them, and working with them.

5. **Show** genuine concern for the unchurched and poverty-stricken by expressing love, offering guidance, and providing assistance.

6. **Show** loyalty by faithful attendance and consistent financial support.

7. **Show** love for the unchurched through encouragement and by inviting them to special events.

BIBLE READING—HEBREWS

8. A New Covenant—8:6-13. The Law was a compelling force from without. The new covenant, based on the ministry of Christ, is performed by God's grace from within by the power of the Holy Spirit. **Pray** that the ministry of your church will not be built solely on outward deeds and actions but also on committed hearts and minds that "feel" and "think" like Christ.

My Journal

FOR THE WEEK

Praise reports, answered prayers, divine provisions, and spiritual plans.

BIBLE READING — HEBREWS

9. Dead Works — 9:14. Under the old covenant, the priests had to perform the same duties — "gifts and sacrifices" (vv. 9-10) — over and over again. We serve a living God. Every day in Christ is new and filled with adventure. **Pray** that your church and pastor will not emphasize "dead works," rituals, and routine, but will highlight serving the "living God" with great expectations and great joy.

SPIRITUAL VITAMINS FOR TODAY

Strength-giving Savior, my heart is filled with Your love, grace, and forgiveness. I also want my life to be filled with adventure, creativity, and aggressiveness. I need spiritual vitamins to maintain allegiance and to stay motivated. It is Your will for these characteristics to be visible and active in my life. Give me the vitamins of . . .

VISION to see Your unlimited resources. In You, Lord, there is fullness of joy, faith for every challenge, and the fruit of the Spirit for total spiritual health. I want to begin my life every day with a clear vision of these holy assets. *Guide me to maintain a clear vision!*

VALUES to stabilize my life. Father, I want what is valuable to You to be valuable to me. I want my values founded on Your Word, to reflect who I am, to whom I belong, and what I am committed to. *Guide me to guard my values!*

VITALITY for high performance living. Motivating Master, today I want to be zestful and aggressive in my lifestyle—worship, work, witnessing. Eliminate sluggishness and backwardness. Endow me, with a spirit of exuberance, extravagant hospitality, and ministry excellence. *Guide me to explode with vitality!*

BIBLE READING—HEBREWS

10. Consider One Another—10:23-25. We are told to "hold fast" our confession of hope in Christ. We do this by standing by one another in "love and good words" and by "coming together for worship." **Pray** for a spirit of faithfulness in church attendance to settle over your congregation and that members would grasp the importance of supporting one another.

STAND AND SHINE TODAY

Never-failing Father, I stand secure in You today. I shine with the brightness of Your glory. I am complete. I am committed. You are in control of my life—the present and the future. I lift my hands in praise because of divine assurance that I can worship with pure intent and walk with pure purpose because . . .

I have been JUSTIFIED. Father, You are just in all Your ways—upright, exact, and equitable. You have vindicated me through Your righteousness, and I stand whole, pure, and innocent before You. There are no marks against my name. I honor You for this!

I am SANCTIFIED. This means I am totally set apart to enjoy Your love, to experience liberty in Christ, and to labor in the white harvest fields that surround me. Thank You, Lord, that I am saved, sanctified, and empowered to serve by the anointing of the Holy Spirit.

I am ready to be EDIFIED. I am open to improvement in my mind (thinking) and morals (acting). Instruct me by Your Word, Lord, empower me by Your Spirit, and secure me through trust in Christ. Lead me to stand and shine as Your yielded servant—to act justified, sanctified, and edified.

BIBLE READING—HEBREWS

11. Hall of Heroes—11:1-40. Verse one provides a description of how faith works. The Old Testament saints mentioned in Chapter 11 obtained a "good report" because they accepted God's promises, even though they could not see them, and acted with obedience and persistence. **Pray** for your church to enhance and exercise faith to attempt great things for God—equip believers for ministry, evangelize the community, and enlarge facilities.

STAND FIRM TODAY

Father, scriptural, Savior-based, and salvation assurance are qualities that constitute a solid foundation on which to build my life—a life that honors You. Thank You for energy, skills, and equipment to build on this foundation . . .

SCRIPTURAL—Instructional Manual. Father, I will build my life and minister in my church according to the instructions outlined in the Bible. Holy Scripture provides a framework for building creatively, impressively, and honorably.

SAVIOR-BASED—Standard for Construction. The completed work of Christ—death, burial, resurrection, and ascension—is the message, motivation, and standard for building. All construction must be Savior-based. Master, I will build my life under Your supervision on the righteousness and lordship of Jesus Christ.

SALVATION ASSURANCE—Guaranteed Performance. Father, I am grateful, indebted, and overwhelmed at the magnitude of Your mercy, grace, and love. You give me the assurance of Your nearness that births unity in fellowship, understanding in mission, and unflinching courage to stand firm on a solid foundation.

BIBLE READING—HEBREWS

12. Endure Chastening—12:3-12. "Endure hardships as discipline; God is treating you as sons" (v. 7 NIV). There will be problems, perplexities, and persecution in church work. God will work during these times to bring you to maturity in Christ—"respect God's chastening love and live." **Pray** for your pastor as he addresses difficulties in the church and in the lives of believers understanding that discipline is based on God's love and laws.

STAND ON THE ROCK TODAY

Father, Your Son, Jesus Christ, is the solid Rock: the Rock of my salvation; the Rock that enables me to stand without compromise; the Rock that gives me life-directing significance; and the Rock that sustains and keeps me. Christ is the rock of my . . .

SALVATION. My salvation, without question, is solid and secure, steadfast! It is founded on the solid Rock, Jesus Christ. I can build a life of unstoppable aspiration, assurance, and remarkable achievements on this Rock. And, by binding trust I will! *I will stand on the Rock!*

SECURITY. Calmness in my spirit! Courage in my soul! Peace of mind! Purpose in life! Master, I am overwhelmingly grateful for the security I have in You; security that empowers me to live a balanced and visionary life. *I will stand on the Rock!*

SIGNIFICANCE. Lord, I feel valuable! You have given me a new life; a life of purpose, adventure, and possibilities. I greet every day with great expectations filled with Your faith, hope, and love. I anticipate the good, holy, and rewarding. *I will stand on the Rock!*

BIBLE READING — HEBREWS

13. Brotherly Love — 13:1-25. The writer of Hebrews concludes his epistle by giving directions in several areas: have brotherly love (v. 1), remember prisoners (v. 3), know that marriage is honorable (v. 4), be content (v. 5), embrace sound doctrine (v. 9), offer a sacrifice of praise (v. 15), do good (v. 16), obey rulers (v. 17), and be confident (v. 18). **Pray** to practice the message of verse 7, "Remember those who rule over you who have spoken the Word of God to you, whose faith follow, considering the outcome of their conduct.

STAND STRONG TODAY

Strong and mighty Father, You are the foundation for a life of security and steadfastness. You supply the spiritual materials to build on this foundation—Holy Scripture, Holy Spirit, and Holy Saints. Anoint the skills You have invested in me so I can build and . . .

Stand on SCRIPTURE. Father, I can stand on Your Word, it is a sure foundation for success. I praise You for a Guidebook that directs me in paths of righteousness, purity, prosperity, and peace. *I will stand strong on Your Word today!*

Stand With the HOLY SPIRIT. Father, You sent the Holy Spirit to be my Comforter, Guide, and Protector. He comforts with solutions to problems, guides into all truth, and protects from the assaults of Satan. *I will stand strong in the Holy Spirit today!*

Stand With Saints. Throughout the years, believers have stood the tests of time and left worthy examples for me to follow—demonstrations of courage, dedication to the Great Commission, and devotion to a lifestyle of honoring Christ. I am thankful for their faithfulness. I am also thankful for true saints who surround me with support and ministry service. *I will stand strong with the examples of saints today!*

BIBLE READING—JAMES

1. Facing Trials—Chapter 1. The people of God were facing trials and temptations. James told them that trials test their faith and produce patience (vv. 2, 3), lead to wisdom (v. 5), affirm a "crown of life" (v. 12), and increase Christian maturity. When facing trials, James said, "Be swift to hear, slow to speak, and slow to wrath" (v. 19). **Prayer:** Let me be a "doer of the word, and not a hearer only" (see v. 22). Let me and my church visit orphans and widows and exhibit the fruit of "pure religion" (v. 27).

My Personal Pledge

TO FAITHFUL BIBLE STUDY

I realize through Bible study I can understand the nature of God, the mission of the church, and the standards for spiritual wholeness. Therefore, I will embrace the value of Bible study!

I pledge to be loyal in consistent Bible study by . . .

1. **SETTING** aside time each day to hear from God through His Word.
2. **SEARCHING** the Scriptures to gain awareness of how God relates, instructs, and blesses.
3. **SEEKING** assistance and directions in applying biblical truths.
4. **STANDING** on God's promises and applying them to daily life and Christian service.
5. **SHARING** the good news of saving grace, heavenly security, and Holy Spirit oversight.
6. **SPREADING** God's love, hope, and happiness through the ministries of my church.
7. **SHOUTING** praises to God for the fruit of His Word in my daily life.

BIBLE READING—JAMES

2. Active Faith—Chapter 2. Faith doesn't show partiality (vv. 1-6), but sets forth the royal law—"love your neighbor as yourself (v. 8). Faith is active—provides clothing, food, shelter (vv. 22-26). **Prayer:** Father, may all people, regardless of background or circumstances, feel welcome at our church. May we affirm them, comfort them, provide for them, and lead them in understanding Your love and plan for their life.

My Journal

FOR THE WEEK

Praise reports, answered prayers, divine provisions, and spiritual plans.

_____

_____

_____

_____

_____

_____

_____

_____

_____

_____

BIBLE READING—JAMES

3. Bridle the Tongue—Chapter 3. The tongue is a little member of the body (v. 5), but it "brags about great things." "The tongue is like a fire." It can kindle a fire of confusion, division, and hurt feelings among church members (v. 6). **Prayer:** Lord, give us Your wisdom to monitor our words, to relate to others in church work with gentleness and purity, and to produce the fruit of righteousness in peace.

STAND TODAY

God of steadfastness and security, You are faithful in supplying whatever I need to live a balanced and blessed life. I am thankful for Your supervision that empowers me to stand firmly in faith. I am . . .

SURROUNDED by Your Presence. Father, You never leave me! Wherever I am, whatever I am doing, whatever I face, Your presence is with me to fortify my faith to fight against my adversaries, and to fulfill my goals of worshiping You and walking daily with You.

STRENGTHENED by Your Spirit. Lord, You sent the Holy Spirit to comfort, to correct, and to keep me on a positive course of commitment. I will depend on the stabilizing and strengthening power of the Holy Spirit to stand by my shepherd, my pastor, as he leads his sheep, the congregation, in fulfilling the mission of the local church.

STANDING on Your Word. Father, Your Word is the foundation for fulfilling Your will and for providing fulfillment in my life. I will stand on Your Word—commands, promises, guidance—and live a life of approval and blessings. I will stand on Your Word for peace, protection, and provisions.

BIBLE READING—JAMES

4. Submit to God—Chapter 4. James asked the question, "What is causing quarrels, fights, and arguments among you?" Then he outlined the route to harmony and church health: "submit to God" (v. 7), "draw near to God" (v. 8), "humble yourselves" and "He will lift you up" (v. 10). **Prayer:** Lord, we need "more grace," and You have promised it to us (v. 6). We need "more grace" to overcome the desires for pleasure, prominence, and personal glory in church ministry. In everything we do at the church we want to say, "Lord, Your will be done."

STAND WATCH TODAY

Protective Master, You stand watch over me today — guarding, guiding, and sending gifts. I feel safe! I feel secure! I feel songs of praise and thanksgiving. I want to follow Your example and stand watch to . . .

Protect CHILDREN. Children in my family, my community, and my city are all precious and packed with possibilities. Satan realizes this and is set to detour their future and destroy their dreams. I want to be a representative for children — praying for them, providing protective safety measures for them, and encircling them with developmental ministries.

Emphasize CHURCH. Father, I will stand watch for my church — faithful attendance, standing by my pastor, and being counted on for ministry support. Satan desires to create conflict and confusion among members. Under Your guidance, I will be a peacemaker, a counselor, and a bridge to connect with the unchurched.

Demonstrate COMPASSION. I can stand watch by standing by my friends and neighbors during failures in reaching desired destinations, in facing financial failure, and in setbacks. I will show compassion, care, and supportive closeness.

BIBLE READING — JAMES

5. Do Not Grumble — Chapter 5. In facing the issues of life, and in the ministry of the church, believers must develop and display "patience" (v. 7). Patience will establish the heart (v. 8), eliminate grumbling (v. 9), and merit spiritual blessings (v. 11). **Prayer:** Lord, You have told me that prayer offered in faith will yield a response from You (vv. 15-16). Today, I sing psalms of praise to You. I pray for the sick of my church, and I lift up those in our congregation who have "wandered from the truth" (v. 19).

STANDING ON THE PROMISES TODAY

Promise-keeping King, I stand firmly without reservations on Your divine promises. Your promises establish my faith, fulfill my dreams, and produce spiritual fruit in my life. Your promises hold me close to You, lead me in paths of righteousness, and open the windows of heaven to pour out blessings. I cherish Your promises of . . .

FLOWING Love. Your love, Father, flowed to me when I was unlovable and undeserving and furnished new life, new meaning, and new directions. Your love guides and guards me every day giving me significance, strength, steadfastness, and a solid foundation to build upon.

FULFILLING Liberty. I am free in Jesus Christ—free from being a slave to sin, free to walk new paths in life, and free to worship in spirit and in truth. Liberating Master, I praise You for liberty today—liberty whereby I can think Christ thoughts and think creatively for Kingdom ministry.

FAITHFUL Longsuffering. Lord, You are longsuffering, You stand with me and support me when I am weak and weary, when I am fainthearted and fall. I praise You for this. I trust You! I will lean on Your everlasting arms and will find peace and provisions in Your promises and presence.

BIBLE READING—FIRST PETER

1. Love One Another—1:22. God's Spirit guides us in obeying the truth which empowers us to "love one another fervently with a pure heart." This verse contains the foundation for church health, growth, and worship that glorifies God—true love for Christian brothers and sisters. **Prayer:** Father of love, we can be a witness to our community and city by sharing Your love with each other—kindness, helpfulness, and generosity.

STEP HIGHER TODAY

Life-building Lord, every day You encircle my life, enrich my life, and expand my opportunities to achieve. This fortifies me to reach higher, to grow stronger, and to see goals clearer. Inspire me to . . .

Step UP — Prayer. Through prayer, Father, I can step up to Your throne of grace and experience fellowship with You — inspiration, impartation, and an investment in eternity. I value my time with You and will protect it, cultivate it, and honor it. *I will step up today!*

Step IN — Study. Through study, Father, I can step in to Your divine plans and experience personal guidance — insights about Your authority and creative powers, Your design for the Church, and how to obediently follow You in spirit and truth. *I will step in today!*

Step OUT — Evangelism. Through evangelism, Father, I can experience Your anointing and favor — to share Your love with the needy, Your forgiveness to the estranged, and Your unfailing promises to believers. *I will step out today!*

BIBLE READING — FIRST PETER

2. Living Stones — 2:4-5. When we come to Christ, the chief cornerstone — He makes us "living stones," and we become God's spiritual house . . . a holy priesthood . . . and we offer up spiritual sacrifices. People recognize the church as God's house as church members live righteously, treat their pastor with respect, and render need-centered service. **Prayer:** I want to be a "living stone" — strong, steady, and showing Your love, gracious Father, in ways that are convincing and Christ-centerd.

STRAIGHT PATHS TODAY

Lord of positive directions, You have outlined paths. If followed, they will lead to personal peace, performance power, and productive ministry. I will use Your compass, Father, the Bible, to follow straight paths — paths that lead to . . .

SPIRITUAL Steadfastness. Christian maturity necessitates spiritual steadfastness. Father, I need both grace and grit to live and serve with steadfastness. Let Your Holy Spirit gird and guide me to be committed and consistent in standing spiritually strong.

SCRIPTURAL Stability. Christian maturity also calls for me to be scripturally stable. Father, I will read Your Word, embrace Your Word, and live Your Word. Let Your Holy Spirit guide me in comprehending divine truths so I will be scripturally stable.

SUPERIOR Success. Christian maturity will generate superior success. Father, it is Your will for me to live a life of abundance, a life of achievement, a life of victorious anointing, and a life of fruitful relationships. Let Your Holy Spirit guide me in expressing daily thanksgiving for superior success in Christ.

BIBLE READING — FIRST PETER

3. Husbands and Wives — 3:1-7. Does the relationship between husbands and wives in the church impact church health, worship, and outreach? We know that it does. Strong relationships create an atmosphere of submissiveness, unity, and love that attests to the truth of God's Word. **Prayer:** Lord, heal marriage hurts in our church. May the couples in our church reflect the love in their relationship that Christ has for the Church, His bride.

PERSONAL AFFIRMATION — ENCOURAGEMENT

All believers need to be foundations of encouragement. I believe I am to be an encourager as well as an equipper to assist others in walking in harmony with the Master and other believers. By Your Spirit,

I Will . . .

- **Manifest** a spirit of contagious zeal.

- **Learn** techniques to convey encouragement.

- **Set** daily goals for sharing encouragement.

- **Make** encouraging family members a priority.

- **Be** an encourager in the neighborhood.

- **Map** methods to encourage church volunteers.

- **Personalize** biblical promises of refreshing joy.

- **Spread** encouragement by example.

BIBLE READING — FIRST PETER

4. One Mind — 3:8-9. When church members are in "one mind," there is compassion, tenderheartedness, and courtesy. This generates strength to bless others and to "inherit a blessing" (v. 9). **Prayer:** Lord, touch my mind so that I can walk and work in harmony with my pastor, ministry leaders, and church members.

My Journal

FOR THE WEEK

Praise reports, answered prayers, divine provisions, and spiritual plans.

_____

_____

_____

_____

_____

_____

_____

_____

_____

_____

BIBLE READING — FIRST PETER

5. Minister to One Another — 4:8-11. Observe the words, "love one another," "be hospitable to one another," and "minister to one another." The church is a family — a caring family, a serving family, a happy family. **Prayer:** In Your family, Lord, I want to be a giver, not a taker. Anoint me to give love, hospitality, and ministry to others.

STRONGER TODAY

Lord of unlimited strength, You provide, protect, and make a pathway for personal fulfillment. I praise You that I am under Your care—daily care, compassionate care, and comforting care. Under Your care, I will grow stronger every day. I will . . .

REVIEW. Today, Lord, I will review my position in You—my salvation, my security, my significance. I will review and rejoice! I will review the flow of blessings in my life—Your guidance, Your goodness, Your gifts. *I will review and rejoice!*

RENEW. Today, Lord, I will renew my covenant to follow You—my sanctification, my service, and my steadfastness. I will renew and rejoice! I will renew my dependence on Your wisdom to lead and Your watchful care to develop me in Your likeness. *I will renew and rejoice!*

RESOLVE. Today, Lord, I will resolve to show forth Your love in my life—my liberty, my longing to make a difference in the ministry of my church, and my loyalty to Kingdom outreach. I will resolve to trust Your Word, embrace Your companionship, and follow Your guideline for living successfully. *I will resolve and rejoice!*

BIBLE READING—FIRST PETER

6. Shepherd the Flock-5:2. The work of your pastor and church elders is to shepherd (care for) the congregation. They must be examples (v. 3), leading the way by being totally surrendered to Christ, sensitive to the needs of the people, and serving with a joyful spirit. **Prayer:** I stand with my pastor! I stand with him in the mission of our church and his personal call from You. Bless him greatly today with a flow of energy and excitement from You.

STRONG FOUNDATION TODAY

Wonderful Counselor, You give me instructions and inspiration to build my life on a strong and secure foundation—sufficient provisions, power to perform effectively, and scriptural building patterns. I'm fully equipped. I praise You for . . .

FAITH to Secure. Father, the doors to heavenly supplies are open to me to secure building materials through faith. I ask You to anoint me to release faith to be, to receive, and to build. I will cherish and follow Your leadership today!

FIRMNESS to Stand. "On Christ the solid rock I stand." Yes, Lord, I will stand on Your foundation with divine assistance and assurance—support, supplies, and supernatural strength. I will depend upon and embrace Your leadership today!

FRUITFUL Service. Father, on the strong foundation You provide I will build an influential image—fruitful, faithful, and fulfilling service. Whatever I need You will supply. I will trust and enjoy Your fruit-producing leadership today!

BIBLE READING—SECOND PETER

1. Add to Faith --1:5-8. Peter outlines seven qualities to add to our faith virtue—knowledge, self-control, perseverance, godliness, brotherly kindness, and love. This will make believers fruitful through living a Bible-centered and balanced life. **Prayer:** Through Christ, You have given us "all things that pertain to life and godliness." Let "grace and peace" be multiplied to our church as we worship, study, serve, and stand with our pastor.

SUNSHINE TODAY

Light of my life, You provide heavenly sunshine that warms, refreshes, and renews. I'm grateful! I speak glorious praise to You. I will keep the windows of my soul open to let in the strength of Your sunshine and to let out a radiant witnessing glow. Your sunshine gives . . .

SOUL Rest. I often get weary in my Christian walk. I let problems, pressures, and perplexities interrupt my peace of mind. Today, Lord, I will seek Your sunshine to drive away these disturbances. You are the sole source for soul rest!

SERENE Relaxation. Today, Father, I trust You to live a calm, unclouded, peaceful, and tranquil life. Your love surrounds me, Your grace fills me, Your unlimited power protects me, Your Word guides me, and Your church stabilizes me. I stand complete in You. Amen!

SECURE Riches. I have riches on earth, and I have riches in heaven. They are secure! I have health, hope, and happiness. They are secure! I have a home in heaven, eternal riches. They are secure! I have open communication with You, Lord, that provides daily completeness. It is secure! I am secure!

BIBLE READING—SECOND PETER

2. False Teachers-2:1-22. There will be false teachers who will try to bring into the church destructive doctrines (v. 1). Their character is lustful, lewd, and arrogant. But, God will deliver the godly out of the temptations of their traps. **Prayer:** Lord, protect our church from false teachers. Let us be true to Your Word, constantly searching the Scriptures with our pastor and standing firm on truth, righteousness, and godliness.

SUPPORT MY PASTOR TODAY

Shepherd, Savior, and Servant-leader Lord, You have provided all three of these in Your Son, Jesus Christ. Through Him, I am equipped to live impactfully today, tomorrow, and for time without end. You have also given me an earthly shepherd, my pastor. I will support my pastor by . . .

SHOWING loyalty to my church—faithful attendance, fruitful service, and financial accountability. Father, I understand that when I show loyalty to my church, I demonstrate loyalty to You and to fulfilling the Great Commission. *I will be a loyal church member!*

STANDING firmly with him in ministry—embracing his vision, promoting church events, and encouraging volunteers. Father, I understand that when I stand with my pastor, I set an example of support for him, for his calling, and for his response to the needs of the people. *I will stand with my pastor in ministry!*

SHARING outreach responsibilities—welcoming newcomers, inviting neighbors to attend church, and personal soulwinning. Father, I understand that when I share outreach responsibilities, I reveal obedience to the command of Christ to "reach, teach, and train." *I will share outreach responsibilities!*

BIBLE READING—SECOND PETER

3. God's Promise—3:1-9. Christ promised that He would return for His people. Many unbelievers say, "Where is the promise of His coming?" (v. 4). The Lord will fulfill His promise but delays His wrath, "not willing that any should perish but that all should come to repentance" (v. 9). **Prayer:** Let us live daily with the expectation of the return of Your Son, Holy Father, and with an urgent desire to "seek and save" the lost.

SURVIVE STRESS TODAY

Mountain-moving Master, I will face stress and strain today—decisions, detours, difficulties. I need help—major help; motivational help—mountain-moving help. You are the answer to my need for help. I will survive today by . . .

SURRENDERING my will to Your will. Father, You have a divine will for my life, a holy plan, and a guiding path to follow. By Your flowing grace, I will embrace Your plan and follow your designated path. *Your will, will be my will.*

STANDING on Your promises. Father, Your promises of partnership, peace, and prosperity are firm, steady, and unmovable. I will walk with You today as a partner in ministry. I will abide in Your peace and enjoy the provisions of Your inexhaustible riches. *Your will, will be my will.*

SHOUTING praise and thanksgiving. Master, You give an anointing for stressful situations. I exalt Your name today. I praise You for acts of mercy. I offer thanksgiving for saving grace, sustaining strength, and steadfast care. *Your will, will be my will!*

BIBLE READING—SECOND PETER

4. Found in Peace—3:14. When Christ returns, He wants to find us, the church, in peace, without spot (united) and blameless (pure in doctrine). **Prayer:** Father, our hope is in the new heaven and new earth. Surround our church with Your strength that we might live according to Your values and under Your control.

PRAYER PATTERN — PRAISE

P — PASTOR. Lord, I praise You for the vision, intense faith, and caring attitude of my pastor.

R — RESPECT. I respect Your call on his life, his recognition of the call, and his total response to it.

A — AFFIRMATION. I ask You to affirm Your presence and approval as we minister together.

I — INSTRUCTIONS. I want to be submissive to his instructions and support him in his ministry.

S — SECOND MILE. I commit to walking the second mile with him in the ministries of our church.

E — ENJOYMENT. I pledge that our time together in ministry will be filled with praise and enjoyment.

BIBLE READING — FIRST JOHN

1. Full Joy — Chapter 1. The life of a believer should be full of joy and the church should be full of joy (v. 4). We have joy by living in the light of God's presence, recognizing the cleansing power of the blood of Christ, and having fellowship with one another (v. 7). **Prayer:** Joy reflects Your nature, Father; let our church share and spread the light of Your Son by being a church of joy, and victory.

My Journal

FOR THE WEEK

Praise reports, answered prayers, divine provisions, and
spiritual plans.

_____

_____

_____

_____

_____

_____

_____

_____

_____

_____

BIBLE READING — FIRST JOHN

2. Influencing the Community — Chapter 2. People are attracted to, and influenced by, the church that keeps the commandments (v. 3), walks the truth (v. 4), reflects the light (vv. 7, 8), loves the brethren (vv. 9, 10), denounces the world (v. 15), and cherishes the anointing (v. 27). **Prayer:** Keeping the commandments and walking in the light begin with me. Father, empower me to be an example in my community and church.

THANKSGIVING TODAY

God of endless gifts, every morning I am greeted with gifts from You — open windows of heaven to receive blessings, opportunities to strengthen relationships, and spiritual oversight to mature in Christ. I am thankful for my . . .

PASTOR — Leadership. My pastor leads me, teaches me, and trains me for Kingdom service. He also holds me accountable to develop and deploy my spiritual gifts. Bless my pastor today, Lord. Give him empowering skills to guide me and other church members in living victoriously, fruitfully, and faithfully.

PROVISIONS — Oversight. Lord, I am thankful for Your daily oversight. You supply all my needs — food for strength, family for companionship, faith for worship, and the Holy Spirit for empowerment to serve. Your provisions feature Your undivided attention and Your unlimited resources.

PROTECTION — Watchful care. Father, I need protection from the attacks of Satan. I praise You, Master, for watching over me and guiding my steps. You lead me around dangerous pits — pressures to conform, persecutions by the Enemy, and predictions of failure. I stand complete in You!

BIBLE READING — FIRST JOHN

3. Sacrificial Love — Chapter 3. Christ is the source of love. We know love, because He sacrificed His life for us. This is why we should live sacrificially for our brothers and sisters in Christ (v. 16). **Prayer:** Father, I know my pastor lives a sacrificial life to guide me. Encourage him today, encircle him with Your presence, and equip him with persevering power.

THAT DAY TODAY

Eternal Father, in Your Word, You refer to "that Day" as the return of Christ (2 Thessalonians 1:10). I believe in "that Day." I anticipate "that Day"! I will be prepared for "that Day" today, by . . .

CONFESSING My Faith. Lord, You loved me and gave Your Son, Jesus Christ, that I might have life—abundant life, extraordinary life, and eternal life. I confess my faith today! I believe! I belong to You! I am blessed with assurance of "that Day"—the return of Christ!

COMMUNICATING My Faith. Father, I am surrounded by individuals—friends, neighbors, associates—who are not aware of Your forecast of "that Day"—the return of Your Son. I have been commissioned by You to communicate the message of Your plan to redeem and restore. I will communicate my faith today by being a living witness, a verbal witness, and a working witness.

CELEBRATING My Faith. Lord, I anticipate "that Day." I will be prepared for it! I am also prepared for today—to celebrate freedom in Christ, to commune in prayer with You, and to cherish and enjoy spiritual gifts. I will activate, radiate, and celebrate my faith today!

BIBLE READING—FIRST JOHN

4. Test the Spirits—Chapter 4. You cannot believe everything you hear. It is necessary to "test the spirits"—carefully examine what people tell you and see if they are of God. There are many false prophets (teachers, doctrines) in the world (v. 1). **Prayer:** Lord of order, direct my pastor in dealing with any claims, teachings, or practices, that do not honor Jesus in a way consistent to the whole truth of the Bible.

THE CHURCH TODAY

Lord of supreme wisdom, You make plans and provisions for the welfare and wholeness of Your children. A major glorious aspect of Your plan is the church—the body of Christ. I believe the church is a place for me to . . .

Meet With Your PEOPLE. When believers come together in Your name, Master, You are always there with them. Your presence brings unity, harmony, respect, and strength. I pray for the health and outreach focus of my church today!

Join in Praise With Your PEOPLE. Father, the Bible admonishes us to come before You with praise and thanksgiving. Together, in the church, we can worship in spirit and truth, sing with joy and adoration, learn and grow, fellowship and serve. I will pray for the biblically-centered worship of my church today!

Hear the Petitions of Your PEOPLE. The church is a house of prayer, a place to commune with You, Father. It is a place to pray about needs and spiritual desires and to believe as a united family that You will answer. I will pray for the intercession ministry of my church today.

BIBLE READING—FIRST JOHN

5. Confidence in Prayer—Chapter 5. John said, "If we ask anything according to His will (v. 14), He hears us" (vv. 14, 15). God's will for your church includes sharing grace, financial giving, good fellowship, scriptural guidance, and numerical growth. **Prayer:** I have confidence in prayer today, Holy Father, because I pray "according to Your will" for my pastor and church. Bless the pastor's preaching, our outreach programs, and the promotion of discipleship ministries.

THE PRIVILEGE OF PRAYER TODAY

Prayer-hearing and prayer-answering Eternal Father, prayer is a wonderful gift-from You. I honor You for this glorious gift. I believe through prayer I can . . .

TOUCH You. Father, touching You is touching deity, holiness, and loving-kindness. I do this through prayer! I feel Your majesty. I sense Your encompassing wisdom. I hear You speak in my spirit. I am empowered with the flow of Your healing mercy in my heart. **I'm uplifted!**

THANK You. Listening Master, I express deep reverent feelings of thanksgiving through prayer. I honor You for spiritual security, soul satisfaction, steady steps, and scriptural stability. **I am blessed!**

TELL You. Comforting Creator, You care about every aspect of my life—my wholeness, my holiness, and my wellness. In prayer I can tell You about my feelings, my faults, and my plans for the future. You listen, You respond, You restore, You renew, and You give me directions. **I am changed!**

BIBLE READING—SECOND JOHN

1. Beware of Deceivers—Verses 9-11. Doctrine, the teachings of the church, must be protected and perpetuated. This means the pastor and the membership of the church must not tolerate anyone who does not teach the truth about Christ—don't invite him in or greet him (vv. 9-11) or show him any hospitality. **Prayer:** Your Word is our light, Master; we must read it, walk in it, confess it, share it, and protect it. By Your Spirit, give us understanding to detect false teachers and holy boldness to denounce them.

THE POWER OF TODAY

Gift-giving Lord of unlimited treasure, I receive Your gifts daily with open hands of thanksgiving and an overflowing heart of praise. Today has power because of Your presence to provide and protect. I will grip the power of today to . . .

Give GLORY for GIFTS. Father, You are righteous, pure, and holy in all Your ways. Today is a gift from You! It is brimming with opportunities to shout praises unto You, share Your gifts with others, and stand in Your presence with uplifted hands of adoration. *Today is a beautiful gift!*

GROW in GRACE. Lord, You give me redeeming grace, refining grace, and refreshing grace. Your grace establishes, energizes, and encircles me. I marvel at Your grace, mercy, and manifold blessings. *Today is a marvelous gift!*

GIVE GENEROUSLY. I realize generous giving requires both inward and outward giving. Inward giving is sharing experiences, conveying compassion, and offering solutions to challenging circumstances. Outward giving is sharing finances, conveying instructions, and offering personal support. *Today is a faith-filled day!*

BIBLE READING — THIRD JOHN

1. Fellow Workers — Verses 4-8. Believers together in ministry (v. 8) is a true picture of the church. As we "walk in truth" (v. 4), faithfully support the pastor (v. 5), and show hospitality to "traveling teachers and missionaries" (v. 5), we become "fellow workers," partners, "for the truth" (v. 8). **Prayer:** Father, I want to be a partner with my pastor in Your holy design for our church. I will pray for him, promote with him, respond to his preaching, and celebrate victories with him.

SEVEN QUALITIES OF BEING A SUPER SUPPORTER OF YOUR PASTOR'S WIFE

1. Spiritual Obedience

2. Authentic Relationship

3. Passion for Ministry

4. Understanding of Partnership

5. Courage to Think Differently

6. Acceptance of Responsibility

7. Visionary Disposition

BIBLE READING—JUDE

1. Build Yourself Up—Verses 20-23. To be a strong believer, to be part of a thriving church, you must build yourself up. Jude outlines several ways to do this: stand on the foundation of your faith (v. 20), pray in the Holy Spirit (v. 20), keep yourself in the love of God (v. 21), show mercy to doubters (v. 22), create fear thereby pulling some out of the fire (v. 23), and don't be contaminated with (smell like) sin (v. 23). **Prayer.** Father, I belong to You. I stand by my pastor, and I stand with other church members to be part of a Spirit-filled, grace-anchored, and love-motivated church that makes a difference in the community and city.

My Journal

FOR THE WEEK

Praise reports, answered prayers, divine provisions, and
spiritual plans.

BIBLE READING — REVELATION

1. Seven Stars — 1:16, 20. The seven stars represent the pastors of the seven churches to whom John is writing. Observe that Christ is holding them "in His right hand." This denotes divine selection, representation, and manifestation. As your pastor must come under God's authority (covering), you must come under your pastor's covering. **Prayer:** Lord, I lift up my pastor to you today. I hold him close as my shepherd and will depend upon him for guidance from Your Word.

THE REALITY OF TODAY

Lord of everything that is real, positive, and possible, shape me and mold me to conform to the image of Your Son, Jesus Christ. Today, I will face the real elements of time, trends, and the principles of transformation. Guide me to understand and to value . . .

YESTERDAY—the past. What I did yesterday brought me to where I am today. Lord, help me to honestly evaluate what I did right and what I did wrong. This will help me to establish constructive patterns and action steps for the future.

TODAY—the present. Yesterday is over, I cannot go back. Tomorrow is in the future, I cannot go there today. I do have Your gracious gifts of today—it is real, brimming with unique opportunities. I will seize the day and avail myself of spiritual and physical resources and maximize the challenges it presents.

TOMORROW—the future. I know what happened yesterday, I am enjoying today, but tomorrow is a mystery. I do not know what will happen, but my faith, Father, is firm in You. I know You will work out the best for me according to Your will. I place my trust and future in Your hands, Lord of glory.

BIBLE READING—REVELATION

2. Seven Churches—2:1-29; 3:1-22. Under the inspiration of the Holy Spirit, John writes to the seven churches who were encountering persecution to give them pastoral encouragement. His letter to each one contains praise, lists problems, provides instructions, and sets forth a promise. **Prayer:** Father, Your promises to the church rest on our obedience to receive, live by, and circulate the good news of life in Christ. Let us always have a clear vision of this scriptural fact.

THE THREE "Ds" OF TODAY

God of great grace, thank You for the privilege to stand in Your presence by being yielded, open, and thankful. I am yielded to Your will for my life. I am open to Your guidance. I am thankful for new life, new hope, and new experiences. Today, I will be . . .

DEDICATED. Heavenly Father, in response to Your call on my life, I will exhibit the characteristics of dedication—singleness of purpose, scriptural purity, and sustained Christ-honoring service. My dedication will be a testimony of my stance in Christ.

DETERMINED. I will face opposition in my walk with You, Lord. Satan will set traps to ensnare and weaken my allegiance. I will depend on You for a Spirit-supported determination—to walk worthy, to work energetically, and to witness boldly.

DEPENDABLE. Through Your equipping grace, Master, I will show forth the fruit of dependability—consistent Christian conduct, church attendance, and honest conversation. I will show You are faithful in all Your ways by the way I depend on You and by the way I show I am a dependable witness of the message of Christ.

BIBLE READING—REVELATION

3. Ephesus, Patience—2:1-7. The church at Ephesus "labored for the Lord" with patience and "did not become weary" (v. 3). Patience and persistence go hand in hand and pay off in spiritual results. **Prayer:** Lord, let us remember our "first love" (v. 4) for You, for the lost, for Your church, and to hear what the Spirit is saying to our church (v. 7).

THINK TODAY

Lord who inspires creative thinking, my mind is open for your anointing to think better, bigger, and bolder. I want to think according to Your will. I know how I think and what I think is what I become (Proverbs 23:7). I want my thinking to be God-centered, Christ-honoring, and Spirit-directed so I can . . .

Think BETTER—Clearly. Father, I do not want fuzzy thinking to dilute my faith. Let my thinking be clear, colorful, and controlled. Every day I want my thinking to be better than the day before—richer, balanced, and guarded by scriptural principles and goals. I will think better!

Think BIGGER—Concisely. I do not want to be a small-thinking believer—limited in scope, controlled by surroundings, and short-circuited by weak faith. Father, I want to think according to Your bigness—unlimited and unrestricted. I will think bigger!

Think BOLDLY—Courageously. Yes, by supportive grace, I will be forward in my thinking—feisty courage, calculated decisions, and next-level ambitions and goals. Father, thank You for the gift of thinking; a beautiful gift that permits me to grow and to boldly serve You. I will think boldly!

BIBLE READING—REVELATION

4. Ephesus, Tree of Life—2:7. The "Tree of Life" symbolizes spiritual strength, sustenance, and supplies to do God's work and to maintain eternal life. **Prayer:** Teach me, Lord—to listen with my ears, to think with my mind, and to receive with my heart, so I can "eat from the Tree of Life" and wage successful combat against the forces of evil.

TIME AWARENESS TODAY

Eternal Father, thank You for the marvelous gift of time. It is a personal gift — precious in nature, packed with powerful potential, and a pathway to please You. I will cherish it and commit to using it prudently. This action will be three-dimensional.

1. AFFIRMATION of priorities. Lord, my number one priority is to use my time to honor and please You. This involves time for daily prayer, for Bible study, and for Christ-honoring service. I pray for strength to stay alert, active, and anointed to remain unmovable in my commitment to You.

2. ADVANCEMENT of goals. Master motivator, You have placed in my spirit honorable goals. These goals include family life, church life, and work life. I want to excel in all three of these. Touch me, teach me, and train me to achieve these goals in a way that reflects the depth of Your grace and wisdom.

3. ALLOCATION of resources. Time and talents are my greatest resources in maintaining a posture of a mature disciple and a motivated worker. Today, Lord, I will check closely on how I am utilizing the resources You have allocated to me. I am open to instructions and corrections and my life is in Your shaping hands.

BIBLE READING — REVELATION

5. Smyrna, Suffering — 2:8-11. The church was suffering from persecution and poor economic conditions. However, John said, "you are rich" (v. 9). They were rich spiritually and secure in God's grace. **Prayer:** Father, let our church accept Your admonition, "Do not fear . . . suffering" (v. 10), and trust You for boldness to show up, stand up, speak up, and send up praise for overcoming power.

TRUE WAYS TODAY

I walk in the brightness of Your guidance today — a true way. Master, You are pure and perfect in all Your ways. Your ways have been tested and tried and always lead to triumph. I will trust You with the development of my life. My faith is founded on . . .

Your RIGHTEOUSNESS. Father, Your kingdom ministry and Your ministry in my life is based on Your righteousness. You are pure in all Your decisions, degrees, and directions. Today, I will look to You to live a life of purity, purpose, and productivity.

Your READINESS. I know You, Lord, are ready to open the windows of heaven and pour out unlimited blessings — provisions, protection, prosperity. I stand ready to receive with praise, honor, and thanksgiving.

Your RESOURCEFULNESS. Master, nothing is too difficult for You! Whatever I need to live an overcoming and victorious life is available from You. I will draw from the resources of heaven today and will honor You with spiritual works and witnessing enthusiasm.

BIBLE READING — REVELATION

6. Smyrna, Crown of Life — 2:10. The "ten days of tribulation" is symbolic of a short period of time. The "crown of life," the victor's crown, represents God's faithfulness and eternal life. **Prayer:** Lord, when suffering comes, let our church stay close to our pastor, hold each other tightly, and keep Your promise of a "crown of life" close and locked in our hearts.

WHEN YOU PRAY FOR YOUR PASTOR

1. It increases **AWARENESS** of his leadership responsibilities.

2. It increases **FAITH** to believe God is with him.

3. It increases **TRUST** in God to meet church needs.

4. It increases **INVOLVEMENT** in ministry projects.

5. It increases **ENTHUSIASM** to recruit others.

6. It increases **TEAMWORK** throughout the church.

7. It increases **LOYALTY** to God, the pastor, and the church.

BIBLE READING — REVELATION

7. Pergamos, Keep the Faith — 2:12-17. The church "kept the faith" when surrounded by heresies, emperor worship, and martyrdom (v. 13). They needed, however, to confront idolatry and immorality (vv. 14-16). **Prayer:** As a body of believers, let us commit ourselves to You, Lord, both emotionally and intellectually, and help us to guard against any form of departure from the faith.

My Journal

FOR THE WEEK

Praise reports, answered prayers, divine provisions, and spiritual plans.

_____

_____

_____

_____

_____

_____

_____

_____

_____

BIBLE READING — REVELATION

8. Pergamos, Hidden Manna/White Stone — 2:17. The Israelites in the wilderness were provided with daily manna — bread for strength and survival. Jesus is "the true bread from heaven" that meets our daily needs. The "white stone" stands for vindication, character of Christ, and a reward for victory. **Prayer:** Our church needs "hidden manna" — the brightness of Christ and the blessings of Christ. Equip us to "keep the faith" and "share the faith."

TRUE WORSHIP TODAY

Ruler of righteousness, You require true worship. Worship is also a holy personal privilege. Through worship, I exalt You and I experience communion with You that conforms me to Your image and will. Today, may my worship be . . .

WORD-centered Worship. Your Word, Father, sets forth how I am to worship You: "true worshipers will worship the Father in spirit and truth" (John 4:23). "Your word is truth" (John 17:17), and I will embrace it to form my structure and standards for true personal worship.

WHOLE-life Worship. Whole-life worship includes whole-day worship—activities, associations, and accountability. In all I do today, Lord, I will recognize Your glory, honor Your gifts of grace, and offer praise for Your life-giving attributes.

WISDOM-founded Worship. Lord, You give scriptural wisdom for acceptable worship—songs of praise, expressions of thanksgiving, instructions from Your Word, and pledges of Kingdom support. I will worship in spirit and truth today.

BIBLE READING—REVELATION

9. Thyatira, Love/Service—2:18-29. The church at Thyatira was busy doing good things. In fact, they were steadily enlarging their deeds and scope of influence (v. 19). They were warned about tolerating false teachers who led people into both spiritual and physical fornication (vv. 20-23). **Prayer:** Sovereign Lord, purity is Your standard in all we do. In serving with You, let our church be known for pure motives, pure methods, and pure ministry activities.

TRUST TODAY

Victory assuring Father, I stand firmly on Your promises through unshakeable trust. I belong to You. I depend on You. I believe You will always come through with whatever I need to live victoriously! Today, I will trust You to . . .

Stand during TESTS. I will face tests; this is reality! I will face tests that will try my faith; tests that will determine my future; and tests that will help form uncompromising standards. Lord, I will face these tests with implicit trust in Your presence, promises, and sustaining power.

Persevere in TRIALS. I will encounter trials, this is an aspect of personal growth. I will face trials in fulfilling work obligations; trials in meeting family responsibilities; and trials in developing durability in my Christian walk. Father, I will face these trials with growing trust in Your Word, wisdom, and divine will for my wholeness.

Praise for TRIUMPHS. Lord, I will experience triumphs based on Your promises that show forth Your grace and glory; triumphs that highlight Your loving kindness; and triumphs that demonstrate Your unlimited authority. Father, I praise You for the trust You have placed in me to trust You.

BIBLE READING—REVELATION

10. Thyatira, Rulership/Morning Star—2:26-28. Observe the words, "Keep My works until the end" (v. 26). This means staying with it, maintaining loyalty, and claiming the victory. The rewards are to rule the nations with Christ and He will give him the morning star (vv. 27, 28). **Prayer:** The purpose of our pastor and our church is to "keep Your works, Lord." Let us be visionary and "do more than we have ever done before" (v. 19), always striving for better, bigger results.

UNCOMPROMISING TRUST TODAY

God of unlimited and unequaled power, I stand today fully trusting in You. My trust is firm, founded on tested, tried, proven, and uncompromising faith. I place my trust in You in all areas of my actions and activities. I depend on You for . . .

DELIVERANCE Trust. Throughout the Bible, You, Lord, delivered Your people from the traps, tests, and tactics of Satan—fiery furnace, fiery battles, and fiery temptations. Today, I trust You for deliverance from every evil force I encounter.

DEVOTIONAL Trust. Father, I am devoted to Your purposes and plans for my life. I realize I will face detours and distractions. Please keep me focused! Let my trust grow and gain momentum every day by exercising faith in Your Word and embracing Your ideal will.

DIRECTIONAL Trust. Sometimes I want to go where I want to go, when I want to go. Keep me under Your control, Master. Give me Your directions every day. I will follow them because I know they will lead to a life of favor with You and the abundant fruit that fellowship with You provides. My motto for today is, "Trust and obey, this is the way to wholeness and happiness in Christ."

BIBLE READING—REVELATION

11. Sardis, Hold Fast—3:1-6. God wants His church to have a positive image, to be recognized as an alive church (v. l). To do this, a church must be "watchful," "strengthen ministries" (v. 2), and "hold fast" the doctrine and principles of righteousness (v. 3). **Prayer:** Lord, bless the leadership and volunteers of our church. Bless them with insight, wisdom, faith, and fortitude to "hold fast" to Your purposes for our church and to "hold us together" in love and unity.

UNDERSTANDING TODAY

All-wise revealing Father, I believe it is Your will for me to understand how You govern today and what Your plans are for the future. My part in the understanding process is to pray for insight wisdom, to read the Bible and study resource material, and to engage in dialogue sessions with other believers. I ask You to guide me in understanding . . .

PROPHECY. Father, nothing catches You by surprise. You have complete oversight of the present and the future. Your Word foretells many aspects of Your plans for the future. Let a spirit of understanding rest upon me as I diligently study about future events.

PARABLES. I enjoy stories that relate to everyday life. In Your Word, Lord, parables and stories are used to illustrate spiritual truths and guidelines for Christian conduct. I want to read parables with an understanding of how to apply them to my life and witness.

PROMISES. Master, You give promises for a purpose — to paint a picture of Your future plans, to prepare for obstacles and opportunities, and to provide assurance of future care, security, and provisions. Today, I am grateful for the light of prophecy, the truth illustrated in parables, and the assurance of Your promises.

BIBLE READING — REVELATION

12. Sardis, White Garments — 3:4-5. White robes represent purity through the righteousness of Jesus Christ and the assurance of eternal life. **Prayer:** Blessed Lord, help our church to be alert, always "pressing forward" — teaching, believing, and practicing.

UNDER YOUR SHADOW TODAY

Always-near Provider, Your shadows represent Your unrestricted power, Your unceasing love, and Your divine understanding of my daily needs. Your shadow covers the entire universe with Your entire presence revealing Your eternal plans for those who are committed to You. Your shadow, Father, according to Your Word . . .

Shows Your PRESENCE. Wherever I am, Father, Your shadow covers me. In Your presence there is complete joy. Your presence brings calmness and assurance in my life. Your presence indicates You will guide me in all truth and fortify my faith.

Supplies Your PROVISIONS. Lord, Your shadow supplies everything I need to serve You with honor and to live a holy life. Your provisions flow from Your goodness and oversight. Father, I live an amazing life under Your shadow, and I shout praises of heart-flowing thanksgiving.

Supports Your PURPOSES. Lord of love, You have a master plan that sets forth Your purposes for all the people of the world. Your shadow hovers over this plan to bring it to fruition. Today, I will live, work, plan, and rejoice under Your shadow that reveals Your gracious gifts and all-encompassing grace.

BIBLE READING — REVELATION

13. Philadelphia, Open Door — 3:7-13. How does a local church have an "open door" from the Lord? The answer — "obey God's Word (v. 8), "do not be afraid to speak God's name" (v. 8), "keep God's command to persevere" (v. 10), and "hold firmly to what God has given you" (v. 11). **Prayer:** Lord, strengthen our grip on grace — what You have done for us, in us, and through us. Set before us an "open door."

My Pledge of Loyalty

TO ESTABLISH TRUSTWORTHY RELATIONSHIPS

I will work with contagious vitality to form relationships that cement partnership in fulfilling the tasks of my church, my home, my career, and my friendships. Therefore, maintaining complete confidence will be crucial!

I pledge to uphold the power of trust in relationships by . . .

1. **MAINTAINING** dependability in keeping my promises, in safeguarding pure motives, and in performing Christian responsibilities.

2. **MANAGING** conflict in ministry by emphasizing Scriptural wisdom, spiritual solutions, and unselfish decisions.

3. **MOBILIZING** support in ministering harmoniously as a steady, sanctified, and Spirit-guided team.

4. **MUSTERING** courage to move forward together without fear, frustration, or friction.

5. **MOTIVATING** consensus, unified togetherness in the various ministries of the church, and in operational patterns and accountability.

BIBLE READING—REVELATION

14. Philadelphia, Pillar in the Temple—3:12. In God's kingdom, we will "go out no more but will be with Him, a pillar in His temple. To be a pillar in His temple in heaven, we need to be a pillar in His church on earth. **Prayer:** Infinite God, I want to be a pillar for my pastor and my church by being dedicated to You, devoted to the mission of the church, and dependable in working with my pastor.

My Journal

FOR THE WEEK

Praise reports, answered prayers, divine provisions, and spiritual plans.

_____

_____

_____

_____

_____

_____

_____

_____

_____

_____

BIBLE READING — REVELATION

15. Philadelphia, A New Name — 3:12-13. In heaven, all things will be new: "And I will write on him My new name (v. 12). Accepted, endorsed by God the Father for goodness and mercy and to "dwell in the house of the Lord forever" (Psalm 23:6). **Prayer:** By Your grace, Master, I will be a yielded vessel so "my cup will run over" with Your blessings.

UNDIVIDED ATTENTION TODAY

Trustworthy King, I want to give You my undivided attention so I can develop and shine as a committed Christ follower. Undivided attention requires that I be focused and stay focused. I must be focused on pleasing You, and I must stay focused on following Your plan for my life. I will focus on . . .

TRUST — undivided trust in God's will and ways. Father, I cherish Your will for my life as revealed to me in Your Word, in prayer, and through the teaching and preaching of my pastor. Regardless of what surrounds me, *I will trust You!*

TRUTH — undivided loyalty to the truth of God's Word. I will depend on Your Word, Lord, as a compass to guide me; a shelter to protect me; a sword to defend me; a banquet table to feed me; and a light to dispel darkness around me. Regardless of what happens, *I will stand on Your truth!*

TRIUMPH — undivided praise for triumph in living a victorious life. In Christ, I stand in the winner's circle. I am a believer! I am an overcomer! I claim victory to live a successful life through Jesus Christ my Savior. Regardless of what I face, *I will triumph in You!*

BIBLE READING — REVELATION

16. Laodicea, Be Zealous — 3:14-22. The church at Laodicea was complacent. They thought they had "need of nothing" (v. 17). They had confused worldly wealth with spiritual wealth, and they were instructed to "be zealous" and to get their values in line with heavenly values. **Prayer:** Lord, our pastor has to preach, emphasize, and stress the values set forth in Your Word. Let our ears be open to hear and our eyes open to see the things You want us to hold dear, practice, and defend.

UNLIMITED POWER TODAY

All-powerful, all-sufficient Father, I stand complete in Your grace today. I can reach my full potential! I can see and seize possibilities! I can make a difference in my church and community! You have placed all of these within my reach.

REDEMPTION. I am a new creation in Christ—a new lifestyle, new thinking patterns, and new involvement priorities. Father, You redeemed me, bought me, and brought me back from estrangement from You. *I am grateful!*

RESOURCES. What matchless love! You have made all the resources of heaven available to me—spiritual strength, daily provisions, and physical necessities. Father, You minister to me when I need healing from sickness, inspiration during times of depression, and encouragement to run the Christian race. *I am grateful and thankful!*

RESOLVE. I have boldness and resolve through Jesus Christ—to demonstrate my faith, to produce the fruit of the Spirit, and to be obedient to embracing the Great Commission. Father, You issue resolve to stand and shine. *I am grateful, thankful, and bountifully blessed!*

BIBLE READING—REVELATION

17. Laodicea, Share Christ's Throne—3:21. There were weaknesses in the church at Laodicea, but God said, "As many as I love, I rebuke and chasten" (v. 19). Then He blesses: "I will let you sit with Me on My throne" (v. 21). **Prayer:** Almighty Father, in You we are made full. Let us be open to Your correction, let us avoid complacency, and let us cherish the promise of sharing the throne of Christ.

UNLIMITED PROVISIONS TODAY

Lord of unlimited provisions, You have provided the resources for me to stand up, speak up, and stand out in difficult situations. Whatever the occasion, You love me and You lift me up. I am grateful for standing-strong strength today. I trust You to lift me up with . . .

Unfailing LOVE. Father, Your love sent Your Son, Jesus Christ, as a sacrifice to redeem me and to release me into a full life of fellowship with You. Divine love lifts me up to heavenly heights, and I am able to walk in newness and wholeness of life.

Spiritual LIBERTY. Father, I have liberty today to grow in Christlikeness; to overcome as He overcame; to please You, as He pleased You; and to serve as He served. Spiritual liberty lifts me up to see clearly, act wisely, and love sincerely.

Compassionate LONGSUFFERING. I am still learning and growing. I am still in the process of becoming. As a result of inexperience, I often slip and slide. Thank You, Lord, for Your understanding nature, Your longsuffering. Thank You for lifting me up, teaching me, and caring for me. I have joy that lifts up today!

BIBLE READING—REVELATION

18. Heavenly Vision, "In the Spirit"—Chapters 4–11. How can we understand the plan of God following the rapture of the church? John was "in the Spirit" when he wrote (4:2). We must depend on the Holy Spirit "to open the Scriptures" so we can grasp the meaning of the seven seals. (6:1–8:5) and the seven trumpets (8:7–11:19). **Prayer:** Father, You do not want the church to be confused about Your plans for the future. Let us trust the Holy Spirit to teach us and to make clear what You have set forth in Your Word.

UNSURPASSED LOVE TODAY

Your love, mighty Master, is unsurpassed—perfect, personal, eternal. Your love liberates, uplifts, and leads into fullness of life. Your love has changed my life—I'm redeemed, renewed, and redirected. According to Your Word (1Timothy 1:5), I will show love from a . . .

PURE Heart. Openness! Acceptance! Affirmation! As You accepted me, Father, I want to accept other people where they are and how they are. This will open doors and hearts to share how You can redeem, renew, and redirect. I will minister with a pure heart!

PERFECTED Conscience. Clear! Secure! Calm! Father, Your work of grace in me has given me a clear mind to think holy thoughts, a secure heart to face every day with faith, and a calm spirit to live with confidence. I will walk with You and worship You with a perfected conscience!

POSITIVE Faith. Established! Progressive! Scriptural! Master of blessings, You have given me the assurance that by faith "all things are possible." In Christ, I am a winner, an overcomer, an achiever. I will live, relate, and minister today with a positive victorious faith!

BIBLE READING—REVELATION

19. The Little Book—Chapters 10–14. The "little book" represents the gospel that John and the two witnesses are to proclaim (10:1-2). The mission of the church today is to share Jesus and the truths of His Word. **Prayer:** Father, we want to understand the events surrounding the Rapture, but our mission now is to unite with our pastor and by every means possible sow the seeds of the gospel and reap the harvest. Equip us and empower us to do this with teamwork and joy.

UPWARD TODAY

Uplifting Lord, You make it possible to move upward every day in rich experiences with You—a stronger relationship, superior service, and scriptural insights. Each day with You is overflowing with empowering grace and offers opportunities to maximize ministry. I am grateful! Yes, over and beyond grateful! Upward mobility requires me to . . .

INSPECT what I am doing and how I am doing it. Father, it is vitally important for my activities and actions to be aligned with what is important to You and what will keep me in the center of Your will. As I inspect my life today, I prayerfully ask for molding instructions from You.

ELEVATE the positive and eliminate the negative. I will elevate characteristics and goals that honor You, Father, and move me upward, closer to You. I will eliminate routines or relationships that hold me down or hold me back from a progressive walk with You.

RADIATE with a glowing Christ-walk spirit. Today, Master and Motivator, I desire to represent You, my church, and my family in a way that will highlight the richness of Your love, respect for Your standards, and gratefulness for the impactful rewards that flow from Your throne of majesty.

BIBLE READING—REVELATION

20. Song of the Lamb—Chapters 15–19. Following the crossing of the Red Sea, Moses sang a song of triumph. This song (15:3-4) is now the song of the Lamb—a celebration of God's works, power, glory, and judgments. **Prayer:** Regardless of what is happening in the world, or will happen, You, Lord, have given the church assurance of triumph—crossing the Red Seas of life. Today, we claim victory for the leadership of our pastor and the advancement of our church.

PERSONAL AFFIRMATION – COMMITMENT

Realizing I am charged to reflect the likeness of Christ in my lifestyle through commitment,

I Will ...

- **Grow** daily in favor with God.

- **Demonstrate** biblical values in conduct.

- **Show** consistency in church attendance.

- **Publicly** confess my faith.

- **Partner** with my pastor in ministry.

- **Share** my experience in Christ.

- **Devote** time to outreach evangelism.

- **Worship** with a pure heart.

BIBLE READING – REVELATION

21. New Heaven and New Earth – Chapters 20–22. God has a perfect plan and place for His people (21:1). He said, "Behold I make all things new" (21:5). **Prayer:** Loving Father, You have promised that we "will inherit all things" (21:7) if we "overcome." And, You have promised to supply whatever we need to overcome. As Your church, we pledge to walk with You, embrace the leadership of our pastor, and unite as a loving body of believers to worship, work, witness, win, and "overcome."

My Journal

FOR THE WEEK

Praise reports, answered prayers, divine provisions, and spiritual plans.

_____

_____

_____

_____

_____

_____

_____

_____

_____

_____

REVIEW MATTHEW

In **Matthew**, Christ is presented as the King of the Jews, the long-awaited Messiah. Throughout the Gospel of Matthew it is stressed that Jesus is Immanuel—God-With-Us. A clarion call to mission is also forcefully presented—to proclaim the Good News to all peoples and to live the Christian life with patience, watchfulness, and bold faith.

USING MY TALENTS TODAY

Talent-bestowing Lord and Master, You give talents as a gift of grace. They are given to individuals for specific purposes—to demonstrate Your excellence, to show developmental determination, and to incite worship, praise, and devotion. I am honored that You have invested talents in my life. These talents are . . .

A TESTIMONY of Giftedness. Talents are a sign of "God on the inside working on the outside." You have gifted me, Father, and my "soul" desire is to use my talents in such a way that attention is focused on You, not me.

A TRIBUTE to Mentors. Many individuals have been mentors in helping me develop my talents, encouraging me, and supporting me with prayer. I am grateful for each one of them and pledge to follow their examples by mentoring others.

A TRACK to Excel. Father, the talents You have given to me place me on a track to excel—to learn, develop, grow, and glow. I must use my gifts now, and I must continue to develop them. I look to You, talent-bestowing Lord, for instructions from Your Word, inspiration by Your Spirit, and guidance by my church.

REVIEW MARK

In the Gospel of **Mark**, Christ is portrayed as a Servant on the move responding to the will of the Father—He came to serve, not to be served. He has commissioned us as His followers to continue His work in His power and to serve, not to be served. This is an excellent study on the pastor and the people, both servants, serving together in the local church.

WALK IN LOVE TODAY

Father of everlasting love, You have admonished me to "walk in love as Christ also has loved me" (Ephesians 5:2). I will embrace Your admonition and the . . .

Pattern of CHRIST. The love of Christ was not, and is not, limited. His pattern of love was to all people—rich and poor, high and low, the unholy and unworthy. His love was all-inclusive providing hope, healing, and transformation. Father, *I will follow the pattern of Christ!*

Pattern for CHRISTIANS. The pattern of Christ is the lifestyle pattern for believers to follow. That is the reason we are called Christians. That is also why I want You, Lord, to implant the love of Christ in me, reveal the love of Christ through me, and portray the love of Christ in my activities and relationships. *I will be obedient to the pattern You have set forth for Christians!*

Pattern for the CHURCH. The church is Your people, Father, united in mission—reach, witness, win, teach, train, and send out. This mission is founded on Your love—"You loved and You sent Your Son to save." *I will be a partner in the pattern You have outlined for Your church!*

REVIEW LUKE

The apostle Luke wrote both the Gospel of **Luke** and the Acts of the Apostles. His purpose in writing is to present "an orderly account" (1:3) "of all that Jesus began both to do and teach" (Acts 1:1). Luke also gives special attention to the prayer life of Christ, setting forth seven occasions where Jesus prayed that are not recorded anywhere else. This will add to our emphasis on praying for your pastor and church.

WILLINGNESS TODAY

Hearing and prayer-answering Master, You are always willing to respond to the cries of Your children. Many times, well, most of the time, I pray for my needs, goals, and desires. Today, I desire to demonstrate a willing spirit to . . .

HEAL Hurts. Father, I am surrounded by people who are hurting—broken relationships, bruised feelings, and financial bondage. I can offer advice; I can give emotional support; I can outline possible routes to take; but most of all I can pray! You have the resources for satisfying solutions. I will pray!

HOLD Together. Satan will try to disrupt unity in the church, divide loyalty in reaching designated goals, and thwart outreach advancement. Father, invest in me the skills to be a peacemaker. Use me to hold people together, to hold down disruptive behavior, and to hold up high standards of Christian ministry.

HELP Restore. Lord of liberty, "let me stand in the gap" (Ezekiel 22:30) and help restore the battered, bruised, and bewildered. Use me to be instrumental in restoring evangelism, excitement, and energy among church members. I have a willing spirit! I have a restoring spirit!

REVIEW JOHN

The Gospel of **John** presents the love of God as demonstrated in the person and work of Jesus Christ—"For God so loved the world that He gave His only begotten Son, that whoever believes in Him should not perish but have everlasting life" (John 3:16). Jesus presents us as His friends before God the Father. A loving relationship with others is dependent on a right relationship with God. As the pastor lifts us Jesus Christ, the congregation is brought together in harmony to reach out to others in sacrificial compelling love.

WILLING SPIRIT TODAY

Life-shaping Lord, I know You want to lead me in paths of righteousness, in paths of spiritual purity, and in paths of productive ministry. I trust Your leadership. I have a willing spirit to follow You and to . . .

GO the second mile. While walking in paths of righteousness I will face challenges. I can stand my ground, or I can go the second mile and set an example of compassion, care, and Christ-exalting convictions. Father, provide me with spiritual fitness to go the second mile.

GIVE time to serve. Father, Christ came "to serve, not to be served." I want to follow His example and serve You, my family, and my church. I will serve You in worship and in witnessing. I will serve my family in devotion and in fulfilling duties. I will serve my church in attendance and in accountability.

GUIDE by example. A holy, daily walk will convince my family and friends that I belong to a holy, heavenly Father. I will serve as a guide by my walk with You and by a willing spirit to go the second mile and to serve unselfishly.

REVIEW ACTS

The Book of **Acts** records the acts of the apostles, or the acts of the pastors. In a key manner Peter, John, Paul, and Barnabas were all shepherds, pastors of the people, leading them in fulfilling the Great Commission through the power of the Holy Spirit—"But you shall receive power when the Holy Spirit has come upon you, and you shall be witnesses to Me in Jerusalem, and in all Judea and Samaria, and to the end of the earth" (Acts 1:8). Apply the principles and prayers set forth to you life and your relationship with your pastor.

WINNING TODAY

Victorious Creator, You promise victory! You provide winning opportunities, winning privileges, and winning power. In Christ, through Christ, and for Christ, I am a winner. All I need to live a winning life is provided by You!

WISDOM for a Winning WALK. Wisdom is a road-map that gives me daily guidance—spiritual and social etiquette, insight to make correct decisions, and standards of conduct that signify I belong to Your heavenly family, Lord. I will walk with winning wisdom today!

WALK as a Winning WITNESS. I am a witness of the love of Christ—new life, new walk, new talk. Father, I will share my story with those who are lost, lonely, and hopeless. Guide me to develop a warm spirit that opens minds and hearts to receive my testimony. I will walk as a winning witness today!

WORK with Winning WISDOM. Father, my goal is to perform Your work, far-reaching ministry with excellence. I ask for wisdom to respond to opportunities, to relate with respect, and to see spiritual results. I will work with winning wisdom today!

REVIEW ROMANS

Romans is commonly accepted as Paul's greatest work and is considered the greatest exposition of Christian doctrine anywhere in the Bible. It sets forth the meaning of the spiritual life and shows how our spirituality should be revealed in our everyday lives. Romans contains powerful pointers on praying for church leaders and performing the work of the church.

PRAYER PATTERN – COUNT

C — Father of grace, I want my life to **COUNT** for You and for the growth of our church.

O — I **OFFER** You and my pastor my skills, my talents, and my schedule to be utilized for ministry.

U — Help me **UNDERSTAND** my potential to perform service and to support my pastor.

N — Let me turn **NEGATIVES** into positives by acting with faith, charity, and accountability.

T — **TEACH** me how to work with my pastor in being a winning **TEAM** for Your glory and the advancement of Your kingdom.

REVIEW 1 AND 2 CORINTHIANS

Paul founded the church at **Corinth** (Acts 18:1-17, and two of his letters are addressed "To the church of God which is at Corinth: (1 Cor. 1:2; 2 Cor. 1:1). Paul addresses the problems and pressures of church life and gives instructions on how the pastor and the people should work together, the functions of the church, and the operation of spiritual gifts.

My Journal

FOR THE WEEK

Praise reports, answered prayers, divine provisions, and spiritual plans.

_____

_____

_____

_____

_____

_____

_____

_____

REVIEW GALATIANS AND EPHESIANS

In **Galatians**, Paul established his authority as a minister with a message from God. He vigorously attacked their stance on the concept of works and defended the gospel of faith — "we are justified by faith and walk with God by faith."

Paul explains in **Ephesians** that the Church is a body formed to express Christ's fullness on earth (1:15-23). The epistle also explains the wealth of the believer's heavenly bank account — citizenship, grace, and the seal of the Holy Spirit; "For we are His workmanship created in Christ Jesus . . . for good works." We see in Ephesians the believer's position and practice in Christ.

WONDERFUL GIFTS TODAY

Gift-giving Lord of glory, You make my life complete and connected—connected with wonderful gifts, generous gifts, life-sustaining gifts. Your gifts spring from Your nature of love, Your forgiveness, and Your care. I praise and honor You for the gifts of . . .

PEACE that provides focus, balance, and contentment. Lord, Your gift of peace lets me focus and give priority to the most valuable things in life. I find balance in believing and in behaving through Your peace. Your peace gives me a spirit of contentment, relaxation, and renewal.

PROTECTION to serve aggressively and to stand firm in faith. Lord, You surround me with the protective forces of heaven so I can live without fear and be free in my spirit. Your protection permits me to minister with authority and to utilize all your weapons for spiritual warfare.

PROSPERITY that opens the windows of heaven for me to receive unparalleled and unlimited blessings—rich, rewarding, and uplifting blessings. Lord, prosperity from You includes faith blessings, financial blessings, and foundational blessings. Thank You for Your wonderful gifts.

REVIEW PHILIPPIANS

The theme of **Philippians** is joy in Christ. Paul outlines the grounds for Christian joy. Ultimately joy arises from fellowship with, and commitment to, the risen Christ. Paul also talks about the joy that comes in the spreading of the gospel. He said, "I rejoice . . . and will rejoice" (1:18), and his admonition to us was, "Rejoice . . . and I will say it again, rejoice" (4:4).

YOUR GLORY TODAY

God of wonder and wisdom, I want to see You clearly today. I want to see You up close in all Your majesty and glory. I seek these insightful experiences with deep humility and with a heart full and running over with expressions of praise and adoration. Your glory represents who You are and what I can become in You. It . . .

Reveals Your NATURE. Father, You are ever-present. You are all-powerful. You know all things. You are not restricted in any way, form, or fashion. Today, I will dwell on Your glory as revealed in Your nature and will live in the full dimensions of all the benefits it offers.

Provides NURTURE. Every day, God of wonder, You set new avenues before me to walk on, new projects to undertake, and new relationships to form. This equals excitement plus! But, I need divine nurture to clothe me, guide me, and sustain me. I trust You to provide nurturing care.

Creates NEWNESS. I am a new creation in Jesus Christ. This means I can do things in new, exciting ways. I will not be blocked or bogged down by outdated, limited practices. I will walk new paths of trust, share my faith, and live victoriously.

REVIEW COLOSSIANS

Colossians sets forth the Lordship of Christ—He is supreme and preeminent. The word "Lord" is used nine times. Chapters one and two are doctrinal and chapters three and four are practical. Christ is Lord over creation, supreme in salvation, and the "Life and Leader" of the church. In Christ we are "rooted," "alive," "hidden," and "complete." The importance of praying for pastors and church leaders is also emphasized, "Meanwhile praying also for us, that God would open to us a door for the word, to speak the mystery of Christ, for which I am also in chains, that I may make it manifest, as I ought to speak" (4:3-4).

YOUR HOLY LAWS TODAY

Gracious and giving Lord, You give life, love, and liberty to those who embrace the laws guiding these gifts. Your nature is characterized by generosity. You want to give—richly, abundantly, regularly. I want to receive Your gifts, and I will observe the laws You have set forth.

The law of new LIFE. Old life; new life—it's a choice! I realize this, Master, I choose new life through the new birth—transformed by the redeeming, sanctifying grace of Your Son, Jesus Christ. *I praise You for new life!*

The law of LIBERTY. Freedom! Liberated to think Christ-thoughts, to think creative thoughts, and to think uplifting, relationship thoughts. Father, I am committed to enjoying the liberty You have provided. I am also committed to prudently protect my unmatchable liberty. *I rejoice in my liberty!*

The law of shared LOVE. Father, I understand I am "to love my neighbor as myself." In obedience to Your law of love, I will love my neighbor, friends, and associates with the accepting and believing love You have deposited in my heart. *I will share Your love!*

REVIEW 1 AND 2 THESSALONIANS, AND
1 AND 2 TIMOTHY

In **Thessalonians** Paul reveals the heart of a dedicated pastor in his letters to the church. He talks about their love, faith, and hope in the face of persecution. He encourages them to continue to develop their faith, to strive for excellence, to increase their love for one another, to rejoice always, and to give thanks.

In the two letters Paul writes to **Timothy**, the young pastor at Ephesus, he gives instructions on mature leadership, safeguarding public worship, and pursuing righteousness and godliness.

YOUR PRESENCE TODAY

God of eternal glory, I bow before You in reverence and adoration! You are holy and unquestionable in all Your ways and acts—I stand in Your presence with awe and holy reverence. Your desire is to see me healthy and prosperous—I stand in Your presence with thanksgiving and pure-heart adoration. You provide . . .

Fullness of PARTNERSHIP. Father, I have been forgiven, freed, and given full partnership in Your kingdom—an heir with You and a joint-heir with Jesus Christ. This partnership gives me access to heavenly riches, to daily interaction with You, and to the flow of grace and mercy from Your throne.

Fruit of PEACE. In You, Master of the universe, there is delicious fruit and peace—inner calmness that surpasses comprehension, assurance in times of adversity, and strength to set standards and achieve goals. I will rejoice and enjoy the flow of fruit and peace from Your throne.

Fortress PROTECTION. Father, the forces of evil cannot penetrate Your divine protection. You have erected a wall of protection around me—a wall that provides security, peace of mind, and freedom to worship and work without fear. I praise You for the flow of gifts and glory from Your throne.

REVIEW TITUS AND PHILEMON

Titus was a valuable coworker of Paul. He was left to direct the work in Crete. Paul wrote him giving detailed instructions about the work of the church and pastoral duties.

Philemon was a wealthy slave owner. Onesimus was a converted run-away slave. Paul wrote to Philemon, a close friend, and asked him to receive Onesimus as a brother in the Lord and to restore him in love.

YOUR VOICE TODAY

Lord of communication and care, You speak to me to safeguard my spirit of devotion, to fortify my faith for deliverance, and to ignite my trust for directions. Teach me how to block out the sounds around me and to lock into Your voice of . . .

DEVOTION. Master, You are devoted to my care and welfare. You do not withhold anything good from me. I will listen to Your voice of devotion today. *Your voice brings comfort!*

DELIVERANCE. Father, when I am pressed, pushed, and perplexed, I will listen for Your voice of deliverance — "My grace is sufficient"; "My provisions are available"; "My power is unlimited"; and "My care provides control." *Your voice brings assurance!*

DIRECTIONS. I need Your guidance today, heavenly Father. I receive directional signals from many different sources that seek to muffle Your voice. I will listen for Your voice of direction today, which says, "I have plans for your life"; "I have a path for your life"; "I will supply your life with provisions"; and "I will partner with you to bring pleasure and spiritual productivity in your life." *Your voice brings steadfastness!*

REVIEW HEBREWS

Most of the early Christians were Jewish. As a result of persecution, many were wondering if they had made the right choice. The writer of **Hebrews** points out the overwhelming superiority of Christ over the law, prophets, angels, Moses, Joshua, Aaron, and the rituals of Judaism. He encourages them to press on in Christ and to claim the riches of His grace.

TWELVE RULES FOR BUILDING RESPECT FOR YOUR PASTOR'S WIFE

1. Don't criticize her to other women.

2. Don't compare her with the wives of other pastors.

3. Don't entertain negative comments about her.

4. Don't minimize her spiritual gifts.

5. Don't expect her to always have the winning ideas.

6. Don't miss opportunities to show her appreciation.

7. Don't be a watcher in ladies ministries.

8. Don't place demands on her family.

9. Don't depend on her to sacrifice more than you do.

10. Don't underestimate the pressure she faces.

11. Don't neglect to include her in your daily prayer time.

12. Don't avoid fellowship with her.

REVIEW JAMES

The theme of the Epistle of **James** is that "faith produces doers;" it puts reality in religion. He emphasizes that you cannot "talk" your way into heaven; you must "walk" your way there practicing "pure and undefiled religion" (1:27). Faith inspires action, endures trials, develops endurance, obeys the Word, prompts obedience, and responds to God's promises.

My Journal

FOR THE WEEK

Praise reports, answered prayers, divine provisions, and spiritual plans.

_____

_____

_____

_____

_____

_____

_____

_____

_____

_____

_____

REVIEW 1 AND 2 PETER

Peter exhorts believers to live godly lives in an ungodly society during trials and persecution. He talks about character and conduct based on submission in relationship to government, husbands and wives, believers to each other, and the "hand of God." Peter warns the church about false teachers. He talks about believers cultivating Christian maturity and keeping a close watch on their personal lives — self-control, perseverance, and godliness.

YOUR WILL TODAY

Willing Master, You are ready and willing to bless me with rich and bountiful gifts. I am ready to receive them with a voice of praise and a heart of thanksgiving. You have a divine will for my life. I am responsible! May Your will . . .

ANCHOR Me. Your will, Father, will keep me steady and unmovable when I face the storms and disruptive forces of life. Your divine will is my anchor — for doctrinal integrity, devotional inspiration, and scriptural development challenges. I will follow Your will and stay anchored in joy-filled assurance and abundant life living.

ANOINT Me. Master, I desire to abide in Your Word and walk in Your will. Anoint me with Holy Spirit power to see clearly the path You have ordained for me, to accept it wholeheartedly, to follow it dynamically, and to experience results fruitfully. I cherish Your anointing!

ADVANCE Me. Lord, I want to advance in Christlikeness, in being conformed to the image of Christ. I am open to the full development of Your will in every aspect of my life, because I know Your will holds me as an anchor, anoints me, and advances me. Amen and glory!

REVIEW 1, 2, 3 JOHN AND JUDE

In **First John** the key word is love — God is love, God is light, God is life. Since we belong to God and follow Him, we must walk in love — unconditional love, giving love, and action-centered love. The test of loving God is keeping His commandments, abiding in truth, and maintaining obedient faith. **Second John** also emphasizes the important of love: "love one another" (v. 5), and "walk according to His (God's) commandments" (v. 5). In **Third John**, John talks about "prospering in all things" (v. 2), "walking in the truth" (v. 3), "showing hospitality" (v. 5), "becoming fellow workers for the truth" (v. 8), and "imitating what is good" (v. 11). Fight for the faith is the theme of **Jude**. You fight the fight of faith by staying "in shape spiritually," "confronting false teachers," "praying in the Holy Spirit," and "making a difference through compassion."

YOUR WORD TODAY

God of grace and guidance, I am thankful for Your daily companionship that guides me in paths of righteousness, in living a life of purity, and in producing the fruit of the Holy Spirit. Your Word serves as a roadmap and compass that . . .

INVITES me to follow You, Lord, with holy convictions. My daily conduct is directed by my convictions about Your calling on my life, the relationship principles You have set forth, and the spiritual lifestyle You have promised to bless. *I embrace Your Word!*

INSTRUCTS me on how to worship You, Father, how to witness about You, and how to work with You. Following this threefold pattern will make me acceptable in Your sight and will advance the mission and message of Your eternal Kingdom. *I honor Your Word!*

INSPIRES me to be creative and to begin each day with excitement and anticipation. Your Word, Father, provides me with fresh, faith-based thoughts, mountain-moving thoughts. *I embrace, honor, and respect Your Word!*

REVIEW REVELATION

Revelation is the book of the ending of time. The name means "unveiling" or "disclosure." Three time frames are set forth in the first chapter: "Write these things which you have seen, the things which are, and the things which will take place after this" (1:19). The devotional thoughts in Revelation will center on the seven churches John writes to in chapters one through three and on how to live victoriously in the last days. The seven churches represent churches of all ages, and the messages should be applied both pastorally and practically.

ONE-YEAR
BIBLE READING GUIDE
JANUARY

1	Genesis	1-3	❑
2	Genesis	4-6	❑
3	Genesis	7-9	❑
4	Genesis	10-12	❑
5	Genesis	13-15	❑
6	Genesis	16-18	❑
7	Genesis	19-21	❑
8	Genesis	22-24	❑
9	Genesis	25-27	❑
10	Genesis	28-30	❑
11	Genesis	31-33	❑
12	Genesis	34-36	❑
13	Genesis	37-39	❑
14	Genesis	40-42	❑
15	Genesis	43-45	❑
16	Genesis	46-48	❑
17	Genesis	49-50	❑
18	Exodus	1-3	❑
19	Exodus	4-6	❑
20	Exodus	7-9	❑
21	Exodus	10-12	❑
22	Exodus	13-15	❑
23	Exodus	16-18	❑
24	Exodus	19-21	❑
25	Exodus	22-24	❑
26	Exodus	25-27	❑
27	Exodus	28-30	❑
28	Exodus	31-33	❑
29	Exodus	34-36	❑
30	Exodus	37-40	❑
31	Leviticus	1-3	❑

ONE-YEAR
BIBLE READING GUIDE
FEBRUARY

1	Leviticus	4-6	❏
2	Leviticus	7-9	❏
3	Leviticus	10-12	❏
4	Leviticus	13-15	❏
5	Leviticus	16-18	❏
6	Leviticus	19-21	❏
7	Leviticus	22-24	❏
8	Leviticus	25-27	❏
9	Numbers	1-3	❏
10	Numbers	4-6	❏
11	Numbers	7-9	❏
12	Numbers	10-12	❏
13	Numbers	13-15	❏
14	Numbers	16-18	❏
15	Numbers	19-21	❏
16	Numbers	22-24	❏
17	Numbers	25-27	❏
18	Numbers	28-30	❏
19	Numbers	31-33	❏
20	Numbers	34-36	❏
21	Deuteronomy	1-3	❏
22	Deuteronomy	4-6	❏
23	Deuteronomy	7-9	❏
24	Deuteronomy	10-12	❏
25	Deuteronomy	13-15	❏
26	Deuteronomy	16-18	❏
27	Deuteronomy	19-21	❏
28	Deuteronomy	22-24	❏

ONE-YEAR
BIBLE READING GUIDE
MARCH

1	Deuteronomy	25-27	❑
2	Deuteronomy	28-30	❑
3	Deuteronomy	31-34	❑
4	Joshua	1-3	❑
5	Joshua	4-6	❑
6	Joshua	7-9	❑
7	Joshua	10-12	❑
8	Joshua	13-15	❑
9	Joshua	16-18	❑
10	Joshua	19-21	❑
11	Joshua	22-24	❑
12	Judges	1-3	❑
13	Judges	4-6	❑
14	Judges	7-9	❑
15	Judges	10-12	❑
16	Judges	13-15	❑
17	Judges	16-18	❑
18	Judges	19-21	❑
19	Ruth	1-4	❑
20	1 Samuel	1-3	❑
21	1 Samuel	4-6	❑
22	1 Samuel	7-9	❑
23	1 Samuel	10-12	❑
24	1 Samuel	13-15	❑
25	1 Samuel	16-18	❑
26	1 Samuel	19-21	❑
27	1 Samuel	22-24	❑
28	1 Samuel	25-27	❑
29	1 Samuel	28-31	❑
30	2 Samuel	1-3	❑
31	2 Samuel	4-6	❑

ONE-YEAR
BIBLE READING GUIDE
APRIL

1	2 Samuel	7-9	❑
2	2 Samuel	10-12	❑
3	2 Samuel	13-15	❑
4	2 Samuel	16-18	❑
5	2 Samuel	19-21	❑
6	2 Samuel	22-24	❑
7	1 Kings	1-3	❑
8	1 Kings	4-6	❑
9	1 Kings	7-9	❑
10	1 Kings	10-12	❑
11	1 Kings	13-15	❑
12	1 Kings	16-18	❑
13	1 Kings	19-22	❑
14	2 Kings	1-3	❑
15	2 Kings	4-6	❑
16	2 Kings	7-9	❑
17	2 Kings	10-12	❑
18	2 Kings	13-15	❑
19	2 Kings	16-18	❑
20	2 Kings	19-21	❑
21	2 Kings	22-25	❑
22	1 Chronicles	1-3	❑
23	1 Chronicles	4-6	❑
24	1 Chronicles	7-9	❑
25	1 Chronicles	10-12	❑
26	1 Chronicles	13-15	❑
27	1 Chronicles	16-18	❑
28	1 Chronicles	19-21	❑
29	1 Chronicles	22-24	❑
30	1 Chronicles	25-27	❑

ONE-YEAR
BIBLE READING GUIDE
MAY

1	1 Chronicles	28-29	❑
2	2 Chronicles	1-3	❑
3	2 Chronicles	4-6	❑
4	2 Chronicles	7-9	❑
5	2 Chronicles	10-12	❑
6	2 Chronicles	13-15	❑
7	2 Chronicles	16-18	❑
8	2 Chronicles	19-21	❑
9	2 Chronicles	22-24	❑
10	2 Chronicles	25-27	❑
11	2 Chronicles	28-30	❑
12	2 Chronicles	31-33	❑
13	2 Chronicles	34-36	❑
14	Ezra	1-3	❑
15	Ezra	4-6	❑
16	Ezra	7-10	❑
17	Nehemiah	1-3	❑
18	Nehemiah	4-6	❑
19	Nehemiah	7-9	❑
20	Nehemiah	10-13	❑
21	Esther	1-3	❑
22	Esther	4-6	❑
23	Esther	7-10	❑
24	Job	1-3	❑
25	Job	4-6	❑
26	Job	7-9	❑
27	Job	10-12	❑
28	Job	13-15	❑
29	Job	16-18	❑
30	Job	19-21	❑
31	Job	22-24	❑

ONE-YEAR
BIBLE READING GUIDE
JUNE

1	Job	25-27	❏
2	Job	28-30	❏
3	Job	31-33	❏
4	Job	34-36	❏
5	Job	37-39	❏
6	Job	40-42	❏
7	Psalms	1-9	❏
8	Psalms	10-17	❏
9	Psalms	18-22	❏
10	Psalms	23-31	❏
11	Psalms	32-37	❏
12	Psalms	38-44	❏
13	Psalms	45-51	❏
14	Psalms	52-59	❏
15	Psalms	60-67	❏
16	Psalms	68-71	❏
17	Psalms	72-77	❏
18	Psalms	78-81	❏
19	Psalms	82-89	❏
20	Psalms	90-97	❏
21	Psalms	98-104	❏
22	Psalms	105-110	❏
23	Psalms	111-118	❏
24	Psalms	119	❏
25	Psalms	120-127	❏
26	Psalms	128-136	❏
27	Psalms	137-142	❏
28	Psalms	143-150	❏
29	Proverbs	1-3	❏
30	Proverbs	4-6	❏

ONE-YEAR
BIBLE READING GUIDE
JULY

1	Proverbs	7-9	❏
2	Proverbs	10-12	❏
3	Proverbs	13-15	❏
4	Proverbs	16-18	❏
5	Proverbs	19-21	❏
6	Proverbs	22-24	❏
7	Proverbs	25-27	❏
8	Proverbs	28-31	❏
9	Ecclesiastes	1-3	❏
10	Ecclesiastes	4-6	❏
11	Ecclesiastes	7-9	❏
12	Ecclesiastes	10-12	❏
13	Song of Solomon	1-3	❏
14	Song of Solomon	4-6	❏
15	Song of Solomon	7-8	❏
16	Isaiah	1-3	❏
17	Isaiah	4-6	❏
18	Isaiah	7-9	❏
19	Isaiah	10-12	❏
20	Isaiah	13-15	❏
21	Isaiah	16-18	❏
22	Isaiah	19-21	❏
23	Isaiah	22-24	❏
24	Isaiah	25-27	❏
25	Isaiah	28-30	❏
26	Isaiah	31-33	❏
27	Isaiah	34-36	❏
28	Isaiah	37-39	❏
29	Isaiah	40-42	❏
30	Isaiah	43-45	❏
31	Isaiah	46-48	❏

ONE-YEAR
BIBLE READING GUIDE
AUGUST

1	Isaiah	49-51	❑
2	Isaiah	52-54	❑
3	Isaiah	55-57	❑
4	Isaiah	58-60	❑
5	Isaiah	61-63	❑
6	Isaiah	64-66	❑
7	Jeremiah	1-3	❑
8	Jeremiah	4-6	❑
9	Jeremiah	7-9	❑
10	Jeremiah	10-12	❑
11	Jeremiah	13-15	❑
12	Jeremiah	16-18	❑
13	Jeremiah	19-21	❑
14	Jeremiah	22-24	❑
15	Jeremiah	25-27	❑
16	Jeremiah	28-30	❑
17	Jeremiah	31-33	❑
18	Jeremiah	34-36	❑
19	Jeremiah	37-39	❑
20	Jeremiah	40-42	❑
21	Jeremiah	43-45	❑
22	Jeremiah	46-48	❑
23	Jeremiah	49-52	❑
24	Lamentations	1-3	❑
25	Lamentations	4-5	❑
26	Ezekiel	1-3	❑
27	Ezekiel	4-6	❑
28	Ezekiel	7-9	❑
29	Ezekiel	10-12	❑
30	Ezekiel	13-15	❑
31	Ezekiel	16-18	❑

ONE-YEAR
BIBLE READING GUIDE
SEPTEMBER

1	Ezekiel	19-21	❑
2	Ezekiel	22-24	❑
3	Ezekiel	25-27	❑
4	Ezekiel	28-30	❑
5	Ezekiel	31-33	❑
6	Ezekiel	34-36	❑
7	Ezekiel	37-39	❑
8	Ezekiel	40-42	❑
9	Ezekiel	43-45	❑
10	Ezekiel	46-48	❑
11	Daniel	1-3	❑
12	Daniel	4-6	❑
13	Daniel	7-9	❑
14	Daniel	10-12	❑
15	Hosea	1-3	❑
16	Hosea	4-6	❑
17	Hosea	7-9	❑
18	Hosea	10-12	❑
19	Hosea	13-14	❑
20	Joel	1-3	❑
21	Amos	1-3	❑
22	Amos	4-6	❑
23	Amos	7-9	❑
24	Obadiah	1	❑
25	Jonah	1-4	❑
26	Micah	1-3	❑
27	Micah	4-7	❑
28	Nahum	1-3	❑
29	Habakkuk	1-3	❑
30	Zephaniah	1-3	❑

ONE-YEAR
BIBLE READING GUIDE
OCTOBER

1	Haggai	1-2	❑
2	Zechariah	1-3	❑
3	Zechariah	4-6	❑
4	Zechariah	7-9	❑
5	Zechariah	10-12	❑
6	Zechariah	13-14	❑
7	Malachi	1-4	❑
8	Matthew	1-3	❑
9	Matthew	4-6	❑
10	Matthew	7-9	❑
11	Matthew	10-12	❑
12	Matthew	13-15	❑
13	Matthew	16-18	❑
14	Matthew	19-21	❑
15	Matthew	22-24	❑
16	Matthew	25-28	❑
17	Mark	1-3	❑
18	Mark	4-6	❑
19	Mark	7-9	❑
20	Mark	10-12	❑
21	Mark	13-16	❑
22	Luke	1-3	❑
23	Luke	4-6	❑
24	Luke	7-9	❑
25	Luke	10-12	❑
26	Luke	13-15	❑
27	Luke	16-18	❑
28	Luke	19-21	❑
29	Luke	22-24	❑
30	John	1-3	❑
31	John	4-6	❑

ONE-YEAR
BIBLE READING GUIDE
NOVEMBER

1	John	7-9	❏
2	John	10-12	❏
3	John	13-15	❏
4	John	16-18	❏
5	John	19-21	❏
6	Acts	1-3	❏
7	Acts	4-6	❏
8	Acts	7-9	❏
9	Acts	10-12	❏
10	Acts	13-15	❏
11	Acts	16-18	❏
12	Acts	19-21	❏
13	Acts	22-24	❏
14	Acts	25-28	❏
15	Romans	1-3	❏
16	Romans	4-6	❏
17	Romans	7-9	❏
18	Romans	10-12	❏
19	Romans	13-16	❏
20	1 Corinthians	1-3	❏
21	1 Corinthians	4-6	❏
22	1 Corinthians	7-9	❏
23	1 Corinthians	10-12	❏
24	1 Corinthians	13-16	❏
25	2 Corinthians	1-3	❏
26	2 Corinthians	4-6	❏
27	2 Corinthians	7-9	❏
28	2 Corinthians	10-13	❏
29	Galatians	1-3	❏
30	Galatians	4-6	❏

ONE-YEAR
BIBLE READING GUIDE
DECEMBER

1	Ephesians	1-3	❏
2	Ephesians	4-6	❏
3	Philippians	1-4	❏
4	Colossians	1-4	❏
5	1 Thessalonians	1-3	❏
6	1 Thessalonians	4-5	❏
7	2 Thessalonians	1-3	❏
8	1 Timothy	1-3	❏
9	1 Timothy	4-6	❏
10	2 Timothy	1-4	❏
11	Titus	1-3	❏
12	Philemon	1	❏
13	Hebrews	1-3	❏
14	Hebrews	4-6	❏
15	Hebrews	7-9	❏
16	Hebrews	10-13	❏
17	James	1-3	❏
18	James	4-5	❏
19	1 Peter	1-3	❏
20	1 Peter	4-5	❏
21	2 Peter	1-3	❏
22	1 John	1-3	❏
23	1 John	4-5	❏
24	2 John; 3 John; Jude		❏
25	Revelation	1-3	❏
26	Revelation	4-6	❏
27	Revelation	7-9	❏
28	Revelation	10-12	❏
29	Revelation	13-15	❏
30	Revelation	16-18	❏
31	Revelation	19-22	❏